Foreword

I met Dick Buck years ago, after I finished playing for the Boston Red Sox. Dick is a serious angler and is totally involved in trying to bring back the Atlantic salmon. However, it looks like we're coming awfully close to losing it all, despite the great strides that have been made. We still have pollution and acid rain. And now more sophisticated fishing equipment makes it easier to intercept schools on the high seas and deplete the overall stock. In a few cases, all this has resulted in the almost complete destruction of the runs in some of our famous rivers.

Dick Buck is a great champion of this fish, and he is working with the greatest ally we could ever have, the United States government. Internationally, he has probably done as much as anyone to help preserve this fish from the ravages of heavy netting off Greenland, the Faroe Islands, and the east coast of Newfoundland as well as uncontrolled and illegal operations in the waters of the United Kingdom and Ireland.

You would have to have fished for the Atlantic salmon to appreciate how great it is; to have studied its life cycle and marveled at the tremendous trip it makes after leaving the estuary and venturing out to sea — in some cases going over three thousand miles to return to its river of origin. The Atlantic salmon is a power-packed, leaping, silver thing of beauty, and God, I hope it lives forever. Everyone who is interested in the outdoors, and in salmon fishing in particular, should be concerned to the point of helping our cause. Anyone who has had the extreme privilege of fishing for this greatest of all fish should get involved in the effort to save it.

A book of this nature is long overdue, and anybody who cares about preserving what remains of our wildlife on this earth should read it. If some of the things that Dick Buck believes can be done by means of conservation and international agreements are accomplished, the future of the Atlantic salmon will be more secure, and the stocks will once again grow to the numbers that will assure its future.

— Ted Williams

Acknowledgments

I take a great deal of pleasure in recognizing those persons who have been of help to me in one way or another in my efforts on behalf of the Atlantic salmon:

• Nick Lyons, my publisher, whose guidance, sound judgment, understanding, and continuing enthusiasm gave me the confidence so necessary to a first-time author.

• Marshall Field, whose perception, common sense, management ability, and encouragement helped immensely with the decision-making process over a period of some twenty-five years.

• Those directors of Restoration of Atlantic Salmon in America (RASA) whose counsel and progressive involvement give meaning, substance, and continuity to the work we are doing, especially David Egan, Robert French, Allen Keyworth, and Ernest Mack.

Over the years, I developed meaningful and effective working relationships with a number of high-level federal government officials: Special Assistant to the Secretary of State Donald McKernan; several assistant secretaries of state (for fisheries and oceans) and/or their deputies — Rozanne Ridgway, Thomas Pickering, Morris Busby, John Negroponte, and Theodore Kronmiller; Larry Snead, Director of the Office of Fisheries Affairs; Secretary of the Interior Rogers Morton; Assistant Secretaries for Wildlife and Parks Leslie Glasgow and Nathaniel Reed; and David Wallace, Assistant Director of the National Oceanic and Atmospheric Administration.

There were also individuals who, at one time or another, had a particularly significant impact on the successful outcome of our special missions and projects: Robert A. Bryan, Frank Carlton, David Clarke, Doris Clarke, Bing Crosby, Philip Crowe, Joseph Cullman, Elliot Donnelley, Strachan Donnelley, Francis Goelet, Thor Gudjonsson, Christopher Percy, Allen Peterson, Gilbert Radonski, Charles Ritz, Svend Saabye, David Scoll, Andrew Stout,

Otto Teller, Peter Thompson, Peter Van Gytenbeek, Royall Victor, Ted Williams, Patrick Wills, and Lee Wulff.

There have also been a number of persons who were helpful to our work in many other different ways: Barbara Anderson, Vaughn Anthony, Robert Applebaum, Palmer Baker, Edward Bartlett, Edward Baum, Kenneth Beland, Doris Berklund, Derek Bingham, Colton Bridges, Nelson Bryant, John Calhoun, Anthony Campbell, Walter Carter, Wilfred Carter, Conrad Chapman, Francis Coleman, Sylvio Conte, Richard Cronin, William Dana, Raymond de Clairville, Gudmundeir Eirikssen, Jack Fenety, Charles Ferree, Edna Fisher, Lewis Flagg, Charles Foster, T. B. Fraser, Marlene French, Kevin Friedland, Stephen Gephard, Ted Giddings, Arnold Gingrich, Leslie Glasgow, David Goldthwaithe, David Goulet, Curt Gowdy, Gardner Grant, Gerald Hadoke, Rafn Hafnfjord, Torrence Hammond, Jack Hanks, Lars Hansen, Tom Hennessey, David Howe, Sydney Howe, Tom Humphrey, Robert Hutton, June Johnson, Robert Jones, Jay Keyworth, Dan Kimball, Al Knight, Robert Korosec, Linda Kosnick, Peter Kriendler, Ronald Lambertson, Albert Lanier, David Lank, Bud Leavitt, Carl Lundquist, A. Theodore Lyman, D. J. MacKenzie, Glen Manuel, Jerry Marancik, Dan Marshall, Thomas J. McIntyre, Alfred Meister, Theodore Meyers, Robbins Milbank, David Miller, John Moran, Grinnell Morris, Arthur Neill, Anthony Netboy, Robert Oden, Leigh Perkins, Thomas Pero, Ralph Peters, John Phillips, Beekman Pool, T. Rex Porter, Michael Price, Paul Rago, David Reddin, Steve Rideout, Ben Rizzo, Ray Robinson, Willard Rockwell, Stephen Saltzman, Warren Schnaars, David Shaw, Jane Sherrill, Jane Smith, Ron Snow, Wilson Stephens, Lawrence Stolte, Peter Stroh, Stetson Tinkham, Clinton Townsend, Conrad Voss Bark, James Weaver, Daphne White, Ted Williams, and Malcolm Windsor.

Introduction

SOME YEARS AGO, several of my friends began urging me to write a history of Atlantic salmon conservation and restoration. They pointed out that my background and experience over the years in all areas of Atlantic salmon affairs would enable me to record and evaluate important events and trends from an overall perspective. After careful consideration, I found myself eager to do this. In addition to a sense of obligation, I felt an inner compulsion to give something back to the salmon because of the pleasure and inspiration this fish had given me over the years. Let me enlarge on this.

In 1921, when I was about twelve years old, my father took me salmon fishing on the Serpentine River in New Brunswick. This was my first experience in learning the ways of the wild. After poling upriver — under canvas each night — we reached Serpentine Pond, the headwaters. We camped out there for several days and then commenced to run the river down, going a short distance each day, stopping every evening by a pool. There were bear and grouse and woodcock. The deer would be snorting at night, and I still have a vivid picture in my mind of a moose, in the early morning mist, feeding on vegetation in the river right beside our camp. And in every one of these pools we would find several salmon and usually a few grilse.

Here was this fish that I had heard so much about. We would usually hook a few, lose some, and keep only what we needed for food. We used wet and dry flies, and my guide started teaching me to do everything myself, such as tying on the leaders and flies and hand-tailing or beaching the quarry.

So that was the beginning of what was to be a lifelong addiction to fishing for the salmon. It soon became apparent that I had come under the spell of a fascinating and special creature, one that was to become for me the epitome of animal courage. Visions of the big jumps and the long runs that the salmon take are indelibly impressed on my mind, and over the years they have brought me through many a long and sleepless night.

To match wits with such a spectacular and skillful adversary answers an inborn competitive urge that seems to exist to some degree in all of us. When I am "into a salmon," as they say, the fish becomes personalized for me, and I seem to be saying: "If I can meet you and beat you fairly and squarely, then I am satisfied and will let you go. And if you break me, then you've deserved your freedom, and you can go your way and I'll try for another."

Years later, when I was in my fifties, I had reached a point where the marts of trade and commerce no longer had any appeal for me. I had enjoyed a successful career in the field of public and distributor relations, yet my heart and soul were no longer in tune with these endeavors. Those were the days when Rachel Carson was singing the song of *Silent Spring*, and conservation was in the air. So why not use such talents as I had in this field? My thoughts naturally turned to saving the Atlantic salmon, which was in serious trouble due to overexploitation in the ocean.

The New England Atlantic Salmon Restoration Program had just been launched. My knowledge of the lifestyle and ways of these fish would be a big asset, but I needed background and experience along other lines, such as working with governmental agencies — the bureaucracies.

I started by organizing the New Hampshire Committee for Better Water, because the rivers first had to be cleaned up to the point where salmon could populate, migrate, and spawn in them. Our job was to work with utilities and the government to get fishways and pollution-control facilities built and operating on major river systems. Governor Thompson supported me by appointing me a commissioner on both the New Hampshire and the New England Water Supply and Pollution Control Commissions. Meanwhile, I had joined Trout Unlimited, at that time one of the leading private-sector sportfishing organizations in the United States. I became involved as a national director and vice president, organizing an Atlantic Salmon committee with the objective of co-ordinating the work of private-sector groups with that of federal and state agencies in support of proposals and projects that would benefit the restoration effort. All this work was high pressure, because time was of the essence, but after about a year or so, our committee felt ready for whatever challenges might arise.

And now, here are some comments about the nature, scope, and substance of the chronicle that follows.

This book sets forth a historical account of the trend-setting efforts of governments and private-sector groups and individuals during the last half of the twentieth century to conserve and restore this creature that we have been ruthlessly exploiting in our headlong rush for material gain, without adequate regard for the protection and enhancement of a valuable and substantially renewable natural resource.

Yet, sad to say, these dedicated attempts have failed to stem the unremitting decline in abundance of the species *Salmo salar*. The principal and overarching issues facing governments in their management of salmon of the North Atlantic have been political and sociological. Humans have the ability to produce artificially any desired number of salmon, but they seem incapable of holding selfishness in check when it comes to exploitation of migrating stocks. The degree of mortality of salmon during these ocean migrations has a direct and compelling impact on the success or failure of domestic programs of conservation and restoration in the rivers.

As is usually the case with historical events of singular importance, after the passing of some little time the archives of those players who were centrally involved are opened up, as succeeding generations seek out the truth. An examination of public and private records and documents, together with a recounting of personal experiences at interviews and meetings with officials at all levels of government and in the private sector, unveils considerations and positions never before revealed to the general public. And these events have not been without their moments of tension, suspense, and drama.

In the United States, we had to restore a creature that we had rendered all but extinct, principally as a result of the building of dams that blocked spawning migrations and the ever-increasing pollution of our rivers. The conservationists among us were not proud of that inheritance. So out of necessity we set a course that was not always shared by the private-sector groups and governments in those other nations whose salmon runs were still intact. Putting it another way, we first had to conserve what little we still had — and then build anew. The other nations had only to conserve. All this translated into not only double trouble but also the necessity of raising substantial amounts of capital for the building of hatcheries, fishways around dams, and the like. And we had to try to protect these fish on their ocean migrations. So the Americans moved naturally and eagerly into the mainstream of the international affairs of the salmon.

In this whole connection, it should be pointed out that if this book seems unduly slanted toward the American involvement in these affairs, this is not by design. I am simply describing what actually happened. There is no intent to minimize the substantial contributions of those throughout the entire Atlantic salmon community who have dedicated their efforts to bettering the lot of the salmon.

Because the Americans were called upon to play a leading role at the green table of Atlantic salmon diplomacy, it therefore seems appropriate and meaningful that the chronicle of the momentous events that have occurred to date should come out of the United States, and at the hands of someone who was centrally involved at all times. Since 1969 — for a quarter of a century — I have been in the unique position of serving in an official capacity at every formal international governmental negotiating meeting (save two) on Atlantic salmon. And President Reagan enhanced my involvement in the decision-making process in 1983, when he appointed me a United States Commissioner to represent the U.S. at meetings of the North Atlantic Salmon Conservation Organization, a position I held until my voluntary resignation in 1990.

Finally, I should emphasize that this work places particular emphasis on the geopolitical and sociological aspects of the conservation effort. Thus it often looks behind the scenes, highlighting and examining the particular issues and positions that motivated the players involved in arriving at trend-setting decisions.

Here then is the story, interspersed with some personal reflections and reminiscences.

PART

I

A SPECIAL
CREATURE

1

Restoration — Genesis

IT IS SPRINGTIME in New England, and along the banks of the lower Connecticut River, white blossoms are falling on the water and drifting lazily downstream on the current. These are the blooms of an old-time and very special shrub, the shadbush, so named because the flowering occurs each year at the very time that the first wave of shad comes in from the ocean.

In early colonial times, this would be the signal for the Yankee farmers and commercial fishermen to get their fishing gear ready, for the silvery salmon — also newly from the sea — always came along right after the shad. They still do.

The Connecticut River from time immemorial boasted the largest Atlantic salmon runs of any river in North America. The 1870 Report of the Commissioners of Fisheries of the State of Connecticut had this to say:

> Records and tradition agree that in olden times salmon and shad filled all our Northern rivers in great abundance. The early settlers frequently alluded to them in letters and public documents. Hendrick Hudson speaks of "the great hordes of salmon" seen by him while ascending the river that bears his name. So common and cheap an article of food were they, that apprentices bound their masters not to serve them at meals oftener than twice a week. In the Connecticut, the salmon were so plentiful that those wishing shad could have them only on condition of taking a like number of salmon. The Housatonic and Thames also abounded with them. The Merrimack swarmed with them, weighing from nine to twelve pounds apiece. The rivers in Maine produced salmon in great numbers, with the Penobscot showing an average annual yield of as many as one hundred fifty thousand of these fish.

The Massachusetts Commissioners of Fisheries four years earlier had reported on the great abundance of salmon in two of the larger river systems, the Connecticut and the Merrimack. It was the habit of the families living in Woodstock, New Hampshire, "to lay in some four barrels of salted salmon, equal to about one hundred fish." At Bellows Falls, fishermen sat in armchairs fastened to ladders, catching salmon with dip nets. And on the Merrimack, a Charles Ramsay of Amesbury, Massachusetts, "customarily would get, with a ninety-yard seine, from sixty to one hundred salmon a day." These fish were "so plentiful in the market that large salmon sometimes sold for only fifty cents apiece."

Those certainly were banner years for the king of the fishes, the Atlantic salmon. It seemed that nature would go right on pouring out its bountiful largess forever. But human beings have an uncanny proclivity for endangering their most valuable resources. And so it would be with the salmon.

Around the beginning of the nineteenth century, the industrial needs of a growing New England population required the building of dams for the purpose of running the mills and hydroelectric stations being built all along the rivers and for providing canals to render river navigation practicable around falls and rapids. On the Connecticut, for instance, a dam erected about 1798 just below the mouth of Miller's River in Massachusetts took only about twelve years to cause the extinction of salmon throughout the entire river system, simply because the major spawning beds were located in the tributaries above that point, which was impassable. On the Merrimack, in 1812, a dam disrupted the runs at Bow, New Hampshire. Finally, by 1848, the closing of the Lawrence Dam in Massachusetts dealt a death blow to any further runs in the whole river system. Thus, with the exception of the Penobscot and a few other Down East rivers in the state of Maine, salmon runs had virtually disappeared in New England.

People still wanted to fish for salmon, however. This common interest brought together the fisheries commissioners from Vermont, New Hampshire, Massachusetts, and Connecticut in

1867 for the purpose of signing an agreement to cooperate in the restocking of the Connecticut River by artificial propagation of eggs from the Penobscot in hatcheries and ponds.

By 1875, about two million fry had been planted, and a small number of returning salmon began to be taken. From then on, the runs increased dramatically, and the fishing pressure became very heavy. Many gill nets were set in the river. And there were some three hundred "pound" nets in operation just between Old Saybrook and Westbrook. (Old Saybrook is in the mouth of the river, and Westbrook is to the west on Long Island Sound; "pound" nets are usually square, set on stakes driven into the bottom, with a funnel entrance and a lead netting along which the fish work.) Yet the fishing was not regulated; no licenses were required, and there were no catch limits. The Connecticut fisheries Commissioners reported in 1879 that "over five hundred full-grown marketable fish were caught."

A salmon river is like a tree, which requires that the sap run freely through the main trunk to the outermost branches before it can be in full bloom. Thus it was feared that the restoration would fail before there was an abundance of fish throughout the tributaries in the northern reaches, where most of the spawning beds were located. So legislation was passed, fining "not less than fifty nor more than five hundred dollars, or imprisoning not less than two nor more than six months, any person taking salmon or grilse, un- less he take such fish unintentionally and immediately restore it to the waters from which it was taken." At first blush, this regulation sounds reasonable, but of course, the easy out was for the poacher to claim that the fish had died while in the net, and there was no sense returning a dead fish to the water.

In truth, the taking of salmon went on as if there were no law. Nearly all the "dead" fish were sent to the New York market, where they were bringing $1.00 to $1.50 a pound — more than any other salmon in the market. With considerable justification, the legislature's Committee on Fisheries took a dim view of this whole situation and denied appropriation of any funds for the restoration, alleging that "it would be useless to propagate salmon if the fishermen were to take all the mature fish on their first return from the sea." From then on, no funding was forthcoming. Over-exploitation always takes its toll, and in this case there was a very steep price indeed — the restoration attempt died a natural death.

Attempts at restoring salmon to the Merrimack River also failed. In 1867, the river was stocked with twenty thousand salmon eggs, and large numbers of eggs, fry, and parr were stocked repeatedly until the 1890s. This project met with some early success, for as many as seventy-five adults were taken in one year to meet hatchery needs at Livermore Falls, above Plymouth, New Hampshire. Salmon did not populate the river for long, however. By 1898, the construction of more dams, severe pollution, and unregulated fishing at the mouth of the river prevented the salmon's passage, and they disappeared entirely.

It is little wonder that after a history of such serious setbacks, there would be no further interest in restoring salmon to these two major river systems for many years.

In Maine, however, the federal government began stocking the Penobscot as early as 1872, and over the years the program met with passable success. In 1947, the state legislature formed the Atlantic Sea Run Salmon Commission, whose objective was to restore runs.

Then, in 1965, the U.S. Congress enacted the Anadromous Fish Conservation Act. An anadromous fish is one — like the salmon, shad, alewives, sturgeon, and most species of eels — that is born in a river, goes to sea to feed and grow strong, and then returns to the river to spawn and renew the life cycle. This opportunity for increased support and funding by the federal government refueled interest in restoring the species throughout the rest of New England. With advanced technology in fish passage facility design, and definite improvements in water quality and fisheries biology, it was now believed that new efforts were warranted in the Connecticut and Merrimack rivers.

On April 20, 1967, top officials of the fish and game commissions of the states of Connecticut, Massachusetts, Vermont, and New Hampshire, and of the U.S. Bureau of Sportfisheries and Wildlife (Department of the Interior) and the U.S. Bureau of Commercial Fisheries (Department of Commerce), signed a Statement of Intent for a Cooperative Fishery Restoration Program for the Connecticut River Basin. It stated: "The intent of this program is to provide the public with high quality sportfishing opportunities in a highly urbanized area as well as to provide for the long-term needs of the population for sea food." This was supplemented on January 17, 1968, by a charter for a policy committee, which would provide direction for a technical committee to manage the resource.

A Statement of Intent for a Cooperative Fishery Restoration Program for the Merrimack River Basin followed on September 29, 1969. The signers represented the official fisheries interests of Massachusetts and New Hampshire and the U.S. Bureau of Sportfisheries and Wildlife and the U.S. Bureau of Commercial Fisheries. The wording of the statement was identical to that of the Connecticut compact, except that in the Merrimack statement of intent the words "for sea food" were changed to: "through development and management of the commercial fishery resources." This was undoubtedly a political ploy to keep open broad options for future exploitation in the ocean and in the river.

These determinations were the beginnings of the current restoration programs now in force throughout New England. They received an enthusiastic response on the part of the general public, and sports fishermen organized conservation and restoration groups in support of restoring a fish indigenous to the region. This result is exclusive to these states, however; attempts to introduce sea-run salmon elsewhere on the East and West coasts have not met with success.

The effort has developed into a coordinated initiative that involves nine states and three federal agencies as well as a number of private-sector organizations. Fish passage facilities around dams have been built, and habitat-enhancement and pollution-control measures have been instituted. There are now ten hatcheries; two of the relatively new federal ones are without peers anywhere. There are also a number of other fish culture facilities, both federally and state owned, throughout the entire region.

These investments of time, money, and labor — reportedly in excess of $300 million — have enabled the wild Atlantic salmon to be returned to virtually all the rivers that were populated in olden times. Great numbers of eggs, fry, and smolts (salmon ready to go to sea) are stocked yearly. Regulatory measures in the New England states do not permit the sale, or the offer of the sale, of Atlantic salmon. Thus there is no incentive for directed commercial operations.

Although the numbers of Atlantic salmon returning to our rivers increased initially, recent results have not lived up to original estimates. Our runs today still number less than six thousand fish annually. With no "hard" past experience to go by, federal and state scientists are having an understandably difficult job determining the causes of these disappointing returns.

The problems are quite naturally divided into two distinctly different areas of concern: in-river and oceanic. The in-river problems should, in time, be overcome by domestic scientific solutions. But the problems of the salmon in the ocean are geopolitical and sociological; on their migrations, the salmon range far and wide, crossing international boundaries to reach their hereditary feeding grounds under jurisdictions of foreign states. Should directed fishing for Atlantic salmon be allowed in the ocean at all? If so, by whom and how much?

Of one thing we can be sure: We should keep in mind that it took nature eons to produce the wild Atlantic salmon. It therefore seems logical to assume that it may take considerably more than the twenty-five years already spent before we will have the full story of how to help the species adjust to the physical impediments and harassments that a modern, materialistic society has heaped on this great fish's hereditary lifestyle.

2

The Life Cycle

WHAT KIND OF CREATURE is this Atlantic salmon, which has captured the minds and emotions of so many people, particularly those of the nations whose shores are washed by the North Atlantic Ocean?

The wild Atlantic salmon is one of nature's most fascinating creatures, with a lifestyle both unique and dramatic. It has a mystique all its own. Here is a fish that undertakes migrations covering thousands of miles in rivers and oceans, encountering and conquering harassments and impediments at every turn — and all under the compulsive drive to grow in size and strength in order to return to its natal river for the ultimate purpose of spawning and renewing the life cycle.

Many writers have tried to explain this mystique, but none has been able to capture completely — much less describe — its full essence. Perhaps you will be able to arrive at your own interpretation of it through a comprehensive view of the Atlantic salmon's life cycle. But first I should explain certain terms:

Salmo salar. The ancient scientific name for Atlantic salmon — the one still in use today — is *Salmo salar.* The Roman armies of Julius Caesar saw great hordes of fish leaping in the rivers of Gaul and called them *Salmo* from the Latin word *salire,* meaning "to leap." In time, someone added the Latin *salar,* in order to define the particular species of the genus salmon. *Salar* is probably from the Latin *salarius,* meaning "of the sea."

Anadromous. All species of salmon — as well as sea trout, shad, sturgeon, herring, and some species of eels — are known as anadromous fish. Such fish are born in fresh water, migrate to the ocean to feed, and then return to fresh water to spawn.

Smolt. A smolt is a juvenile salmon in fresh water ready to go to sea.

Grilse. A salmon that has spent only one winter at sea before returning to its natal river to spawn is referred to as a grilse. They weigh between two and six pounds, depending on the nature, size, and geographical location of their native streams or rivers. Grilse on the angler's line are scrappy fighters and great leapers. They are sexually potent and will spawn with other grilse or with larger salmon that are repeat spawners.

"Wild" salmon. The question is often asked, what is a "wild" salmon? The simplest and most understandable definition is one I received back around 1972 from Colton "Rocky" Bridges, then Director of the Massachusetts Division of Fisheries and Wildlife, who had referred my question to a panel of his biologists: A wild Atlantic salmon is a free-living (my own contribution to the definition) fish, hatched and reared in fresh water — a river, stream, or lake — that migrates to salt water to grow strong in an ocean or sea, then returns to fresh water — usually its natal stream — to spawn and renew the life cycle.

To be sure that it is accurate and appropriate in today's salmon world, I referred this definition to Allen Peterson, Director of the Northeast Fisheries Science Center at Woods Hole on June 26, 1992. He put it up to the other scientists there and wrote me on July 25, 1992, that "all agreed that your definition is fine just the way it is worded. It is clear, direct, and to the point."

*Pacific salmon.** In the Pacific Ocean, there are five different species of Pacific salmon, all of which die after spawning. In sharp contrast, Atlantic salmon have the capability of renewal. Significant numbers — estimated at up to 10 percent — survive the stress of spawning, make their way back to the ocean, recondition themselves in salt water, and return one or more times to spawn again.

*For purposes of this book, the word *salmon* — when used alone — refers to Atlantic salmon.

Gender. In fishery circles, a male salmon is referred to as a cock salmon, a female as a hen salmon.

Now let us take a kaleidoscopic journey through the life cycle of one such Atlantic salmon. To add to the pace and flow of the narrative, I have anthropomorphized this salmon, giving him the name "Salar."

EARLY LIFE IN THE RIVER

Salar is a cock salmon parr, momentarily resting alongside a large rock embedded in the middle of a long, broad run of smooth water usually referred to as the Home Pool, one of the historic salmon spawning grounds of the Wild Ammonoosuc River, a tributary of the Connecticut River. The Home Pool rises in Beaver Lake, a part of the Lost River Reservation, hard under Mount Moosilauke in the White Mountains of northern New Hampshire.

A little over three years ago, on an early November day, Salar was one of some eight thousand eggs deposited by a wild ten-pound hen salmon — and fertilized by a cock salmon — on a redd, or spawning bed, which the hen salmon had constructed in the gravelly bottom of the river. After some eight weeks, he emerged as a tiny alevin, receiving nourishment from a yellow yolk sac on his belly, upon which he fed for several weeks before freeing himself from the loose gravel to begin swimming on his own. Then, as a fingerling, or fry, Salar began to forage for himself on the minuscule insects, crustaceans, and zooplankton that populated the bottom of the river.

When a fry reaches nearly three inches in length, it becomes known as a parr, appearing very much like a small trout, except for eight vertical, brownish stripes on its sides. Salar now begins to feed in the current on midges, mayflies, caddis, and stoneflies, often rising to take these tiny insects as they seek to emerge from the surface.

So here Salar is now, in his accustomed lie, always facing

upstream, usually alongside or just above this large rock just off the main current. This is his territory, which he defends aggressively against all challengers unless, of course, they are larger than he, in which case he flees.

He must constantly be on the lookout for predators such as large trout, bass, mink, otter, kingfishers, and, in particular, the red-headed merganser with its long, thin rasplike beak—perfect for grabbing small fish. This is perhaps the most deadly and voracious of all his enemies—in sharp contrast to our accustomed image of this duck as a handsome and charming decoration on the river, with the hen sailing down the rapids, often with young chicks on her back peering ahead around her neck.

This early training makes Salar "river-smart," acquiring the impulses and reactions to strengthen him for a life of continual vigilance and struggle.

In the late fall, Salar and other parr are present as the big mature salmon return to the Home Pool to engage in the spawning ritual. These parr are precocious and even try to get in the game, darting in and out between the cock and hen salmon. Many of these parr will not live to see the spring. Studies reported in April 1984 by Ken Beland, Chief Aquatic Biologist of the Maine Atlantic Sea Run Salmon Commission, show that lack of forage and severe environmental conditions result in overwinter survival rates of only 40 to 65 percent each year.

So nature has already taken a terrible toll on this year-class of young salmon. Of the original eight thousand eggs, half were immediately swept away by the currents, leaving four thousand in the nest of small rocks and gravel. Half of these were not fertilized by the cock salmon's milt, so only two thousand hatched into alevins. The surviving fry, about sixteen hundred, became parr, which will suffer high rates of mortality during each of the next several years.

DOWN TO THE SEA
It is now late April, and Salar is restless. He takes to cruising around the Home Pool—the waters that he has come to know so well over

the past three years. But, for the first time, he now occasionally turns and faces downstream — with the current instead of against it.

A striking change has come over Salar and his companions in recent days. Their scales have taken on a silvery hue. Along with this, their fins and tails have grown larger in proportion to their bodies, and the fin margins have become black.

The whole process by which a young salmon changes from a parr to a smolt has puzzled scientists for years. It is one of the special wonders of nature and is referred to as *smoltification.* Probably under genetic control, it is generally taken to mean the physiological, endocrinological, and behavioral changes that prepare salmon for migration and adaptation to life in the ocean. It is believed by some scientists that environmental factors such as light and water temperature may trigger the process within the endocrine system.

Nature's purpose in all this seems quite clear. In rivers, salmon lying on the bottom or swimming in the current are seen against a changing background of banks and rocks; here their coloring of mottled greys, browns, and blacks is an advantage. In the ocean, however, salmon are seen both from above, against the dark background of the bottom — hence a dark head and back — and from below (the direction from which predators usually attack), against the bright surface and the sky above — hence the silvery sides and white belly. This is advance camouflage — pelagic coloring.

Changes in behavior are also required. As parr, the salmon are individuals — living on or near the bottoms of streams. But in the ocean they will become pelagic, that is, they will swim in open water and often near the surface. So smolts build up larger amounts of air in their swim bladders than they needed as parr, making them more buoyant. Scientists have postulated that this may also be a factor in originating the desire to migrate downstream.

Salar's metamorphosis is now complete. Some five and a half inches in length, he weighs about three ounces. He is in new raiment. He is a silver swimmer.

Today, the wind comes off the northwest, and the sky lies clear and blue over New England. Salar, now impelled by some unknown force, makes his move. Down he goes, over the ledge that contains the waters of the Home Pool, and into the fast-running rapids. The other salmon follow — only about forty-eight out of the original eight thousand. They commence to run the river down.

Atlantic salmon probably have genetic direction-finding techniques that lead them in the general direction of the salt water. And all the while they are receiving an indelible imprint of the "bouquet," or aroma, of the particular waters through which they pass. This imprinting process is made possible by the salmon's sense of smell, its olfactory system — said to be over a million times more acute than that of humans. While drifting downstream, the fish imprint the entire length of the river on their memories — as if it were a road map. This will stand them in good stead one or more years hence on their return spawning runs, because it will compel the salmon to return unerringly to their rivers and streams of origin.

Salar covers about twenty miles the first day. The Wild Ammonoosuc is indeed wild, and rocky. It is canopied by trees, with big rapids through narrow gorges, calling for all his skills in navigating. He then comes out into smoother water just below the town of Bath, at the river's confluence with the main Ammonoosuc. It is then but a short run to the main stem of the big Connecticut River.

Here Salar swims lazily along with the strong, deep currents, a practice he will follow for the rest of his trip to the mouth of the river. He rests and feeds occasionally. Atlantic salmon do not school tightly like herring, for example. They travel as a loosely integrated group, but they usually close ranks when faced with some new experience or hazard, or when resting.

Several days later, they arrive in the slow-moving water above the Wilder Dam, the first of five major dams on the Connecticut, all of which impound water for the operation of hydro-electric generating stations. At each one, there will usually be four different means of negotiating the barriers. If the spring runoff water is still high, they can be swept over the dam. Or they can descend the fish ladders that have been built principally for fish on upstream migrations. This option is not always available because the ladders are poorly designed for downstream travel; they are not normally opened for this purpose, due to insufficient volumes of water for descending salmon. A third option would be for the salmon to choose the sluiceways designed to carry off logs, trash, and ice. One guiding and often compelling consideration for the fish in the selection process is the pull and volume of the current. Another is the configuration of the river channel just above the dam. In most cases, these two factors combine to lead the fish to the fourth option — the large penstock intake units, which carry heavy volumes of water to the turbines.

Turbines take a terrible toll. It is estimated that mortalities from the whirling blades vary from 4 to 20 percent of any run of salmon, with an average figure of 15 percent generally accepted. Yet these mortalities are only the immediate and visible impacts. Amputations of fins can occur; scale losses may have even more damaging long-term effects. It has been estimated that if a fish loses as much as 30 percent of its scales, ultimate mortality can be expected due to bacterial infections after the fish enters salt water. And "impaction" from different levels of high and low pressures caused by the blades of the turbines can cause internal injuries, with a resultant weakened condition. There is no means of measuring the numbers of chronic illnesses or delayed mortalities that result from these types of injuries.

Salar instinctively follows the main channel, and this draws him into the penstock. It is dark inside, and the water is swift. In spite of losing all control, he is fortunate in not being swept onto the curved blades of the wheels that operate the turbines. Propelled to the exit, Salar is discharged into the lower river. Disoriented, he rests behind a large rock in the streambed. Not all of his siblings are so fortunate. Seven are nowhere to be seen, presumably cut to pieces. Others show evidence of lacerations and loss of protective scales.

The salmon slowly resume their downstream migration. After several days, they come to the next impoundment, the dam at

Bellows Falls, Vermont. Here they go through roughly the same procedure as at Wilder, and there will be three more such obstacles to negotiate—the dam at Vernon in Vermont, and then those at Turners Falls and Holyoke in Massachusetts. Each episode will be a nightmare in itself, with essentially the same grim results.

Finally, the whole experience is over, but at what cost? The odds against coming through alive remind one of a game of Russian roulette, for the cumulative effect of the mortalities alone is staggering. With an estimate of 15 percent average mortality attributable to each hydro location, there will have been a total reduction of some 56 percent of any school of salmon that originally commenced to negotiate all five dams.

And as a result of these hazards, what happened was that out of Salar's original band of forty-eight salmon, only twenty-one are left.

The next hazard occurs in the Springfield-Hartford area, where the water quality is not up to the standard of the rest of the river. Even after substantial cleanups in recent years, industrial wastes here have a high concentration of pollutants and toxicity, contaminating the water. Salar gasps for breath, gills working overtime due to oxygen deficiency. He moves as rapidly as possible to put this area behind him.

He must also be on the lookout for the dangerous resident largemouth bass, whose numbers have increased markedly in recent years since the improvement in water quality of most of the river. One seeks to do him in, but misses.

In the lower Connecticut, conditions are now more relaxing. There are new kinds of fish that Salar never encountered during his early life: shad, alewives, herring, eels, even sturgeon, all up from Long Island Sound. And Salar also encounters a number of big Atlantic salmon—his own kind, but going the other way, commencing their upstream passage to the spawning grounds.

Newly from the sea, these are splendid creatures, silvery, vibrant—sure of purpose, with power and grace of movement. Most weigh between six and seven pounds, yet there are some two sea-winter salmon of ten pounds, and even a few multiple spawners weighing eighteen to twenty-five pounds.

Several, however, give cause for concern. They have suffered deep wounds or gashes on their sides — evidence of attacks by predators such as seals and sharks. A number also have the telltale lines and lacerations from monofilament nets, indicating escapes some weeks ago from the commercial fishermen operating nets off Labrador and west Greenland. In time, these wounds should heal.

Here the Connecticut is smooth-flowing, deep, and heavy, running through fertile farmland and wooded shores. These last few riverine days, however, are not without a special hazard — exposure to one of the most skillful and deadly of all piscatorial predators, large striped bass. They were not present in the river in olden days, but the slight warming of the Long Island Sound in recent years has brought these fish into the Connecticut regularly each spring. These rapacious stripers often travel as far as five to ten miles upriver. And their quarry? The sleek young salmon smolts. The stripers choose to lie in shoals off the mouths of tributaries such as the Salmon River on the lower Connecticut and Roaring Brook in Glastonbury. They are the heavy hitters among predators, gulping down their prey.

And for the first time ever, seals have begun to appear in the Connecticut. They prey on the same small salmon smolts.

In their earlier days, Salar and the others were harassed by all kinds of predators, so by trial and error they have become river-smart. For the most part, they escape, losing only two of their remaining number.

They are now in the estuarine area at Essex, near the mouth of the river. Here, for the first time, they experience a buoyancy due to the admixture of salt water that was not present upriver. So, moving in and out with the tides, they spend a week to ten days acclimatizing themselves to all these invigorating changes.

To recap, back in the Home Pool, only forty-eight of the young salmon had escaped the hazards of upriver predation and pollution and changed into smolts. On the downstream migration, twenty-seven of these smolts perished at the hydro plants, and two became forage for the largemouth bass, the striped bass, or the seals. So these nineteen survivors at the mouth of the river now represent only about one-quarter of 1 percent of the original eight thousand eggs.

This is nature's way — her historic means of ensuring that an adjustable ecological balance among all the creatures of this earth is maintained. This was all well and good — until humankind's intrusion for commercial gain and private profits. We have upset this precarious balance, endangering the survival of many species of wildlife and causing the extinction of more than a few.

Finally, on another clear moonlit night, about one month after leaving the Home Pool, Salar and his small band swim with the ebbing tide out into Long Island Sound. He is embarking on an ocean odyssey — one that will direct him to strange and distant waters.

A NEW WORLD

Salar gives expression to the buoyancy and astringency of salt water by moving out swiftly from the shore, through Plum Gut off Montauk Point, then out past Block Island.

This is a new life — in completely new surroundings: an endless expanse of water; free and easy movement — not constricted by the banks of a river.

This scenario presents a whole new range of adjustments for Salar. He swims mostly in the upper part of the water column, because that is where he finds the best foraging. At first he feeds on insects and small crustaceans, but as he moves along he includes a fish diet that is predominantly juvenile launce (sand eels).

There is a whole new set of potential predators that would do him in: sharks, cod, pollack, silver hake, tuna, and striped bass; and the salt-water mammals, the porpoises, grey seals, and harbor seals — particularly the seals. Since the banning some years ago of the annual seal hunt off Newfoundland, stocks of seals have proliferated to such an extent that the center of population had to move southward, seeking new feeding grounds. They have now populated Cape Cod in great numbers and, for the first time ever, are present off Montauk. And as we have seen, they also visit the Connecticut River.

Large seabirds such as cormorants, shags, and diving ducks also specialize in the taking of smolts.

Salar has to learn how to become ocean-smart, so he constantly moves on, traveling up to twenty-five miles a day, depending on weather conditions and the availability of forage fish. He has now passed Rhode Island and Martha's Vineyard. After rounding the fishhook tip of Cape Cod, he comes along Stellwagen Bank, the shallow sandbar running between Cape Cod and Cape Ann, a prime feeding ground for all kinds of fish. Salar and the other salmon move slowly here, feeding heavily.

And here he encounters a number of specimens of the largest animals on earth, humpback and finback whales. These two species of whales, and others, migrate north in the spring, after wintering in the warm waters of the South Atlantic Ocean for the purpose of giving birth to their calves. They will spend the summer along Stellwagen Bank and off the New England coast.

HEADING DOWN EAST WITH A BUILT-IN COMPASS

Gorged from several days of feeding on Stellwagen Bank, Salar takes off on an easterly course. Interestingly enough, this is the very same direction that was followed many years earlier by the old-fashioned sailing ships, the square-riggers, on their way to ports in Maine, Canada, and Europe. This course gave rise to the popular expression "Down east," and to "state o' Mainers" being called "Down-Easters." The prevailing winds were — and still are — generally southwest, so a square-rigger would follow an easterly course, setting its sails for a following wind. With luck, it would not have to alter direction for the whole trip. Thus, a ship was said to be "running her easting down" — hence, Down East.

Salar, following the same course, was obviously operating

under a different set of controls — one that has long puzzled scientists. What has directed or pulled the Atlantic salmon — from time out of mind — to follow a navigational course leading ultimately to the Labrador Sea, bounded on the south by Newfoundland and the north by Greenland?

To put such a trip in clearer perspective, the ocean distance between the tip of Cape Cod and Cape Race at the eastern tip of Newfoundland is roughly the same as that between New York City and Miami, Florida! This has to be considered another of the great marvels of nature.

In an article in the May 12, 1982, issue of *The Field* magazine (London), Dr. Andrew Allen of Brighton, England, a world authority on migrating animals, pointed out that "scientists have not only found a biological compass built into the animal brain — they have found out an embarrassment of compasses.... Homing pigeons, robins, butterflies and bees all have a magnetic compass built into their brain in the form of micro-crystals of the iron oxide magnetite: the lodestone of the old-time mariners.... The eel has three: astro, magnetic and electro magnetic." In a letter to me dated July 6, 1982, Dr. Allen suggested that "salmon are born with some sort of inherited compass bearing, probably magnetic, on Greenland (this bearing might vary appropriately from breeding region to region).... Salmon probably possess compass senses equivalent to those of the eel — i.e., one or more celestial compasses, a magnetic compass perhaps, and an electromagnetic compass."

Since that time, the work of scientists has continued on this fascinating puzzle. Although a great deal of substance has been added to the scientific literature, so far no one has been able to solve the mystery in a manner completely acceptable to all.

THE GRAND BANKS OF NEWFOUNDLAND

Salar's journey during the late spring and summer months has taken him through New Hampshire and Maine waters, across the Gulf of Maine, and along the Nova Scotia coast. Then from Cape Breton he crosses the Cabot Strait and passes the islands of Saint Pierre and

Miquelon, reaching the St. Pierre Bank and, further on, the Grand Bank, both of which are part of the large feeding-ground complex generally referred to as the Grand Banks of Newfoundland, off the eastern and southern coasts of that island. He lingers here.

In the area of the Grand Banks, the Labrador current and the North Atlantic current (an extension and split-off from the Gulf Stream) meet. Their interlocking fingers of cold and warm water create upwelling conditions favorable to plankton growth, and the resulting rich sea pasture provides one of the world's greatest fishing grounds.

THE LABRADOR SEA

Of salmon in the ocean, it is often said that what we don't know outweighs what we do know. Over the years, however, considerable scientific research has been undertaken with respect to salmon in the northwest Atlantic Ocean.*

The Labrador Sea lies generally north of the Grand Banks and Newfoundland and off the east coast of Labrador, extending to the Davis Strait off the west coast of Greenland. Most people interested in the Atlantic salmon usually refer only to the Davis Strait or the waters off west Greenland as the prime sea feeding grounds of the fish. Yet this is far too narrow a delineation of the boundaries of the salmon's feeding range. It is actually in the whole of the Labrador Sea that salmon are found feeding throughout the

* I wish to acknowledge the substantial contribution of David G. Reddin to the sections "The Grand Banks" and "The Labrador Sea." A scientist with the Canadian Department of Fisheries and Oceans in St. John's, Newfoundland, Dave Reddin is a recognized authority on migrations of Atlantic salmon in the ocean. With his permission and with the benefit of his helpful advice, I adapted much of the substance of several of his many published documents to provide an understanding of this particular — and very important — stage in the salmon's life cycle. See the Bibliography for a listing of the documents used.

year, even though it has been demonstrated that different areas are frequented at certain times on a seasonal basis.

It is a vast expanse of ocean, roughly twice the area of New England, New York State, and Pennsylvania combined, and at least three times larger than Great Britain. The distance from Cape Farewell at the southern tip of Greenland to St John's, Newfoundland, is approximately the same as that from New York City to Key West, Florida.

Great numbers of Atlantic salmon are found here, both of North American origin and from most of the European salmon-producing nations. And here they will stay for at least one winter; many stay for several years. The principal exceptions are salmon of Norwegian origin, some of which prefer to feed off the Lofoten Islands in the Norwegian Sea, as well as around the Faroe Islands. Russian salmon forage in the Arctic Ocean and also come down around the North Cape. Salmon from Iceland are not known to frequent the northwest Atlantic in great numbers; they feed on and around the continental shelf and in the waters off the Faroe Islands.

Here in the Labrador Sea, the salmon commingle indiscriminately and come in all sizes and configurations. These variations are particularly noticeable among the big salmon, the repeat spawners who have returned two or more times to their natal rivers for spawning.

Natural selection is practical, choosing qualities that will be useful for the purpose intended. The nature and requirements of different river habitats have dictated and molded the body structures of the fish over many thousands, perhaps millions, of years, proof of Charles Darwin's theory of the inheritance of acquired characteristics. To give just a few examples—we find here the large and powerful salmon from the Grand Cascapedia River in Quebec, reflecting the qualities of that river. The Sevogle, a small branch of the Northwest Miramichi in New Brunswick, sends small but very stocky fish. The Serpentine River, a tributary of the Tobique, also in New Brunswick, produces strong, wiry fish from its shallow, rocky stream. From Scotland, the heavy and relatively slow-moving

Tweed contributes bulky salmon, with a particularly big one being referred to by the English as a Portmanteau. Salmon from Scottish highland rivers, however, such as the Dee with its upstream rapids, are lean and well-formed. In the United States, the large Penobscot River has good-sized, muscular salmon. And for beauty and grace, none surpasses the sleek, well-proportioned fish of the big Connecticut River. Rivers as far distant as the Eo and Narcea in Spain also send salmon to the Labrador Sea. So this is the kind of company in which Salar finds himself as the first winter of his ocean migration approaches.

The question keeps arising in people's minds: What are the special characteristics that set the Labrador Sea apart from other regions of the northwest Atlantic and make it the feeding grounds of choice for the salmon? And for so long a stay? There appear to be at least two such reasons.

The Labrador Sea Gyre. Conditions throughout the entire Labrador Sea are strongly affected by a set of extraordinary circumstances that combine to form a huge ocean gyre — a dramatic example of one of nature's many phenomena. In effect, what happens is that, perhaps under the influence of the earth's rotation, a circumferential flow of merging currents — counterclockwise in direction — shapes an irregular boundary around the edges of the Labrador Sea. And, as was the case in the Grand Banks area, the conflict between the joining flows of water — some cold or icy and some warmer — continues here and there around the gyre and causes a series of eddy systems, which in turn encourages an abundance of nutrients and thus salmon and other fish. It is fascinating to let one's imagination drift with this gyre — this circular motion — and visualize the infusion of new currents that merge to send the whole upon its way.

The relatively warm North Atlantic current runs in a northeasterly direction from the Grand Banks of Newfoundland and soon forms a spinoff known as the Irminger current. Irminger ultimately bends in a long curve westward toward Greenland. There

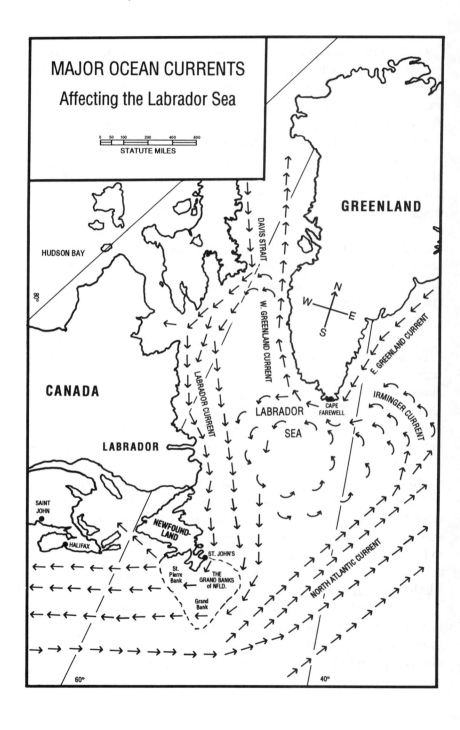

MAJOR OCEAN CURRENTS
Affecting the Labrador Sea

0 50 100   200   400   600
STATUTE MILES

GREENLAND

DAVIS STRAIT

HUDSON BAY

80°

W. GREENLAND CURRENT

N
W — E
S

E. GREENLAND CURRENT

CANADA

LABRADOR CURRENT

LABRADOR

CAPE FAREWELL

IRMINGER CURRENT

LABRADOR

SEA

SAINT JOHN

NEWFOUND-LAND

HALIFAX

ST. JOHN'S

St. Pierre Bank

THE GRAND BANKS of NFLD.

Grand Bank

NORTH ATLANTIC CURRENT

60°

40°

it gives up its direction of flow as it meets up with the big, strong east Greenland current, which courses southerly and is so cold that in July it is still carrying icebergs that calved from the glaciers far to the north in the Denmark Strait and beyond. Off Cape Farewell, at the tip of Greenland, these two flows — now merged — form the west Greenland current, which moves northerly up the coast. Before entering the Davis Strait, however, part of this current — continuing the gyre system — veers off westward to join the strong Labrador current. This flows southerly, having originated far up north in Baffin Bay. The Labrador current is cold and can also carry icebergs; it drifts southward along the long Labrador coast and then moves across the northeast coast of Newfoundland, where a part of it splits off in an easterly direction to join the North Atlantic current, thus closing the circle — and preserving the integrity, so to speak — of the whole gyre complex. The remaining main part of the Labrador current curls on down around Cape Race into the Gulf of St. Lawrence.

Migrating salmon of Canadian and United States origin enter the gyre and eddy system from the south in the area of the Grand Banks. Then, after one or more winters spent feeding in the Labrador Sea and its environs, these fish leave for their return migration by reentering the gyre and using the counterclockwise drift to the point of departure, perhaps from the St. Pierre Bank off the southern coast of Newfoundland. Similarly, salmon of European origin enter the eddy by joining the Irminger current in the area to the southwest of the Faroe Islands and leave to return to home waters at or near this same entry point.

The Temperature Factor. It would be natural to assume that migrating salmon would always seek out those ocean areas where the quality and quantity of food meet their requirements. Yet David Reddin's research indicates that satisfactory sea surface temperature is the determining factor and that salmon are opportunistic feeders, preying on whatever organisms are available. In this connection, Dave has this to say:

Salmon are a cold-blooded species in that their body temperature will be about the same as the sea water surrounding it. All body functions are to a certain extent temperature controlled and all species have temperature ranges over which their metabolism functions best. For salmon, this is in the range of 4–12°C. Temperatures above and below this result in a slowing down of body functions including growth and maturation and if it is too much above or below then death results. Thus, most species including salmon will go to some efforts to ensure they remain in their optimum temperature range. This is why the Labrador Sea is so important to North American salmon as all the year round there are always areas with suitable sea surface temperatures for the salmon's life and growth.

It has been shown that perhaps as many as 80 percent of the salmon are located mainly in areas with these sea temperatures. Research vessel catches indicate that in spring, salmon are commonly found in the area of the Grand Banks; in summer, they move northward off West Greenland and up into the Davis Strait. It is believed that in winter they frequent those parts of the southern Labrador Sea where the appropriate temperatures can normally be found. Dave Reddin also points out:

> The presence of sea ice, which lowers sea surface temperatures, probably acts to modify salmon movements, and water of low surface temperature appears capable of deflecting salmon from their recognized migrational pathway, as they are disinclined to pass through it, even though warmer water may be beyond. And since most fishing gear set to catch Atlantic salmon is passive, and depends on the fish moving into it, any changes in the pathway of the fish can have a major influence on catch rates.

LIVING IT UP

Salar has spent September and most of October on the southwestern part of the Grand Banks, feeding particularly on those two staples of a salmon's diet — capelin and sand eels. In late fall he moves on, up into the southern part of the Labrador Sea, where the interactions of the cold Labrador current and the warmer waters of the North Atlantic current produce an abundance of nutrients, fostering a rich food chain.

We know about the diets of salmon from analyses of stomach contents, reported from catches of research vessels. Salmon in the southern Labrador Sea prey on a wide variety of organisms indeed: herring; squid; barracudina (a fish closely related to lantern fish); a type of krill called euphausiids, closely related to the shrimplike organisms that form the bulk of the diet of whales and other creatures in the Antarctic; and amphipods, another shrimplike crustacean, reddish in color and — interestingly enough — credited with imparting the reddish-orange color to a salmon's flesh.

Salar will remain here in the relatively warm waters, for he is one of those salmon genetically programmed to remain in the ocean for more than two winters. So in the spring he returns and feeds over the Grand Banks. Here his food will be 93 percent sand eels and capelin, and occasionally shrimp larvae and barracudina. He will even venture out over the oceanic depths to the east of the Grand Banks, where his diet changes to only about 68 percent fish, such as barracudina and black smelt, and 32 percent invertebrates, almost entirely amphipods.

In his second summer at sea, Salar moves up off the Grand Banks and into the North Atlantic current. Coming under the influence of the gyre, he soon finds himself in the flow of the Irminger current, where it bends over toward Greenland. Once off Cape Farewell, he follows the west Greenland current, close up against the land. Salmon concentrate here in the summer and early fall months, with their feeding range extending from the inner coastal fjords out to as far as twenty-five to thirty-five miles offshore. Their principal forage is capelin and sand eels. Some of the salmon venture up into the Davis Strait, depending, as usual, on environmental conditions, particularly satisfactory sea surface temperatures.

It is now well over a year — some sixteen months — since Salar first started down the Connecticut River. He has grown considerably in size, now weighing over seven pounds.

By late summer, Salar has drifted with that part of the west Greenland current that veers off toward Labrador and finds himself moving down the coast with the Labrador current and then out beyond the entrance to the Strait of Belle Isle and off the northeast coast of Newfoundland. Here he slows his progress and moves in and out of the Twillingate area of Notre Dame Bay, where, for some reason not fully understood, salmon of U.S. origin have been found concentrated in considerable numbers at this time of year. He stays here until well into November, feeding on capelin and sand eels.

CAPELIN

Capelin and sand eels are the food of choice for the salmon wherever these forage fish are found in the northwest Atlantic. The capelin, in particular, warrants some special attention, for a number of reasons.

Almost everything that lives in the ocean feeds extensively on capelin. To name the principal predators: among the fishes — tuna, cod, haddock, salmon, herring, and flounder; among mammals — whales and seals; and among the seabirds — puffins, kittiwakes, gannets, murres (a diving duck), terns, and gulls.

Newfoundlanders have always fished for capelin, using them as fertilizer for gardens, bait, and food for dog teams, as well as for human consumption.

A member of the smelt family, a mature capelin is long and thin, averaging a little over six inches in length. It is ferocious looking, like a big barracuda, with big eyes. Its hue is silvery green.

The nature of its spawning ritual is weird and exciting. It takes place on the beach, a custom shared by only one other fish that we know of — the grunion, off the Pacific Coast of North America. Some twenty years ago, it was my good fortune to be able to witness this drama one July day near Corner Brook, Newfoundland. We went out to a small fishing village near the entrance to Humber Arm, where there is a smooth, sandy beach. It was late afternoon, and a number of townspeople were already present on the beach—in rubber boots and with buckets in hand. Thousands of capelin were in the small bay; they were on their spawning run. The annual "capelin scull" was ready to begin, for these fish make a tasty meal.

The male capelin wait close to the beach. When the female feels that her time is at hand, she comes in, riding a large wave, where she is joined by one or two males. Together they swim up the beach as far as possible and then settle in as the wave runs out. Ridges along the sides of the males hold the smaller females in place. A small depression is hollowed out by the fins and tails; each hen fish deposits thousands of eggs, and the males ejaculate their milt. The hen fish then attempt to ride a retreating wave back to deep water. Some make it. The males continue to spawn with other hen fish and then are so worn out that most of them die.

Capelin eggs are tough and sticky, attaching themselves to grains of sand and gravel. Without this glue, waves would quickly wash the eggs away. The larvae emerge after only a few days, and at high tide they make their way out into the bay.

In the 1970s, a large offshore capelin fishery developed off Labrador, northeastern Newfoundland, and on the Grand Banks, using midwater trawlers and purse seiners. The Soviet Union and Norway were the big operators, taking about 80 percent of the total, with Iceland, Poland, Spain, Japan, Portugal, and East Germany joining in the harvest. Total offshore catches by foreign vessels continued to rise until 1976, when they peaked at 266,000 tons. Small wonder that catches dropped sharply thereafter. The Canadian government had to restrict the catch so severely that the fishery virtually disappeared.

The Japanese know a good thing when they see it, and in recent years, they have been buying capelin from the Newfoundlanders. They want only the roe, which is a gourmet item in Japan, so the males are discarded from the nets. The prices offered by the Japanese buyers have kept everyone else out of the market. Fortunately, capelin stocks were able to support landings considerably higher than the amounts caught. The local inshore fishery has been managed by Canada in terms of the size of the Japanese market, which is well within the conservation levels required to ensure the health of the resource.

Yet the abundance of capelin can swing wildly from one year to the next. In 1992, the biomass estimates were so low that the offshore capelin fishery was closed for 1993 by the North Atlantic Fisheries Organization (NAFO). Thus the question will always remain as to how much and in what way the capelin resource can be reduced by a commercial fishery without serious detriment to all those predators that rely on this little fish for a major share of their sustenance. This calls for continual vigilance, and so far the government of Canada seems keenly attuned to this problem.*

THE RETURN MIGRATION

As the second winter of his ocean migration approaches, Salar leaves the Twillingate region and moves once again to the relatively warm waters of the southern reaches of the Labrador Sea. He remains in a general area some three hundred miles east of the Strait of Belle Isle, where large concentrations of salmon customarily overwinter.

Then, in late January, along with thousands of other salmon, Salar seeks out the southwestern part of the Grand Banks, using it as a sort of staging area for what is to come.

Salar is now technically classed as a "two-plus sea-winter salmon." He is strong, streamlined, and agile.

Now he responds to a new urgency. Something has taken over his purpose, his direction. Salar and the others move along the south shore of Newfoundland and pick up, in reverse, the migration route that they followed several years ago on the way up to the Labrador Sea. Traveling easily and steadily, they average about

* Portions of this information about the capelin and its commercial fishery were excerpted from "The Science of Capelin," published by the Communications Branch, Department of Fisheries and Ocean, St. John's, Newfoundland, Canada.

twenty-five miles a day, depending on the weather, oceanic conditions, and the time spent feeding.

As they pass along Nova Scotia, New Brunswick, and Maine, small runs of salmon peel off to return to their natal rivers.

SEALS

Further down the coast of Maine, off Monhegan Island, as the school is feeding on shrimps along a rocky ledge, Salar is attacked by a large grey seal, seeking to cut him in half and then quietly enjoy a big repast. Luckily, Salar is quick enough to avoid the full impact. Even so, the seal comes away with a rich morsel, which seems to satisfy it. Once he has fled to a safe distance behind a ledge, Salar, exhausted and in semishock, languishes for some time without moving. Then he joins the other salmon, still feeding on shrimps. He is left with a long, narrow gash on his left shoulder, but he is strong and healthy, and the wound begins to heal quickly with scar tissue. He will carry a scar from this experience.

A few years ago, the public's general impression of seals was based on an image of cute little white-coated, puppy-faced, bewhiskered animals being cruelly slaughtered by Eskimos and Newfoundlanders for their fur to make coats and hats. Such a hue and cry was raised by conservation groups that the government of Canada was forced to call a halt to what had been a legally mandated and controlled culling of the seal herds.

There is now a need for a broader perspective on this whole problem. As expected, due to the ban on their harvest, stocks of seals have proliferated exponentially — to such an extent, in fact, that their forage requirements may be an important factor in the steep decline of world stocks of valuable fish such as cod, haddock, salmon, and other species.

What is certain is that populations of seals have become so great that they have had to seek new sources of forage fish, spreading out from their normal feeding grounds and migrating northward along the rocky shores of Labrador and Greenland as well as southward into the waters off the Maine coast. Several years ago, for the first time ever, seals began to populate Cape Cod; in the last few years, they have been seen regularly off Martha's Vineyard and Montauk Point. And, as noted earlier, they go up the Connecticut River to prey on the thousands of young salmon smolts on their first trip down to the ocean.

Actually, the public's image of seals as doglike and charming belies their nature and lifestyle. They are among the most skillful predators in the animal kingdom — efficient and deadly. Seals are also among the most wasteful of predators; once they have gorged on their victims, they continue to kill just for the sport of it. I have witnessed several such exhibitions, and one such occasion is vividly etched in my memory.

I was on a salmon trip to the Big River, about a third of the way up the Labrador coast. Just before it meets the bay, the Big River splits up into a delta of three or four small tidal streams. I was fishing there one evening, and, not having had even a rise to my fly, I decided to sit down on a rock to relax and enjoy the sunset. Almost immediately, it became apparent that there was something unusual going on out there in the bay. The commotion turned out to be a herd of twenty grey seals rolling and turning as they came in toward the river. And then it became obvious what was happening.

A salmon run was on, and the seals were in a feeding frenzy. They barred the way to the delta, slashing at the salmon, sometimes killing them. They scarcely paused to gulp down one chunk of meat before they moved on to attack another fish. Although the appetites of some of the seals were already satiated, they continued the plunder, simply playing with the fish, taking the salmon in their jaws, tossing them in the air, and cutting them in half as they fell.

All this carnage attracted a horde of seagulls. They got into the act, climbing, wheeling, and swooping as they snatched for leftovers — all the while shrieking.

I watched, mesmerized, for about half an hour. And then suddenly the raucous clamor died down just as quickly as it had started. The gulls left, and the seals took off down the bay. It became quiet. The spectacle was over, but never to be forgotten.

This was another reminder — and a rather grim one — of nature's way. It was an example of the predator and prey relationship at its most dramatic. From that time on, I lost most of the affection that I had ever had for the seals. Here they had revealed their true nature.

Seals are obviously a problem. If present trends continue and the imbalance increases, governments will simply have to find acceptable ways of culling the seal herds. Scientific research needs to be undertaken now to determine how to accomplish this rationally and humanely.

THE OLFACTORY IMPRINT

The homing route of the salmon now takes them off the shores of New Hampshire and then around Cape Cod and on to Nantucket Sound, Vineyard Sound, and Rhode Island Sound.

Salar has another nasty experience off Block Island. A two-foot lamprey fastens onto his flank with its rasping teeth. It is a vicious, bloodsucking predator, slowing down his progress for over a day. Salar finally shakes free of this creature, after he has lost considerable blood and the lamprey is finally satisfied. This round wound, about the size of a U.S. quarter, will heal slowly, with Salar bearing the scar for some months.

Somewhere along this route, the genetic olfactory imprint of the Connecticut River takes over Salar's direction and that of the rest. Guided and buoyed by this inner driving force, the salmon quicken their speed, traveling higher in the water column and nearer the surface. They overtake several other loosely integrated schools of Atlantic salmon heading in the same direction — west. Perhaps they were all of the same year-class but from one of the other main tributaries of the Connecticut.

There have been many theories about what directs salmon to return from ocean migrations to their rivers of origin. Arthur D.

Hasler, the early and still acknowledged authority on this subject, in his book *Underwater Guideposts*, points out:

> Speculations on the functions of homing bring up the difficult question of whether heredity or conditional response is the factor which determines to what breeding ground an individual migrates or whether perhaps the two work in concert. Thus, while we can appraise the results of homing, the fundamental reasons remain in the realm of conjecture.

It is widely believed, however, that when a salmon comes within a few miles or so of its natal river or stream, some kind of olfactory memory bank takes over, recalling for the fish the aroma or bouquet of that particular water, which was imprinted on its brain during its juvenile stage and its original downstream migration to the ocean. Apparently, a salmon follows that bouquet not to just any part of that river but to the exact same tributary and stream where it began as a fertilized egg.

Hasler has this to say on the subject:

> We have demonstrated that fishes are able to discriminate effectively between natural waters and that the distinguishing characteristic in each water is perceived by the olfactory organs, indicating that the factor is an odor.... The final and crucial test of the odor hypothesis, then, is to show whether fishes are capable of "remembering" imprinted odors over a long period of time.

Further experiments by Hasler indicate that certain odorous substances are probably carried into a stream by runoff from the vegetation and soil of a watershed. These combine with the bouquet of the aquatic flora and fauna to give the stream a distinctive scent that can be perceived, learned, and recognized by fish even after a long absence, such as the year or more an Atlantic salmon spends in the ocean.

There's an interesting sidelight having to do with this odor business. Scientific tests indicate that the salmon's keen sensitivity to odors enables it to detect from some distance the presence of certain predators, such as seals and other mammals — including humans. The particular odor that all mammals produce and give off through their skin is said to be an amino acid. Hasler cites an instance in which the odors given off by children swimming well upstream from a salmon pool excited the salmon sufficiently to send them elsewhere. Thus, it is not at all farfetched to remind salmon fishermen wading downstream, or fishing from a canoe, to avoid putting their hands in the water!

THE NATAL RIVER
Passing by Montauk Point, Salar finally pulls up with the others just off the mouth of the Connecticut River, relishing the feel of fresh water once again as its cool column mingles with the salt currents. He and the other salmon, making up a school of about fifteen fish, tarry for a few days as the tides take them in and out of the Connecticut River estuary, allowing them to undergo the physiological changes that will acclimatize them back to fresh water.

The whole run of salmon has been plagued by sea lice, tiny horseshoe crab–like insects that attach themselves at the base of the salmon's ventral and anal fins. These parasites take minuscule amounts of blood from their hosts and remain attached for about forty-eight hours — even as the salmon enter fresh water. Thus, if anglers take salmon well upstream with sea lice still attached, they know that the fish are truly fresh-run.

Finally, a high tide brings water levels that tempt the run to move into the main stream of fresh water. As he leaves the ocean, Salar now weighs over ten pounds. When salmon enter a river on their final spawning runs, they stop feeding. They live on the body fat that they have stored up after one or more winters feeding in the ocean.

We know that roughly 90 percent of the Atlantic salmon will die after spawning. Those that survive the stress will experience one of two fates. If the spawning grounds are located not far from salt water, they may be able to make their way down to the ocean to rehabilitate and recondition themselves. If the spawning grounds are well upriver, the fish will probably be forced to undergo the tribulations of spending the winter under the ice.

"BLACK" SALMON

By next spring, after a winter under the ice, what kind of condition are these spawned-out salmon in? Emaciated, lean, and weakened from lack of nourishment, they have probably lost over 25 percent of their body weight. Now known as black salmon, or kelts, they are ravenous and start moving downstream, their purpose being to reach salt water once again and feed heavily. They range along the riverbanks or in midstream, anywhere they might find sustenance.

In this condition, they are an easy catch for poachers and meat-hunting fishermen. Although black-salmon fishing for Atlantic salmon is frowned upon by most anglers and prohibited on rivers in North America, there is one exception — an early spring fishery for these salmon on the Miramichi River in New Brunswick. It has long been a subject of controversy, and there appears to be no excuse or justification for the government of Canada or the province of New Brunswick to permit it. On scientific grounds alone, it is not warranted. The Canadian government has reported in recent years that the spawning requirements for Atlantic salmon have not been met on the "index" (i.e., major) rivers — such as the Miramichi — with respect to multi-sea-winter (large) salmon. Therefore, every single black salmon that can make its way back to the salt water and recondition itself for another spawning run would be a plus for the future.

DESTINY

Salar's initial run upstream is free and easy. He presses against the strong, heavy current and even jumps clear of the current, as if to express a new jubilation.

Fortunately, Salar avoids the shad nets that have been set

upriver from the mouth. These are gill nets and take an estimated 4 percent of returning salmon. This shad fishery is a holdover from the past, with licenses from the state of Connecticut passed down from one generation to the next.

The shad resource itself has been restored as a byproduct — and a very valuable one — of the salmon restoration. In fact, stocks are now greater than ever because the fishways built for the salmon have opened new shad spawning grounds upriver. In recent years, for instance, upwards of 400,000 shad have passed over the Holyoke Dam.

Further on, the Connecticut Yankee Atomic Power Plant at Haddam poses no problem at present. A heated effluent of water is used to cool the turbines; after running through a mile-long canal, this discharges into the main stream at 20°F warmer than the main stream and influences water temperatures for as much as two miles downstream. Fortunately, the deepest part of the river channel, which the salmon always use, is along the other side of the river. Migrating fish are safe for the time being, unless the channel should seek a different course.

The salmon run halts momentarily at the Enfield Dam above Hartford, a "low-rise" dam originally some six feet high. Now in disrepair, the dam is breached in several places, so the salmon surmount it with ease.

Along the way, significant numbers of the run have been moving off into tributaries such as the Salmon River and, later on, below Springfield, Massachusetts, the Farmington River.

The first big barrier is the hydroelectric dam at Holyoke, with its elevator for raising migrating fish over the dam. This Holyoke operation can be described as sort of a Rube Goldberg affair, principally because it was the first fish-passage facility on the river, and the design has had to be modified from time to time. The best that can be said for it is that it gets the job done.

Salar moves into the "attraction water," which flows along a concrete abutment designed to produce the fast water to which salmon always gravitate. This leads him up into the "crowder," which pushes him from behind into the elevator cage. Here he is herded in with other salmon as well as shad, river herring, eels, and any other fish that happen to be around. They are lifted some forty feet up and deposited in the lake impounded behind the dam. A few of these fish do not make it as a result of the banging around they get and being part of a mass of thrashing, squirming fish. Shock and stress do them in.

After this experience, Salar seeks out a restful spot in the reservoir above the dam. This is deep water, so he positions himself in front of a huge boulder on the bottom, around which there is a smooth flow of slow-moving water. Several days later, he resumes his travels.

Next, Salar comes up to the Turners Falls fish ladder, which bypasses the next dam above the one at Holyoke. It is modern—a concrete stairway with resting pools between steps. Salar completes this trip with apparent ease.

A RIVER REVERSES ITS DIRECTION

It seems that harassments are a way of life for salmon migrating upstream. Now the salmon run comes up against what must be the most bewildering experience of all, passing by the Northfield Mountain Pumped Storage Facility several miles above Turners Falls.

A huge pipe (large enough to hold a subway car) pumps water from the Connecticut River (at the rate of ten thousand cubic feet per second) up to the top of Northfield Mountain, then sends it back down again in order to generate electricity, with any excess filling a giant reservoir. The long-term plan calls for this reservoir to act as a backup for Quabbin Reservoir (a principal source of water for the city of Boston many miles away). This massive extraction of water, taken out of the lake formed by the Turners Falls impoundment below, actually makes the river current run upstream during peak periods of pumping.

This is extremely disorienting to Salar and the others. Because salmon always face into a current in order to ingest the oxygenated water, they momentarily turn about and face downstream. Fortunately, the pumping was at the end of its cycle, and the river current soon resumes its normal course. Once turned around again, the salmon regain the normal steady flow of the river. Obviously, it is not possible to measure just how much stress an experience of this kind can inflict on fish.

The full story of the effect of this pumped storage facility on Atlantic salmon (and shad and other fish) has yet to be told. Already, young salmon smolts migrating downstream have been entrained in the pipe and deposited ignominiously into the reservoir near the top of Northfield Mountain. The possible intake of grilse and salmon migrating upriver is also awaiting assessment.

And if mortalities turn out to be high, what is to be done about that? It seems incredible that problems of this nature were not anticipated early on, addressed, and resolved by federal and state authorities and the utility company involved.

THE FINAL HURDLES

Now Salar lazes along, for it is late July, with the dog days of August approaching. The river temperature can reach 65–70°F, an enervating climate for cold-water fish like the salmon, which prefer cool, oxygen-rich waters.

In late summer, as the salmon run approaches the fish ladders that will facilitate their passage over the dam at Vernon, Vermont, they are momentarily confused and slowed by a sudden rise in water temperature. This situation is similar to that which occurred at Haddam and is caused by the heated effluent of water that is used to cool the turbines at the atomic energy plant. This is stressful and tiring, so after surmounting the ladders, they spend several days relaxing before resuming their laborious journey.

There are only two more fish ladders to negotiate — those at Bellows Falls and Wilder Dam in New Hampshire. This they accomplish with ease, for the experience has become almost a way of life.

The fish hole up whenever they reach rapids and riffles in the main stem of the river, now markedly smaller and faster-

flowing. Arriving in late October at the confluence of the Ammonoosuc and the Connecticut, Salar, still impelled by his olfactory
senses and followed by other cock and hen salmon, chooses the
smaller tributary.

FULFILLMENT

Early one afternoon, they all reach the big Home Pool. The hen fish
move ahead. Slowly circling, each looks the place over carefully, apparently seeking quiet, shallow stretches, often near the banks.
Some of them check the remains of last year's redds and then move
on to build their own.

Anyone who has witnessed the spawning rites of salmon
will never forget it.

Atlantic salmon do not pair bond. They are polygamous,
with the hen salmon accepting any cock salmon that can dominate
her and fend off challenging rivals.

Each hen fish "cuts" her redd in slow-moving water that is
generally between twelve and twenty-four inches deep and often off
the edge of a riffle. Turning on her side, she vigorously propels jet
streams of water with her strong tail, scooping out the loose gravel
underneath. The redd will be roughly horseshoe-shaped, with the
open ends facing upstream and the gravel higher at the tail end.

Salar is now attending one particular hen fish, weighing
about ten pounds. He is soon challenged by another cock salmon
that attempts to draw close. Salar repulses the intruder by vicious
attacks and chases him all over the river. Other cock fish engage in
similar kinds of activity; at times, the whole place is a melee of
thrashing fish. It continues until sunset.

The next day is spent quietly resting. The hen fish is on the
redd, waiting only for an impulse to achieve her purpose. Salar is
positioned alongside. Every now and then he still has to repulse
some competitive lone male. Then, in the late afternoon, his partner
feels that her time is at hand. She turns on her side.

The spawning is elegant and vibrant—two bodies quivering
rhythmically. There is no actual physical union, but the act suffers

FIVE PHOTOGRAPHS OF SPAWNING SALMON FROM OLD STREAM, 1980. Courtesy of K. Beland, Atlantic Sea Run Salmon Commission, Bangor, Maine.

1. *Male salmon* (left) *approaches female prior to spawning.*

2. *Female salmon* (right) *digging redd prior to spawning.*

3. Male (left) *and female immediately prior to spawning.*

4. The spawning act. Male salmon on left.

5. *Female salmon* (right) *burying eggs after spawning.*

no loss of drama because of this. It expresses a simultaneous joining, an ecstasy all its own. Salar ejaculates his milt at the exact moment that she spills forth her eggs. The eggs sink into the nest of
gravel with a cloud of white milt enveloping both of them.

What kind of mental telepathy, or extrasensory perception,
has triggered Salar's response? Or is it perhaps an olfactory message
— a pheromone — given off by the hen salmon when she is about to
bring forth her eggs? It is another of nature's mysteries.

All the while, a few young salmon parr are darting in and
out, trying to participate. Several actually ejaculate milt, for, as tests
have shown, they are sexually potent. The parr then finally turn
cannibalistic and eat some of the eggs floating downstream that
failed to find lodging in the redd.

Salar and the hen fish repeat the action several times until the hen is fully spent. She then covers the eggs, some eight thousand of them, with gravel in the same fashion — jet water propulsion — that she used in building the redd to begin with.

Salar and his partner now become completely indifferent to each another. They split up, with the hen slipping slowly downstream.

Salar moves to take up a position alongside a rock in the slow current near the bottom lip of the pool. His great strength has ebbed. He rests, and total weariness overtakes him. It is all over. No longer is there any incentive to continue the fight for survival. He has fulfilled his mission — the renewal of the life cycle. Salar just drifts away — perhaps into some Nirvana of his own.

Sic transit gloria mundi.

II

OVEREXPLOITATION

1962 – 1969

3

Storm Clouds

THE WILD ATLANTIC SALMON is the most valuable fish that swims, offering a wide range of benefits to society. Aesthetically, we thrill at the sight of salmon leaping falls and big rapids in their compelling desire to reach the spawning grounds. Recreationally, fishing for Atlantic salmon has always been considered the most exciting and demanding of all piscatorial sports. As a food, it is without peer; cooked or smoked, it is considered a gourmet item at the table as well as a nutritionally valuable protein, for it contains Omega 3, the polyunsaturated fatty acid that appears to be effective in decreasing the risk of heart disease and may even retard the growth of tumors. Economically, fishing for salmon generates a tremendous amount of income for the tourist trade, sportfishing equipment manufacturers, and outfitters.

Yet human beings often have the curious habit of endangering those things they treasure most. Nations generally have failed to discharge the principal obligation incumbent upon any government that permits the exploitation of renewable natural resources for personal pleasure or private profit: the responsibility of maintaining the resource at least at the level of abundance that existed when the exploitation commenced. As far as salmon are concerned, these governments, with a few notable exceptions, have failed to limit commercial fishing operations to ensure that adequate and sustainable numbers of salmon escape upriver to spawn and renew the life cycle. This has led to the predictable effect of reducing the catch for all harvesters of Atlantic salmon, commercial and sport fishermen alike. Let us take a look at how this sad state of affairs began.

TYPES OF FISHING OPERATIONS

For the purposes of this chronicle, the methods of conducting commercial fishing operations for salmon in the ocean can be defined in general terms. Actually, these operations fall into only two general categories: those on the high seas or offshore, and those that are inshore or coastal.

High seas fishing is done from boats in the ocean that set either driftnets or long lines. Driftnets are usually gill nets (salmon swim into them and are caught by the gills) with one end attached to a boat. These boats may be small, handled by one or two fishermen, in which case the nets are only about thirty feet long. Driftnets can also be rolled out to a distance of thirty miles or more from drums on large oceangoing fishing vessels requiring larger crews. Long-lines are what the name implies, a long line usually suspended between buoys in the water and sunk a few feet below the surface, from which baited hooks are hung at regular intervals.

Inshore fishing calls for fixing one end of a net to the shore, using either a set gill net or mesh netting that directs the fish into a trap. There are also "stake" nets, "bag" nets, and other different designs that are peculiar to certain nations or regions. Coastal netting usually operates on the same principle but from headlands, with long nets set out from the shore and wound in by engines. In Great Britain, these are referred to as fixed engines.

DRIFT NETTING COMES OF AGE

After World War II, drift netting and long-lining for salmon began in earnest on both sides of the North Atlantic Ocean. These pursuits burgeoned into a new means of livelihood for great numbers of commercial fishermen.

By the 1960s, government agencies in Scotland had determined that drift netting had depleted stocks to such a point that it had to be prohibited by law, under an order issued September 15, 1962. At the same time, a committee, under the chairmanship of Lord Hunter, was named to study and recommend ways and means of controlling the taking of salmon. The Hunter committee's first report of July 1963 — identified as HMSO (Her Majesty's Stationery Office) 2096 — reported on progress and defined the various types of nets. The committee's second report (HMSO 2691) of August 1965 recommended that (1) "drift net fishing at sea should not be resumed," (2) "coastal netting by fixed engines should be ended," and (3) "the commercial catch for a river should be made at a single point, preferably by a trap or by a concentrated net fishery associated wherever possible with a counting device."

It is important to note that these findings by the Hunter committee were soon recognized by the entire Atlantic salmon community as being of landmark importance. And indeed, the third recommendation by the committee was to become (as we shall see later) the foundation upon which many organizations would base their opposition to driftnetting on the high seas.

In Norway, the local fishermen had been driftnetting for years in the fjords from small boats close inshore. By the late 1960s, this fishery reached its peak, with over five hundred boats participating. A bulletin (No. 190) put out by the Sport Fishing Institute (SFI) of Washington, D.C., reported that Norwegian officials were concerned that the nation's salmon stocks were being depleted. Because salmon spawn only in streams, they believed that the rivers should be assured of a sufficient share of the annual run, yet during the past decade, the river part of the catch had declined from 15 percent to only 10 percent of the total.

Offshore, however, it was the Danes who became the big operators. As the SFI bulletin also pointed out:

> In 1967, about twenty Danish long-lines, one or two Swedish boats, and some Faroese and Norwegian vessels fished salmon out to 200 miles off the Norwegian coast. And the Danes were planning to convert a large steel cutter to mothership operations, saving many trips from the fishing grounds back to Denmark, because Norway does not permit the Danes to land their catches for transshipment.

Thus it had become obvious that the Danes were planning to get into high seas fishing for salmon in a big way.

The Danes have a natural affinity with the sea. It is a small but fertile country, consisting of the large Jutland Peninsula and some five hundred islands, sticking up from Germany like a sore thumb, with the North Sea on one side and the Baltic Sea on the other. With a total population of only some five million people, the Danes, from time immemorial, have put out to sea. Adventuresome by nature, they had no place else to go. And they took what they found — which was more than just fish and mammals from the sea. They also gained sway over some of the lands that gave them shelter, food, and trade. This ultimately brought islands such as the Faroes and Greenland under Danish rule.

4

The Greenland Escalation

THE LAND AND ITS PEOPLE

GREENLAND is not particularly green. An ice sheet 11,100 feet thick depresses five-sixths of the surface of the world's largest island far below sea level, and a mountainous, glaciated rim surrounds this great ice mass.* Yet the southwestern part of the island is ice-free, even in winter, since it is bathed by the warm west Greenland ocean current. Here there are deep fjords and green valleys. This is where the population of Greenland lives, some 57,000 inhabitants, over one-fifth of whom have been imported from Denmark.

It was also in these green parts, uninhabited at the time, that Eric the Red, banished from his native Iceland for murder, hit upon the name Greenland when he established a colony some one thousand years ago. At about the same time, another people, this time from North America, were landing in the far north, founding what was called the Thule culture. They were Eskimos — the people from the sea. Their descendants, intermingling with European colonists, are the Greenlanders we know today.

Early in the eighteenth century, the Danes took possession of the country, and the Greenlanders were converted to Christianity. Political reform came in 1953 when Greenland changed its status from colony to county, thus becoming an integral part of the Kingdom of Denmark. It is often referred to as a province of Denmark.

With county status came progress. Thousands of Danish workers invaded western Greenland over the next few years, blasting

* Source: National Geographic Society, Atlas of the World, rev. 6th ed.

and dynamiting sites for hospitals, schools, housing, power stations, and roads. Housing standards rose, and the great Greenland illness — tuberculosis — was wiped out. Thus a bulldozer culture had rolled out a path for the development of Greenland. But these sudden sociological changes took their toll. The natives just about buckled under, and the only medicine that could help was education and job training, so thousands of young Greenlanders were sent to Denmark for further education.

Educational improvements and radical changes in social conditions brought in their wake a demand for greater self-determination. A commission, appointed in 1972, turned its attention to the issue of home rule for Greenland. In 1979, after a Greenland referendum on self-government had been passed, the Danish Folketing (parliament) relinquished part of its powers and invested them in self-government legislation — in effect, a Greenland constitution. Greenland then came — and now remains — under the Danish crown and continues to have the administrative status of a Danish county. A legislature, still subject to the Danish constitution, appoints a governing body, with a chairperson elected for the same four-year term of office as the national government. Greenland sends two representatives to the Folketing in Copenhagen. The new Greenland government exercises all powers except those of defense and foreign relations, which are handled by Denmark.*

THE GREENLAND SALMON FISHERY

By the middle of the twentieth century, the climate of western Greenland had become warmer, which led the seal population to move north to colder waters. This effectively brought an end to seal hunting, which had been the only important local industry for native Greenlanders.

* Much of this information was excerpted from Erik Erngaard, "Fact Sheet/Denmark," Press and Public Relations Department of the Ministry of Foreign Affairs of Denmark, 2 Stromgade, DK-1470 Copenhagen K, Denmark.

Fortunately, however, the warmer waters had already brought an influx of cod to the west coast, and this led to the growth of a permanent stock of Greenland codfish. Thus about a third of the population became engaged in codfishing, using set nets attached to the shore or gill nets let out from small motorboats.

Soon there was to be an annual invasion of yet another species — Atlantic salmon — into west Greenland waters. They came on feeding migrations, generally from late July to the middle of November. This would turn out to be a bonanza for the Greenlanders, and by the early 1960s they were into salmon fishing in a big way.

By 1965, the big oceangoing trawlers out of Denmark had joined the fishery, operating on the high seas off west Greenland, outside the territorial limits of the islands, thus leaving the inshore fishing grounds largely to the local Greenlanders.

It did not take long, however, for the native fishermen to resent the intrusion by their own countrymen, who were harvesting salmon from waters that the Greenlanders had traditionally considered their own domain. This tension festered over the next few years and became a critical issue back in Copenhagen. Political infighting had been going on within governmental agencies and in the Folketing over the whole matter of the Greenland fishery, both high seas and inshore.

Meanwhile, scientific improvements in fishing gear helped the lot of all fishermen immeasurably. It was now possible to obtain nylon nets, which were far more efficient than twine nets, because monofilament is invisible to the fish. Also, the native Greenlanders had learned how to construct quick-freezing plants, which made for greatly improved storage and marketing practices.

MURRES

There was one aspect of salmon fishing, that threatened to do damage to an important way of life for the Greenlanders. The salmon nets took large quantities of seabirds known as murres, which feed in the sea on capelin and other fish, as do the salmon. Next to the eider duck, the murre is the most important bird in the economy of Greenland. The flesh and eggs are eaten, and the skins and feathers are used for blankets and capes. Murre eggs are said to contain about as much vitamin A as domestic poultry eggs and have far more calories per unit than cow's milk. Aside from the short period spent on land for breeding and nesting, murres spend their entire lives in the sea. Their excrement is rich in phosphates and nitrates, without which the phytoplankton, the basic life in the sea, cannot exist. Murres have been referred to as the fertilizer factories of the northern seas and are thus an important link in the ecological chain.

This species was being endangered, because as many as 400,000 were being taken in the high seas nets, according to an early report by an Audubon official.

THE PRIVATE SECTOR GETS INVOLVED

By 1965, the salmon exploitation had begun to assume important proportions. The total catch from inshore nets and driftnets had grown to 861 tons, an estimated 237,200 salmon. In 1966, the total catch ballooned to 1,370 tons, some 394,000 salmon. The meteoric growth of this Greenland fishery sent a shock wave through Atlantic salmon conservationists all over the North Atlantic.

The Atlantic Salmon Association, at its 1966 annual meeting in Montreal, Canada, became the first private-sector organization to express its deep concern for the future of Atlantic salmon stocks. T. B. "Happy" Fraser, its president, called for "the prohibition of taking salmon by any means on the high seas outside of the Baltic Sea" and for "the abolition of taking salmon with gear other than shore nets within territorial waters."

By 1967, the high seas fleet off Greenland had grown to eleven vessels — four Danish, three Faroese, and four Norwegian — taking some 314 tons. Together with the inshore native Greenlander catch of 1,287 tons, this totaled 1,601 tons.

The extent of the escalation is best understood from a report by the International Council for Exploration of the Seas

(ICES)* on the total catch — high seas and inshore — for each year since catch figures were first reported in 1960:

YEAR	TONS	POUNDS	NUMBER OF SALMON (Approx.)
1960	60	132,240	16,500
1961	127	279,908	35,000
1962	244	537,776	67,200
1963	466	1,027,064	128,400
1964	1,539	3,391,956	428,000
1965	861	1,897,644	237,200
1966	1,370	3,183,760	394,000
1967	1,601	3,528,604	441,000

In 1968, joint concern by newly formed Atlantic salmon organizations in the two principal producing nations, Great Britain and Canada, led to the first international Atlantic Salmon symposium, held at Fishmonger's Hall, London, on May 15, 1968. This meeting concerned itself principally with setting forth for the record an outline of the present status of salmon stocks, scientific evidence as to the nature and extent of the fishery, the political aspects of the situation, and the consequences of allowing the exploitation to go unregulated. Other organizations that were represented included the International Atlantic Salmon Foundation, which had been organized in 1967 in the United States by a private group headed by Francis Goelet of New York City, and the Atlantic Salmon Research Trust, founded in England in 1968.

Thus, a beginning had been made in bringing together organizations that could coordinate actions designed to focus on problems standing in the way of the rational management and conservation of Atlantic salmon stocks.

* The ICES is the scientific arm of the Food and Agriculture Administration, United Nations. ICES is widely used as the research authority on fisheries matters by leading nations.

REFLECTIONS

It seems important to note today that the destiny of salmon conservation some twenty-five years ago rested in the hands of unusually capable and knowledgeable individuals who devoted their entire energies to the job: people like Happy Fraser in Canada, Jock Menzies and Peter Liddell in the United Kingdom, and John Olin in the United States.

I knew Happy Fraser during the few years just before his retirement. We coordinated our efforts on salmon matters, and I stayed at his salmon camp on the Etamamiou River in Quebec. Perhaps the most unrelenting of all the early Canadians in the struggle to stop the high seas carnage, he was tough, persistent, and fervent. The others I knew only slightly, because I had only just commenced my commitment to salmon work.

Sadly, all these forerunners left us some years ago. They were champions of a special sort — individualistic, to be sure, but each in his own way pioneered the cause. The question that comes to mind is, where do we find the likes of these champions today? Such are needed — badly.

5

The ICNAF Convention

IN THE 1960S, the only institutional arrangement authorized and equipped to propose management measures for fish of all species in the northwest Atlantic Ocean was the International Commission for Northwest Atlantic Fisheries (ICNAF). ICNAF was the operating mechanism of the International Convention for the Northwest Atlantic Fisheries, which had entered into force July 3, 1950.

MEMBERS
The seventeen members of ICNAF were Bulgaria, Canada, Denmark, France, Federal Republic of Germany, German Democratic Republic, Iceland, Italy, Japan, Norway, Poland, Portugal, Rumania, Spain, United Kingdom, United States, and USSR.

It should be emphasized that of the seventeen member nations, only five produce Atlantic salmon that migrate to, and feed off, west Greenland in substantial numbers. Thus the salmon-producing nations have difficulty securing a majority vote of nine members to support new conservation measures.

ICNAF—1968
At the June 6, 1968, meeting of ICNAF in London, the Canadian delegation proposed the stabilization of the west Greenland high seas fishery for Atlantic salmon in the ICNAF area. They made the point that the Atlantic salmon was in danger of becoming extinct because of the rapidly growing fishery, the greatly improved techniques and fishing gear, and the increased number of powerful fishing boats of advanced design taking part.

The Canadian proposal was strongly supported by the United Kingdom and the United States delegations. The Soviet delegates expressed their conviction that, based on their experience with Atlantic salmon, the protection of this species on the high seas was necessary to its survival.

The Danes would not agree to the proposed regulation, claiming a lack of evidence regarding the effect of the fishery on home water and total salmon yields. The Icelanders agreed with the Danish position. Norway, which had prohibited commercial fishing for salmon in its own territorial waters but could not prevent Norwegians from fishing on the high seas, could not support the Canadian proposal. Apparently, there was a division within the Norwegian government.

In the end, the required two-thirds majority vote could not be obtained. But the commission did unanimously adopt a resolution recommending that member governments "consider urgently the desirability of preventing an increase in high seas fishing for salmon...for the time being, and that high priority be given to studies of the effects of such high seas fishing on the resources." The Danish delegation agreed to bring to the attention of the Danish government the grave concern of other delegations over the consequences of high seas fishing.

On April 19, 1969, in London, the Atlantic Salmon Research Trust held an international conference concerning the problems presented by high seas salmon fishing. This meeting, to which Denmark did not send a representative, resolved that there should be a suspension of high seas salmon fishing for ten years.

ICNAF—1969

At the June 1969 ICNAF meeting, the United States made a statement that set forth the "Basic U.S. Position" on high seas fishing for Atlantic salmon. It was extremely important not only because it accomplished its objective for that particular meeting, but also because it became the rationale for all major moves on Atlantic salmon made by the United States in international forums. The Committee on the Atlantic Salmon Emergency and its successor organization, Restoration of Atlantic Salmon in America, Inc., both adopted it as their basic position, using it and parts of it for years to come in connection with important occasions, such as giving expert testimony before committees of the U.S. Congress.

The position is all-embracing and compelling, and its precepts are as valid today as they were nearly a quarter of a century ago. Here it is:

BASIC U.S. POSITION

High seas fishing for salmon is wasteful and contrary to principles of conservation. Continuation of this practice opens the real possibility that coastal nations will abandon their stream preservation and improvement programs and their hatchery programs, and thus prepare the way for extinction of this valuable species. Salmon can be maintained on the high seas only if the coastal nations maintain the streams in which they spawn in a suitable condition. Not only does this represent a significant expenditure by the coastal nations, but they must often forgo alternate uses of these streams to maintain them in suitable condition for salmon, for example using them for power or irrigation. If the salmon runs have been depleted, restoration is even more costly. This work will be difficult to continue if coastal countries cannot be assured of some benefits to their domestic fisheries, whether sports or commercial, and without these special efforts by the coastal nations it is doubtful that salmon could survive. Even the best conservation program by the coastal state can be completely nullified by indiscriminate salmon fishing on the high seas. Fishing on the high seas is applied indiscriminately to various salmon runs which intermingle in the ocean. Thus fish are harvested without regard to the condition of different runs, and excess numbers may be taken from the very runs needing special protection. The productivity of salmon runs from different rivers varies, and individual runs fluctuate from year to year, usually independent of each other. Coastal fisheries can be managed to allow adequate escapement for all runs, but this type of conservation can not be practiced on the high seas. High seas fishing for salmon is also wasteful because fish are taken before they attain full growth and ocean netting oftens injures or kills fish without capturing them. It has been estimated that the salmon killed by ocean nets and then lost may equal half the total harvested by this method. By far the most preferable way of managing the salmon resources is to ban high seas salmon fishing; salmon fishing should be restricted to the mouths of the streams and the streams themselves where the catch can be regulated to ensure the proper escapement for each run. This kind of limitation does not have implications for most high seas fishing, since most species found on the high seas do not depend on returning to the stream of origin for spawning as does the salmon. This aspect of the salmon makes a prohibition on high seas salmon fishing a unique conservation tool which cannot be applied generally to other fisheries. Immediate action is needed which will ensure coastal states that their careful efforts to conserve limited salmon resources will not be defeated by lack of conservation in ocean waters.

At this same meeting, under the influence of considerable U.S. pressure, a proposal for a complete ban on high seas fishing for Atlantic salmon passed by a majority vote of eleven. Two nations, Denmark and West Germany, were opposed, and Portugal abstained.

During the 1969 salmon season, the Danish government paid scant attention to the 1968 resolution — to which it had agreed — and proceeded to increase its salmon fleet in the West Atlantic, resulting in a substantially increased high seas catch (exclusive of the inshore Greenlanders' catch) of 1,358 tons (up from 595 tons in 1968). It was apparent from the outset that the Danes' intention was to take every available salmon they could find, with little regard for the future health of the salmon stocks.

REFLECTIONS
ICNAF was not an effective mechanism for protecting Atlantic salmon for the following reasons:

1. ICNAF is commercially oriented. Its members are interested solely in maximum economic yields from pelagic and demersal species of fish such as cod herring, flounder, and haddock. There is little interest in conservation, and the Atlantic salmon is completely out of place in this company. Sportfishing means nothing.

2. Countries such as Denmark, Rumania, and Spain, which make no contribution to salmon propagation and management, have a vote on salmon measures and thus can control the fate of countries that do.

3. The ICNAF convention lacks the authority to control dissenters. A unanimous vote and ratification by each member government are necessary to secure complete effectiveness for any measure.

4. Atlantic salmon decisions (and other fishery decisions) are subject to trade-offs. For instance, the United Kingdom might make a deal with Denmark for some benefit on herring in return for agreeing to go along with the Danish position on salmon.

So, what could be done? It was obvious that ICNAF would not alter its structure or change its procedures to accommodate the Atlantic salmon, which was small potatoes in the huge field of international fisheries problems. Besides, the bureaucracy was nicely settled into ICNAF. It served the purpose but accomplished very little.

In spite of its inherent weaknesses, however, ICNAF was the only medium available for negotiating any protection for migrating salmon. For the time being, we had to live with it and operate within its narrow confines. But other means would have to be found — and soon.

PART

III

THE SALMON WAR

6

The Committee on the Atlantic Salmon Emergency

I MET OTTO "Mose" Teller on a beach during a holiday stay in Jamaica. Our initial acquaintance ripened during the next few years into a close friendship, nurtured by our common addiction to fly-fishing and hunting birds with dogs.

Mose was a guiding light in Trout Unlimited (TU), which, with about fifteen thousand members, was already the leading trout conservation organization in the United States. TU wanted to get into Atlantic salmon work, so Mose began pressing me to join, probably because of my background in public relations and my life-long devotion to Atlantic salmon fishing. I acquiesced and soon had a seat on the board of directors; in 1969, I became a vice president in charge of organizing and directing an Atlantic salmon committee.

The initial objective was to undertake, through our councils and chapters, a nationwide public information program highlighting the U.S. restoration efforts. Also, we wanted to tell the story of the devastating commercial netting off Greenland principally by the Danes but also by the Norwegians and Faroese.

The program caught on immediately, and other fishing organizations soon evidenced a keen interest in joining the under-taking. I now realized that we had a bear by the tail and that it would be necessary to set up an entirely separate organization to lead the private sector in coordinating the efforts of all the leading Atlantic salmon organizations. It would be no easy job because of the differing objectives and rivalries that had built up over time, but I thought that it would be possible to weld these groups together at least for a common front and an ad hoc effort. By this time, I had even dreamed up a catchy name for such an organization. It would be the Committee on the Atlantic Salmon Emergency, or CASE for short. I have always been a believer in the value of acronyms and had chosen this title carefully (we had a "case" against the Danes).

I next met with Francis Goelet, President of the International Atlantic Salmon Foundation (IASF), and described my concept to him. He was interested and referred the matter to his people. At that time, IASF had more background and experience on the salmon than any other group in the United States. This is what IASF could give to TU. For its part, IASF recognized that TU had a national organization that could give broad expression to the foundation's purpose and objectives. As a result of further discussions, IASF elected me to its board in December 1969.

Finally, in a letter dated January 16, 1970, Goelet asked me to form a Committee on the Atlantic Salmon Emergency, which would be an IASF committee designed to activate and operate Project CASE, a public information and educational program to inform the general public about the dangers facing the Atlantic salmon as a species. I accepted this invitation and proceeded to appoint the committee, which included Goelet as well as Joseph E. Cullman, President of the Philip Morris Company, and Theodore Bensinger, President of the Brunswick Company. I also appointed the following as special advisors: Otto Teller, Bing Crosby, Lee Wulff (author and renowned fisherman), Curt Gowdy (the sportscaster), and Roderick Haig-Brown (also an author and renowned fisherman).

The main thrust of Project CASE would be to highlight the facts surrounding exploitation of the salmon. The public relations firm of Grey and Davis was retained by IASF to use the media to tell the story.

To publicize our work and raise funds, I organized a "Save the Salmon" dinner, which was held at the River Club of New York on January 27, 1970. President Donnelley of Trout Unlimited and Francis Goelet spoke about the public information program, and I announced the formation of CASE. Guests were invited to make financial contributions to our program, and the substantial sum raised was later augmented by a special grant of $15,000 from the Philip Morris Company in the name of IASF to cover operational expenses.

This public relations effort succeeded far beyond our expectations. Assistant Secretary of the Interior Leslie Glasgow, with whom I had been working closely, stated that it "played a very important part in causing the Danes to begin to listen to the weight of world opinion in favor of abolishing their high-seas netting operations." This success was now leading our original Trout Unlimited component of CASE to promote a more active involvement. This involvement would be international in scope, coordinating with other groups in the United States and elsewhere as well as undertaking meetings with fisheries officials of other nations in order to mount a unified effort.

But here we ran into a serious stumbling block. The IASF directors on the committee were becoming increasingly uneasy about what they considered to be an overly high-pressure approach to solving the Danish problem. And they had different perspectives from ours, as well as special positions to protect. IASF was a nonprofit organization, and its tax-exempt status must not be jeopardized. In those day, tax-exempt organizations were subject to much stricter constraints than they are today. The Internal Revenue Service's particular caveat was troublesome in that it stated that a foundation may not "carry on propaganda or otherwise attempt to influence legislation or affect the opinion of the general public other than making available the results of non-partisan analysis, study, or research."

Another restriction on IASF's operations was that it needed to sustain a posture of rigorous scientific objectivity in order to maintain its credibility in the scientific world. Further, most of the IASF directors, about thirty at that time, had Canadian interests to protect. Nearly all of them either owned or leased, or were members of clubs or groups that owned or leased, valuable real estate in the form of salmon camps with fishing rights on the finest salmon rivers in Canada. Also, their base of operations was in St. Andrews, New Brunswick, and their executive director, Wilfred Carter, was a Canadian. Thus, the directors would have to be careful not to alienate the government of Canada by supporting programs that would, in principle, restrict commercial netting operations for salmon, because high seas driftnetting and inshore fixed netting operations were ongoing and important industries in Canadian waters.

For our part, we members of the original Trout Unlimited group were not about to be deterred from our long-term objective, which was to stop the high seas slaughter of the salmon by whatever means necessary. And we sensed — rightly, as it later turned out — that to do so would involve all kinds of stratagems. Furthermore, looking down the road a bit, we could see that this work would be highly specialized and that a self-contained or autonomous unit would be the best mechanism for producing the efficient and hard-driving force necessary.

At our committee meetings, these opposing points of view about how to proceed were often strongly expressed, and every now and then things got pretty sticky. The commitment to Atlantic salmon conservation on the part of the directors of IASF was every bit as sincere as that of anyone else, yet they always had this tax-exempt baggage to carry on their backs, and it held their motivation on a very tight rein indeed. Anyway, we all knew that we must survive these differences, and we brought Project CASE to a highly successful conclusion.

In his letter of May 19, 1970, announcing the completion of the CASE Project, Goelet extended, on behalf of the board of directors of IASF, "our most sincere thanks and congratulations for the splendid job the CASE Committee has done in bringing the Atlantic salmon crisis before the general public." He then drew attention to the constraints on IASF's operations and added this:

> Restrictions lead us to a somewhat frustrating position where we can develop and disseminate facts, define the problems and in

limited areas, make modest recommendations, but must leave the thrust of developing practical solutions to other persons and organizations.... The CASE Committee has defined and publicized the problem, and the logical next step would be toward a sharper focus on the Greenland fisheries and perhaps toward recommendations for a practical means of curtailing those operations. It is the feeling of the Board that the IASF should leave this next step to individuals and organizations who are not inhibited by our requirements of objectivity.

This was, of course, an accurate assessment of the situation, and we were happy to have his assurance that the directors of IASF understood and were perhaps even sympathetic with our objectives. So CASE was disbanded.

On June 7, 1970, CASE II was organized by our key group. We did not want to lose the public image value of the original name that I had invented, because it was under that banner that we had already engendered so much momentum for the cause. It was only a matter of time before we and everyone else dropped the roman numeral in correspondence and conversation and reverted simply to CASE.

The new Committee on the Atlantic Salmon Emergency was an ad hoc committee organized under the laws of the state of New Hampshire. I was elected chairman, and David E. Scoll (a New York lawyer and official of the Federation of Fly Fishermen) was elected secretary-treasurer. Our members included Bing Crosby, Joseph Cullman, Marshall Field, Arnold Gingrich (publisher of *Esquire* and a noted fisherman and author), H. Peter Kriendler (part owner of The 21 Club), Willard F. Rockwell, Jr. (President of Rockwell International), Otto Teller, Peter S. Thompson, R. P. Van Gytenbeek (Executive Director of Trout Unlimited), Ted Williams (baseball Hall of Famer), and Lee Wulff. Others were added later.

Although CASE was a nonprofit organization, there was no intention of trying to qualify for income-tax exemption. We wanted to be able to exert pressure wherever and in whatever manner was necessary or desirable.

Trout Unlimited made a special grant of $5,600 to cover our administrative costs for six months. From that point on, we raised our own funds for operating expenses and were answerable only to ourselves. Considering the tremendous job that had to be done — meeting with top U.S. governmental officials and agencies in Washington and with state fish and game commissions; meeting with other private-sector organizations; meeting with the media; paying administrative costs for the printing of press releases and position statements; and paying travel costs connected with meetings in Ottawa, Halifax, Montreal, Copenhagen, London, Edinburgh, Paris, and Oslo — we operated on a very small budget indeed. Actually, during the entire period of our existence — a little over two years — we required only about $120,000. This was raised principally by donations from our membership, which grew to nearly 600 members.

Our public announcement included the following:

> The objective of the Committee on the Atlantic Salmon Emergency is to restore the Atlantic salmon to the rivers and waters of the United States and to protect the species as far offshore as the stocks may range in the ocean.
>
> CASE is embarked on a comprehensive campaign of unremitting pressure to accomplish this formidable task. We marshal United States and world opinion through public information programs. We also provide guidelines to effective action, encouraging commitment by individuals, organizations and governments to attack critical problems, such as overexploitation in the ocean, with a sense of urgency and priority.

7

Enlisting Public Support

OUR INITIAL PURPOSE was to make the salmon's plight so well known that a ground swell of informed public opinion would be the lifeblood from which would flow a many-faceted campaign to get the Danish government to stop the high seas slaughter. We would pull out all the stops.

CASE entered into a new contract with the public relations firm of Grey and Davis, with whom we had worked previously. They had already gone through the indoctrination and education that are necessary in such a complicated project, and Carl Lundquist of the firm specialized in getting wide coverage of the salmon emergency in sports magazines and sports columns of newspapers. In fact, under the first contract — the period January through May 1970 — the newspapers carrying such stories had a combined circulation of 13,979,399 persons — a very satisfying audience.

We planned a new action campaign that would guide Grey and Davis in a positive and affirmative direction, under strict standards of good taste and dignity, thus avoiding any articles that might have a negative effect on the entire effort. The objectives would be to put salmon spokesmen such as Bing Crosby, Ted Williams, Curt Gowdy, Lee Wulff, and others on network television and radio; to place topflight features with the wire services such as Associated Press, Reuters, and United Press International; to place stories with outdoors editors, women's page editors, and feature writers on key metropolitan daily newspapers, with special emphasis on the northeastern quarter; and, finally, to produce an outflow of special stories to leading magazines and weekly newspapers.

How well this second public information effort succeeded can best be illustrated by quoting part of Grey and Davis's report of April 1, 1971, to CASE:

> It has been an upstream fight, not unlike that late-in-the-game home-stretch battle of the regal salmon itself, but your committee has scored a resounding victory in the second phase of the public information campaign now nearing completion. . . .
>
> Very few of the sports fishermen and conservationists... had any real knowledge of the tragedy that was impending for the entire species throughout the North Atlantic nations.
>
> Now, nearly a year later, it is fitting to cite the comments of Anthony Netboy, one of the world's foremost authorities on the subject, and author of the book, *The Atlantic Salmon, a Disappearing Species?* Writing in the *Portland Oregonian*, Mr. Netboy said that "CASE's success is phenomenal. Many people who were never interested in the Atlantic salmon ... are now telling their friends, 'Don't buy Danish goods — the Danes are killing off the Atlantic Salmon.'"
>
> High point of the CASE campaign was the oversubscribed Save the Salmon Dinner attended by more than 500 persons at the Hotel Waldorf-Astoria on Jan. 20. This was the fulcrum for a massive publicity thrust involving subsequent network radio and television coverage in depth for CASE spokesmen on the David Frost show with Bing Crosby, Garry Moore's "To Tell the Truth" show with Lee Wulff as central guest, Dick Cavett on ABC with Ted Williams, NBC Monitor Radio with Joe Garagiola and Bing Crosby as guest, and Mark Sosin's CBS radio ecology program with Curt Gowdy. Additionally, there was wire service news and feature coverage of the event by both Associated Press and United Press International, plus syndicated picture layouts by both services to all daily newspapers in the U.S. Several syndicated columnists gave the event extensive coverage and the nation's two foremost sports publications, *Sports Illustrated* and *The Sporting News*, gave it full treatment.
>
> Two other major media placements deserve special emphasis. The first was the eight-minute segment by Walter Cronkite in his CBS evening news on what amounted to a

Thanksgivng night special before a mammoth at-home audience on Nov. 26 over 180 stations.

The second special was the Sunday, April 4 story of the Atlantic salmon problem on ABC's "The American Sportsman." This 24-minute film, capturing the true enchantment of salmon fishing, leads off with remarks by Curt Gowdy, Bing Crosby, Ted Williams, and Lee Wulff at the Waldorf dinner and pursues the story at Montrose, Scotland, described as "a town with one foot in the ocean and one in the river."

Grey & Davis, on behalf of the committee, is gratified at the results and is hopeful that the campaign not only has brought awareness to concerned Americans, but that it will give our friends, the Danish people, pause for thoughtful consideration about bringing to a halt the deep seas netting operations in the Davis Strait.

CASE records show that thirty-nine of the leading East Coast newspapers and most of the prominent outdoors writers ran or contributed special articles from October 1970 through April 1971. In addition, a United Press International article by Connie Ryan ran in 1,200 newspapers on January 27, 1971, and an unsigned Associated Press story from Elsinore, Denmark, ran in 1,400 newspapers on March 19, 1971.

Thus, by the fall of 1971 we knew that our publications program had fulfilled its mission; the American public were now adequately informed about the salmon emergency. We could set in motion our tactical offensives, secure in the knowledge that we had a sound base from which to operate.

HIGH SEAS FISHING OFF GREENLAND

During the late summer of 1971, CASE treasurer David Scoll was able to arrange for a television crew to film a sound and color movie, *High Seas Fishing Off Greenland*. It was made possible by a grant from the Philip Morris Company and is the property of that company. Directed by Lee Wulff, it was produced and distributed under the supervision of CASE.

Dave flew up to Greenland with the film crew and somehow persuaded the skipper of a big Danish trawler to take them aboard to photograph a fishing trip offshore. Dave told us that the captain indicated that he would "have Scoll's neck if the film was for propaganda purposes." But the film was made, and Dave wryly admitted that he didn't ever expect to visit Greenland again!

The trawler was the *Polarlaks* (*laks* meaning "salmon" in Scandinavian languages), out of the island of Bornholm in Denmark. These trawlers are the most sophisticated in the business, capable of freezing and storing 750 tons of fish, with sonar equipment almost as valuable as the ship itself. In the trade they are called distant oceangoing vessels. The film shows seventeen miles of monofilament driftnets being set one day and taken in the next morning, with not only salmon but also great numbers of seabirds (mostly murres) hanging limp in the nets.

It is of interest to point out here that the National Audubon Society had come out in strong support of CASE's work, principally because of its concern over the excessive loss of seabirds in the Greenland netting. Here was proof positive that such concern was warranted.

Nylon netting is invisible to fish and seabirds and is illegal in most countries. When the salmon swim into it and try to push through the webbing (with a mesh size of 5 to 5 ½ inches) to free themselves, their gills get caught and the fish drown. Most of the salmon die while the nets are still in the water. Many escape but are badly damaged; these perish later from infections attacking their wounds.

This film, *High Seas Fishing Off Greenland*, turned out to be an important adjunct to our work. We used it to great advantage at many meetings with both governmental officials and private-sector groups to give a vivid picture of this deadly drift net fishery.

8

Engaging Denmark

THE OPENING SKIRMISH of what was already being referred to in Denmark as The Salmon War actually took place in Washington on March 2, 1970. It was my intention to give clear notice to the Danish government that CASE was in this business for keeps — it was no fly-by-night, one-shot deal. This way, CASE's future excursions and actions would come as no surprise, and Denmark couldn't claim foul. So, in a February 16 letter to the Danish ambassador to the United States, the Honorable Mr. Torben Rønne, I requested a meeting to discuss with him the concerns of our committee about "the recent escalation of the netting of salmon on the high seas." After several telephone calls from Vice Consul E. Hulgaard, commercial fisheries attaché for Denmark to North America — presumably to ferret out our qualifications and probably to try to avoid getting into this business at all — the ambassador finally agreed to meet with us. I would be accompanied by Syd Howe, chairman of The Conservation Foundation, and Bob Hutton of the American Fisheries Society. (I had long ago learned the value of having witnesses at important meetings — insurance against future counterclaims.)

Inasmuch as the ambassador was ill, we met on March 2 with Hans Christensen, Minister Counselor in the Political Section, and Carlo Christensen, Cultural Counselor. The whole meeting, which lasted over an hour, was notable for its spirit of friendly exchange of positions and ideas.

First, we identified the various groups participating in the overall Atlantic salmon effort, such as the International Atlantic Salmon Foundation and its directors, international advisory group, and scientific advisory group. Then we stated CASE's present purpose: to acquaint the general public with facts pertaining to threats to the conservation of the Atlantic salmon. We next took up the two principal objections to high seas fishing for Atlantics: that the rapid escalation, if continued at its present rate, would endanger the species; and that the salmon-producing countries have the primary responsibility for ensuring the overall health of this valuable renewable resource.

It soon became apparent that the Danish embassy had very little information or concern about these basic problems of conservation. The counselors pointed out that the Danish fishermen, particularly the Faroese, were poor people who needed this income. Our reply was that although we understood this, there were many more underprivileged persons in Canada alone, particularly Indians and Eskimos in Labrador and Quebec and the other Maritimes, who from time immemorial also have depended on fishing for their livelihood.

The matter of the desirability of securing indisputable scientific evidence of the depletion of stocks through netting was only lightly touched upon by them, because we dismissed it right away, on the grounds that the samples were too small to mean anything.

They mentioned that their government might consider some controls such as mesh sizes, forbidden zones, and closed seasons. Our reply was that all these half measures, which had been brought up before, were impractical because they required policing on the high seas, which was far more difficult than inshore and inriver policing, and considerable sums of money, which were not available. We further pointed out that these compromises would not solve the principal problem, which was that the salmon-producing countries would still be losing salmon that were predestined to escape upriver, spawn, and renew the life cycle.

Finally, they made the point that the Nordic nations were planning to discuss this whole problem soon. This was new and encouraging information.

The meeting closed with my stressing very clearly that our

views represented the position of not only our group of conservation organizations but also of the United States government. A complete ban on high seas fishing for salmon was in the best interests of conserving and restoring the species as a valuable food resource and for recreational purposes.

We left with the feeling that the meeting had cleared the air and opened up the opportunity for dialogue.

THE BRITISH ADOPT A MILITANT MOOD

The indignation in America over the Danish overexploitation was paralleled in Great Britain. Here is an excerpt from an editorial in England's leading country magazine, *The Field*, in the March 12, 1970, issue:

> On the Danish interception, one repercussion of the increasing anger in Britain was the surprising but welcome intervention of Mr. Harold Wilson, who sent a personal letter to the Danish Government. The brush-off which he received caused no surprise. But the Prime Minister now knows what others had earlier discovered about the Danish attitude on salmon on the high seas, which is that escalating is a matter of principle. This attitude would be unimaginable if it were not actually happening. That nation seems oblivious of the discreditable image which it is projecting of itself. To be unrepentant about reaping a crop which others have sown (not merely in Britain but elsewhere on both sides of the Atlantic) may eventually prove to have been as imprudent as it is contemptible.

ICNAF 1970—MAKING A REGULATION STICK

CASE's next active involvement was in the diplomatic arena, at the June 1970 annual meeting of the International Commission for Northwest Atlantic Fisheries in St. John's, Newfoundland, which I attended as an adviser to the U.S. delegation.

At its 1969 annual meeting, ICNAF had adopted by majority vote a total ban on high seas fishing. But contracting member governments that opposed specific proposals were not required under the ICNAF protocol to put such regulations into effect. Denmark had opposed the 1969 ban and not only continued to operate in the Davis Strait off Greenland but also steeply escalated its takings. The Danes were joined by the Norwegians, and the total 1969 high seas catch was in excess of 1,200 metric tons (about 2,650,000 pounds of salmon), up from 547 metric tons (about 1,200,000 pounds) for 1968.

The compromise amendment finally agreed upon contained the following main points: It recognized that the proposal adopted at the 1969 annual meeting prohibiting salmon fishing outside national fishery limits had not been fully effective. It determined that interim measures were desirable in order to avoid the escalation of fishing for Atlantic salmon throughout the convention area. It proposed that contracting governments that had participated in high seas fishing for salmon limit the catch taken by its nationals to a level not exceeding the 1969 catch and prohibit fishing for salmon outside national fishery limits before July 31, 1971, and after November 30, 1971.

Voting on the proposal was recorded as follows: for the compromise amendment, ten nations — United States, Denmark, Norway, Rumania, France, Italy, Portugal, Spain, United Kingdom, West Germany; against the compromise amendment, four nations — USSR, Iceland, Poland, Canada.

In voting for this compromise, hold-the-line amendment, the United States in no way retreated from its basic position that high seas fishing for Atlantic salmon is wasteful and contrary to principles of conservation. But we realized that a proposal for a total ban would not carry, and stopping the escalation would at least conserve very important stocks of fish. The United States stated that it was "not at all satisfied" with this compromise action and that during the one-year holding period it would continue "to urge governments which engage in high seas fishing to refrain" from doing so. Dr. Leslie L. Glasgow, Assistant Secretary of the Interior and head of the U.S. delegation, also made an urgent plea for more research efforts to secure scientific evidence of the effect of this fishery on the conservation of Atlantic salmon stocks.

Those countries that voted against the amendment — the most important being Canada — did so solely on the grounds of principle; they were committed to a total ban on high seas operations. There was no conflict of interest or lack of cooperation between, for instance, Canada and the United States; the ultimate goal was still no high seas fishing.

Although the Danes had agreed to a one-year pause in escalation, they were adamant in their refusal to adopt the total ban desired by all the major salmon-producing nations. Thus an analysis of the overall result told us that the compromise was at best a stop-gap measure; the polarization would continue, and any permanent solution would be very difficult to achieve.

EXERCISE IN POLEMICS

Back home, the CASE public information program was drawing attention to the escalated catch for 1969. In an attempt to answer the outcry in the United States against this rapacious fishery, the Danish embassy issued a statement in July 1970 on the North Atlantic salmon fisheries. CASE was not favored with a copy until September 14, perhaps on purpose?

The Danish statement pointed out that "a solution to this problem was reached" at the ICNAF meeting and proceeded to attempt to justify this ridiculous claim. CASE issued its own Statement on October 1, 1970, rebutting the Danish one. We enlarged on the U.S. position at the ICNAF meeting that the United States was not at all satisfied with the compromise and that it would continue to urge governments that engaged in high seas fishing for salmon to refrain from doing so. We pointed out that Canada had voted against the motion, being unwilling to compromise its stand against high seas fishing. So how could the Danish government claim that these firm positions by the United States and Canada constituted a solution to the problem?

The Danish statement also claimed that "the statistical and scientific information available does not indicate any trend towards a significant reduction in home water catches that could warrant restrictive measures." In reply, CASE had this to say:

> It will be many years before research will come up with a complete and accurate answer on this point. The life cycle of the salmon — five to six years from egg to ultimate spawning — complicates estimates. If the 36 tons taken by the Danes in 1965 removed a potential 11,000 fish from the spawning beds, what may be the result in 1975 of the 1969 steeply escalated destruction of some 600,000 salmon? The proper way to deal with a depletion problem is to restore total stocks to abundance, and then, with all facts at hand, consider the feasibility of a controlled commercial harvest. Yet the Danes prefer to set sail on a catastrophe course, a strange position for a country which professes a belief in conservation.

The CASE statement went on to say:

> The Danes have had a habit of overlooking, in their formal releases, any reference to a major consideration with respect to high seas fishing for Atlantics. Unless there is a maximum economic yield, it becomes unprofitable to fish commercially or by angling for salmon. So, a substantial overexploitation, let alone complete exhaustion, of the resource would destroy the livelihoods of thousands of people.... The people who inhabit the shores of the Canadian Maritimes, the coasts of Norway and England, Scotland and Ireland have tended salmon nets at the mouths of rivers. There are more than 16,500 nets in operation in the Maritimes alone. Then throw in the numbers of people employed by sport fishermen as guides, cooks, and maintenance personnel, to say nothing of those employed in the fishing tackle business, and you know that the total families affected would run to high figures. And loss of income? Certainly in the millions. Compare with this the Danish high seas salmon fleet in the Northwest Atlantic of about 34 trawlers (in 1969) with perhaps about 300 fishermen involved! And these people have only

lately come into this fishery. It is only a three months' part-time operation for them, and the boats, not being designed exclusively for this purpose, could easily be used for other types of fishing. . . .

So the situation is that all the work, all the development, all the sheer hard cash which has been poured into the salmon fisheries of the salmon-producing countries during the past generation is going in a rapidly increasing part to the lining of pockets of high seas netsmen, processors and marketers from countries which make no contribution whatever to this rich fishery. At enormous expense in terms of human effort and money, we sow the seed. At great profit to themselves, others reap the harvest.

An ever increasing world population requires more fish, not less. It starts with conservation in its most basic sense — the preservation of a marginally endangered species. Denmark must be made to realize that the salmon-producing countries are deadly serious in their determination to stop high seas fishing, the first and basic step towards proper management and an increase in world-wide stocks of this most valuable of ocean species.

The above exchange of positions by CASE and the Danish government specialists is but one example of the unremitting campaign of letter-writing upon which CASE embarked throughout the whole course of the Salmon War. These letters were principally from CASE to those Danish officials who were responsible for the Danish position on high seas fishing. Such letters went all the way to the top, including one to the Honorable Hilmer Baunsgaart, Prime Minister of Denmark. It was not answered!

THE "SAVE OUR SALMON" DINNER

On January 20, 1971, CASE put on one of the largest and most successful parties ever held in the interest of Atlantic salmon conservation — the "Save Our Salmon" dinner at the Waldorf-Astoria Hotel in New York City. Its purpose was twofold — to give the greatest possible publicity to the cause and to enlist more individuals in the support of it.

SAVE THE SALMON *Dinner—Waldorf-Astoria, New York City, January 20, 1971. The dinner was sponsored by the Committee on the Atlantic Salmon Emergency.*
Left to right: *Lee Wulff, the author, Bing Crosby, Curt Gowdy.*
Shortly after this picture was taken, Bing Crosby and the author went on national television, also beamed to Denmark, to protest the overkill off West Greenland by this Danish province.

It was a big undertaking, and many people volunteered to help us with the arrangements. Of particular note was Joe Cullman, who assigned some of the Philip Morris personnel to the arduous chores of getting out the invitations, arranging the table seatings, and other incidentals. Although this was not conceived as a fund-raising effort, we did charge a reasonable subscription price of $25 a head. We cleared costs, leaving a small amount for the coffers of CASE, which were always at low levels. We invited everyone known to man who had any connection whatsoever with the Atlantic salmon, and our records show an attendance of well over 500 persons.

With Curt Gowdy as the master of ceremonies, the dinner went off without a hitch. I made a few opening comments about the critical nature of the salmon problem and was followed by several other speakers, including Lee Wulff and Sydney Howe, president of The Conservation Foundation. We were in for a special treat when Curt Gowdy called on his good friend Ted Williams to say a few words. Ted, in his own inimitable style, related how, for him, the salmon had come to personify strength, courage, and beauty. It was a sincere, emotional, and unforgettable appeal. He hit a real home run that brought the house down, concluding as follows: "I think it's a crime that anything on this earth should be expedited toward the exodus of its extinction." The final feature was Bing Crosby, showing his movie *Salmon Fishing in Iceland* and singing a song about the salmon that he had composed for the occasion. As usual, the audience was enraptured.

At the conclusion of the evening, the Danish TV representative (whose team had taped the dinner) requested that I be interviewed and insisted on including Bing Crosby and Lee Wulff. This was just what we wanted. It actually turned out to be a big tactical mistake for the Danes to let Bing talk to their people. He was very popular in Denmark, since he was part Danish. Mr. Hulgaard, attaché from the Danish consulate, was present as an observer.

The interview, in the Louis XVI Room, lasted approximately half an hour, and we believed that we had fielded the questions well. No matter what parts might be cut, the official CASE position on the high seas fishery was very clear. We placed particular emphasis on the hope that the Danish public understood the situation. On the subect of a possible CASE visit to Denmark to discuss the problem with high-level government officials, I commented that we might not be welcome. The interviewer asked Hulgaard whether this was possible, and Hulgaard's reply was "no comment."

The next day, Hulgaard reported that the TV taping had gone out over a Danish national network, and the newspaper report had hit the front pages in Copenhagen. He said that the topic was discussed by the cabinet and was also brought up in parliament. We couldn't have asked for more!

Then, on Thursday, January 28, Hulgaard telephoned me. Hulgaard's suggestion that the consulate and CASE keep each other informed had been flatly rejected by the Foreign Office. Hulgaard was told that the Danish consulate was not supposed to get involved, and that the whole question was referred to the embassy in Washington. Hulgaard, reading between the lines, felt that a hard stand had been taken against CASE, and that he could offer us no conciliatory message. He stated that this hard stand against us, and in fact against any country or organization pressing for a total ban, came from the Minister of Fisheries, A. C. Normann. (*Note*: Hulgaard had implied at the Save Our Salmon dinner that there is a severe difference of opinion in Denmark over the high seas fishery and that it was possible that, after the next election, in the fall of 1971, Normann might be replaced.) In conclusion, Hulgaard stated that since he had not specifically been told not to communicate, he would like to be helpful, though he could not be so officially.

So there we had it. There was more official opposition than we had expected, all along the line.

REFLECTIONS
A few words and personal reminiscences about Bing Crosby: I had persuaded Bing to be the key attraction at the salmon dinner, and my wife and I had Bing and his wife Kathy staying at our club with

us in New York. Bing was a wonderful person, and I was privileged to have known him, particularly during the two years he was most involved in helping CASE. It all came about simply. I had felt for some time that we needed several nationally known and respected figures who would lend distinction and charisma to the salmon effort and to CASE. I knew that Bing was a salmon fisherman. Once, when I happened to be holding some meetings in San Francisco, I decided to call him at his home in Hillsborough, California, and tell my story. It took some detective work, but I was able to get the telephone number of his house, and I called. The butler answered and asked what I wished to speak with him about. I told him, and the butler said, "Wait a minute." After about a minute, Bing came on and spoke of his interest in salmon fishing. So I told him the story, answered a few questions, and then asked if I could see him. His reply was "Yes, what about tomorrow morning?" We met the next day at his home and had a long discussion. He was very natural, asking intelligent questions, and then closed our meeting with a friendly, "Please keep me closely informed." Thus began a productive association that ripened into a friendship. Once he accepted you, he more than held up his part of the relationship.

Bing was part Danish, and I'll never forget the time we first heard that the Danish government had banned the sale of his records and movies throughout Denmark. This was certainly the biggest blunder made by the top Danish officials during the whole salmon war. They just didn't understand that the general public — out of their genuine affection for Bing — would have more confidence in his judgment than in that of anyone in government! This affair hit newspapers all over the English-speaking world, and it was a front-page story in many of the European ones. It produced a tremendous amount of publicity for our cause, and the sympathy was all for Bing — and the salmon! As a byproduct of all this, CASE acquired a number of new members.

Just the same, this loss in income amounted to big bucks. I called Bing from my home in the East, with the intention of telling him how sorry I was. I didn't get very far, though; right away he said, "Hell, Dick, that's not important — it's the salmon that count. And besides, I can stand this. I'm not exactly a poor man, you know." That was Bing. I believe that he took setbacks with a shrug of the shoulder and went on with the business at hand.

The fine thing about Bing Crosby was that he enjoyed helping people. He gave himself unsparingly to causes in which he believed, so he worked very hard at trying to save the salmon. With contacts all over the world, he told the story of the indiscriminate high seas netting off Greenland whenever and wherever he could. We elected him a special adviser to CASE, and he was appreciative and proud of this recognition.

Bing Crosby

Hillsborough
August 28, 1970

Dear Dick:

I happened to be in Copenhagen about a week ago, and I thought as long as I was there, I would dig around a little and see what I could do in behalf of CASE.

The Ambassador, Guilford Dudley, is an old friend of mine, and I called on him and had dinner with him, and he, of course, is well aware of the program, and is losing no opportunity to ascert the point of the view of sportsmen who are concerned about the situation.

I also spent a day with Count Carl-Johann Bernstorff. He is a great sportsman, and although he was partially acquainted with the nature of the crisis, I filled him in on additional details, and he has promised to do some missionary work among sportsmen in Denmark in our behalf.

He avers that most of them are aware of the situation
and are already doing something.

His address is Gyldensteen, Bogense, Fuen, Denmark.

He gave me the name of another man who he says is
really militant about the thing, and a great sportsman.
He's a painter by vocation, and lives in a town called
Odense. His name is Svend Saabye.

Count Bernstorff was of the opinion he could be very
helpful.

From conversations I had in Denmark, I can only tell
you that most of the sportsmen there are well aware
of the situation's urgency. Possibly you know all
about this already, but I just thought I'd tell you
what I encountered.

The article I wrote for the NASHVILLE BANNER has been
very widely syndicated, notably through Jack O'Brien,
New York columnist, and other syndicated writers.

I didn't realize until I read the article myself how
liberally I had borrowed from all the other material
you sent me by other writers. I hope the various
writers whose material I've borrowed will forgive me.
I was in a great hurry to get away, and I wasn't too
familiar with all the facts, so I took this liberty.

Incidentally, someone in the United States had sent
our Ambassador, Guilford Dudley, a copy of the article

All best wishes,

Bing Crosby

BC:lm

Mr. Richard A. Buck
Old Dublin Road
Hancock, New Hampshire   03449

9

Mission to Copenhagen

IN THE LATE FALL of 1970, I proposed to Lee Wulff and David Scoll that a visit to Copenhagen might further our cause, and by early winter 1971, it appeared that an ideal time for such a trip might be in April. The reasoning was that the volume of publicity that we felt we needed — in Denmark as well as in the United States — was reaching its peak. By now there might be some cracks in the Danish armor. For instance, Anker Nielsen, Washington correspondent for the important Danish newspaper *Politiken*, told me in a telephone conversation on February 16 that for the first time the Danes were "taking a critical view of their own attitude."

We knew that the matter of a possible American boycott of Danish goods was the number one concern of the Danish government. The dangers of overfishing the salmon didn't appear to be receiving much attention. The export business was very important to the Danish economy. The United States was the third largest importer (after Great Britain and Norway) of Danish goods. The principal exports to this country were meat products (about 33 percent of the total), such as hams, bacon, and smoked salmon; dairy products (about 5 percent of the total), such as bleu and other cheeses; contemporary furniture; lager beer and cordials; snuff; and manufactured goods, including hair curlers.

The objective of such a mission to Copenhagen would be twofold: to secure further publicity in the Danish press and on radio and TV, and to acquaint the Danish government, in a friendly manner, with our determination to bring about a total ban on the high seas fishery.

Our committee approved my recommendations along these lines, and a letter was sent to A. C. Normann, Minister of Fisheries, on February 22, 1971. It included the following points:

> Several members of our Committee would like to visit Copenhagen in April, for the purpose of discussing with you and other Danish officials the problem of high-seas fishing for Atlantic salmon.
>
> We should state that the entire efforts of this Committee are focused currently on finding means of bringing an end to the recently steep escalation of the catch of Atlantic salmon off West Greenland.
>
> There apparently still is some misunderstanding in your country as to the source of concern in the United States, with your people still feeling that interest stems in this country from "monied special interests." Nothing could be further from the truth. Our Committee represents all classes of Americans — citizens who believe that the conservation of valuable renewable resources should not be endangered. Our cause therefore appeals literally to millions of people.
>
> As you undoubtedly are aware, some Americans have already adopted their own informal family "Don't-Buy-Danish" regimen, in protest against your high-seas salmon fishery. This Committee, however, has not issued a formal call for an all-out boycott of Danish goods. We hope that this will not be necessary, but if present trends continue, we may be forced into a position of having to place it under active and serious consideration.
>
> A visit to Denmark would be a serious mission on our part, and we would therefore want to know in advance of the visit, first, that we could have meetings with you, and also that you would arrange some time for us with the heads of other ministries and organizations. We naturally most particularly would like to have a brief audience with the Prime Minister.
>
> Please let us know as soon as possible whether or not you feel that such an exchange of ideas would serve a useful purpose.

Some nervousness was apparent among those at the State Department when I informed them of our plans, but after assurances that we would clearly state that we were not negotiating for the United States, they approved. They really had no other choice, because they knew that if they refused to give our mission their blessing, we would let that be known, and widely so. And we certainly had gained the confidence of the State Department, because I was now included as an adviser at all the important meetings on salmon.

Our CASE delegation would consist of committee members David Scoll, Otto Teller, Willard F. ("Al") Rockwell (chairman of North American Rockwell), and myself, as well as our special advisers Robert F. Hutton (American Fisheries Society) and J. Peter Kriendler (one of the owners of The 21 Club). Kriendler was a key man for this trip, for he imported large amounts of beer, cordials, and food from Danish exporters, and he also had important contacts at high levels of government and with leading food manufacturers.

Before we left, Joe Cullman (head of Philip Morris), Pete Kriendler, and I met with Baron Wedell, the largest American importer of Danish foods (Plumrose hams and other products), and Knuds Sorenson, President of the Danish-American Trade Society. They gave us names of persons to see and, as expected, urged a policy of friendly appeal rather than the taking of an aggressive position. We assured them that we were already committed to such an approach.

Meanwhile, Danish Fisheries Minister A. C. Normann had replied to my letter, saying that "such a visit could contribute to eliminate some of the misunderstandings which I feel have arisen as to the Danish fishing and its effects." A further exchange of letters had brought an acceptance of my suggestion that we meet with Poul Hartling, Minister for Foreign Affairs (who some years later was to receive prominence as the head of NATO). All this indicated that the Danish government was by now deeply concerned over the possibility of a formal boycott.

The Danes put out the welcome mat for our arrival in Copenhagen. Peter F. Heering, chairman of the Danish Tourist Board and a leading Danish industrialist—his family's company manufactured the then very popular cordial Cherry Heering — and Peter Kriendler were good friends. He had set up a first-day luncheon of about ten people in the village of Fredensborg, to be followed by a meeting at the extensive farming and forest (hunting) estate of Baron Jens Wedell-Neergaard.

At this luncheon we were able to exchange views on salmon fishing — to which most of the Danes were addicted, as was our own group. Later, at the meeting, there was a full discussion of the existing conditions — the high seas fishery. As was usually the case, the Danes were not at all knowledgeable about the Greenland fishery, the extent and escalation of the high seas catches, and the present standoff situation. We gave them much to think about.

At the time, I didn't realize how valuable these connections — two in particular — would turn out to be for the American cause. I had already heard from Bing Crosby about Svend Saabye, an ardent salmon fisherman and the leading painter in Denmark, with paintings on display in the Louvre in Paris. His specialty these days was large murals for public buildings all over Denmark — he was now working on one for the front hall of the largest hospital in Copenhagen. Much admired and well-known throughout this small nation, he immediately offered to help save the salmon, provided he did not have to call a boycott on his own people. Although he was some ten years older than I, we became close friends, a rewarding relationship that lasted until his death some fifteen years later.

The other very valuable and helpful contact — one that we were also to hear a great deal from in the future — was Jorgen Paldam. He was a salmon fisherman but, more importantly, he was also head of the Economic Administration of the City of Copenhagen (which, in effect, meant almost the entire nation, since the city was so vital to the economy). Thus, he had a special reason to be involved; his responsibility was to keep economic conditions on an even keel — especially exports, the major activity of Denmark. A boycott would disrupt that.

Our first meeting with Minister Normann used up the whole afternoon of April 21. As might be expected, it was a working group meeting, in preparation for the following day's meeting with Minister Hartling. That evening we were royally entertained at dinner, with little opportunity for getting down to business. There were many toasts, designed to try to soften us up. The Danes were masters at this art.

The next day, April 22, 1971, we met with Minister Hartling. There were about eight persons present for their side, and seven for ours. Here is the text of the memorandum I wrote the next day, for the record, covering our meeting:

At the outset, I explained that our mission was to express to the Danish government and the Danish people the deep concern of the American people over what might be the unhappy consequences of the continued fishing on the high seas for Atlantic salmon in the North Atlantic Ocean off West Greenland.

Also, I right away made it clear that we did not come to Denmark to negotiate — this, of course, being the province solely of the two governments involved.

We informed the Danish government of the rising tide of resentment in the salmon-producing nations against the devastating and indiscriminate overexploitation of salmon stocks. We stressed another highly disturbing point, namely, that Russia, Japan, and Sweden had indicated an interest in joining this high seas fishery, on the grounds that it now was "discriminatory." The result of such an escalation would most certainly endanger the very existence of the species.

We presented to the Foreign Minister eighteen official letters of protest, addressed to him, that I had been able to secure from leading broad-based conservation organizations and state governmental authorities in the United States, with total membership rolls in excess of four million people.

We repeatedly asked if there was any assurance that could be reported back to the American people that this fishery might be phased out over a period of time.

The statement was made by Fisheries Minister Normann that the government was committed to a continuance of high seas fishing for Atlantic salmon.

In this particular connection, it is to be remembered that the Baltic high seas salmon fishing is very important to the economy of Denmark. This fishery is commercial, the fish coming from Sweden, by artificial stockings of hatchery smolts, with limited return to rivers for natural reproduction. Thus, the Danes contribute nothing to this Baltic fishery, yet benefit greatly from it — the same situation that obtains off West Greenland. We surmised, and I believe correctly, that the Danish government was concerned about the possibility that a ban in the North Atlantic might weaken this structure in the Baltic.

We made a serious attempt, therefore, to separate the problem of the *Northeast* Atlantic from that of the Northwest Atlantic, pointing out that the *Northwest* Atlantic was important to us, and particularly so to Canada, from a sportfishing as well as a commercial standpoint.

Also, we emphasized that a ban on high seas operations conducted by distant oceangoing trawlers out of the Danish ports would act to increase the stocks available to the inshore West Greenland native fishermen, about whose economic status the Danish government has expressed so much concern.

The Fisheries Minister placed great emphasis on the establishment of a fund that would enable Danish salmon fishermen to convert to shrimp or other types of fishing. He claimed that the salmon fishery is no longer economical due to the fact that limitations on seasons prohibit continuous operation. Why he brought this up was not at all clear, because it weakened his argument. He perhaps was throwing out an implication that the United States might contribute to such a fund. If so, we didn't fall for this ploy.

The Fisheries officials pointed out that a number of vessels were being converted for other purposes this year, and that this should act to reduce the tonnage taken to a figure below that allowed by the 1970 Compromise Amendment. I couldn't resist this opportunity of expressing the thought that, in view of this likelihood, there should be no reason why the Danish government should not be willing to formalize this as a limitation, at the upcoming ICNAF meeting this June. The reply to this was that, before formalizing anything for the future, the government would wish to review actual tonnage figures that would be produced by the fishing in 1971, as a result of the compromise agreed to in 1970.

Foreign Minister Hartling expressed his concern over the recent publicity in America about the Danish high seas fishery, holding that any economic pressure against Denmark would act to damage the friendly relations of our two countries. Our reply to him was that many of our citizens were in favor of a boycott. Throughout this meeting, however, we repeatedly pointed out that CASE does not favor a boycott, and we hope that we may not have to take such under active consideration.

At the conclusion of this meeting, which had lasted over several hours, the Foreign Minister, with an air of finality, turned to me and said, "Mr. Buck, you hold the future of friendly relations between Denmark and the United States in your hands." I drew myself to my feet and replied, "Mr. Minister, *you* hold the future of our relations in *your* hands. Thank you for listening to our side of the story." We shook hands and our delegation retired.

Danish television was nationalized, and it and the newspapers gave considerable coverage to this meeting and the CASE story. We had had to set the record straight on several points, and the publicity we gained certainly made the public aware that their government had embarked their country on a voyage that was encountering stormy sailing in foreign waters. The subject was discussed almost daily in the Folketing (the Danish Parliament).

It was our opinion that, to stay in power, any Danish government had to give important consideration to the political pressure that could be exerted by the commercial fishermen, mostly from the island of Bornholm, who constituted a powerful labor force. This could be a serious roadblock in the future.

We did accomplish to our complete satisfaction the objective of our mission — publicity in the Danish press and on TV and radio and meetings with top government officials. Our delegation concluded that CASE's ultimate objective — the elimination of high seas salmon fishing in the northwest Atlantic — was one step closer to achievement.

10

Embargo Legislation — The Pelly Amendment

TODAY, VERY FEW PEOPLE realize that the most powerful weapon protecting salt-water fish and mammals populating and migrating in the jurisdictional waters of the United States originated in legislation pushed through the U.S. Congress by CASE. It's a fascinating story.

In 1971, it had been widely — and falsely — rumored that CASE had called for a boycott of Danish goods. As we had informed Foreign Minister Poul Hartling, we hoped that it would not be necessary to take such drastic action. In reality, we in CASE were under no illusions as to the effectiveness of boycotts — they rarely worked. It was the threat of a boycott that sometimes did the job. Embargoes, however, are entirely different. Properly organized, directed, and supported, they can be very effective, for they carry the weight of government law.

During the Salmon War, it was standard operating procedure for CASE officials to keep in close touch with key senators and congressional representatives with respect to any bills that might either help or hurt our programs for restoring the Atlantic salmon. On February 2, 1971, Congressman Thomas M. Pelly, of the state of Washington, introduced Bill H.R. 3304 in the House of Representatives "to amend the Fisheries Protective Act of August 27, 1954, to conserve and protect Atlantic salmon of North American origin." The congressman's basic interest was, of course, in salmon of Pacific Coast origin, particularly the protection of the commercial salmon fisheries there — a billion-dollar industry. Yet he apparently felt that he could best achieve his objective by riding the wave of public concern that had been built up over the Danish Atlantic salmon overkill. It would therefore be appropriate — and perhaps easier — to get legislation on the books to address the needs of both the Atlantic and the Pacific salmons.

This proposed legislation was right down our alley. CASE would see to it that, when it was finally passed into law, it would include embargo language. The Pelly bill was worded to accomplish this. The proposed legislation received so much initial support from the Atlantic salmon community that cosponsors in the House, mostly New Englanders, put up two additional and identical bills, H.R. 3305 and 3841.

Marshall Field, David Scoll, and I had met with Congressman Pelly early in the year for the purpose of planning the strategy of the conservation groups, and I had been in touch with him constantly. He now proposed that I coordinate the appearance of representatives from several salmon organizations to give expert testimony at a May 24 hearing on these bills before the House Subcommittee on Fisheries and Wildlife Conservation. All this was arranged and carefully orchestrated in advance.

The *Congressional Record* of May 24, 1971 on Commercial Fisheries, Serial No. 92–4. (p. 303) contains the following:

> Statement of Richard Buck, Chairman, Committee on the Atlantic Salmon Emergency.
> Our committee is in support of House Bills 3304, 3305, and 3841.
>
> The Committee on the Atlantic Salmon Emergency, popularly known as CASE, was organized in 1970 to develop programs designed to increase worldwide stocks of Atlantic salmon, focusing particularly on the threat to conservation of the species on account of high seas fishing, principally by the Danes.
> In 1965 the Danes moved in on a newly discovered major feeding grounds in the Davis Strait off West Greenland. Each year, they steeply escalated nettings, so that by 1970 they

were taking an estimated four hundred thousand salmon. The principal salmon-producing countries, such as the United States, Canada, the United Kingdom and Ireland, and others, have repeatedly protested this ruthless plunder, in the proper international assemblies, and through diplomatic channels.

In the high seas feeding areas, salmon stocks are inextricably intermingled. They come from different spawning streams, different river systems, different nations, different hemispheres. No man, and no type of fishing gear yet known to man, no method of control, can separate them out. Thus high seas fishing takes indiscriminately from perhaps the very river runs needing particular protection, and results in absolutely no rational or scientific means of conserving basic stocks or ensuring adequate escapements for spawning.

Danish fisheries authorities and the Danish government profess great interest in conservation measures, and it is assumed therefore that they certainly understand this basic tenet of proper management of salmon stocks. Yet they never acknowledge this basic principle, probably because to do so would place them in an indefensible position.

There are important reasons for supporting a total ban on this fishing. The coastal states have substantial investments in propagating and managing the fish. Severe depletion would cause loss of livelihood to tens of thousands of commercial fishermen all around the North Atlantic shores. It would bring an end to sport fishing for Atlantic salmon.

The only international body set up to work towards conservation measures in this feeding area is the International Commission for Northwest Atlantic Fisheries (ICNAF), but this convention lacks the authority to control dissenters. For three straight years, against the weight of world opinion, Denmark has refused to agree to cease high seas operations. There is no law that can stop her.

In the opinion of CASE, only political and economic pressure will cause Denmark to cease this ruthless plunder.

Our CASE Committee has not yet issued a formal call for an all-out boycott by Americans of all Danish products, but we have it under active and serious consideration. No one wants a boycott, but, as a last resort, people historically have arrived at this frame of mind. Many Americans have already taken this route, and adopted their own informal family boycotts. This CASE Committee, with complete confidence that it enjoys the respect and following of leading conservation organizations and substantial numbers of private citizens, feels that the Atlantic salmon crisis today is either at, or very near, this point of determination.

A delegation representing our Committee has just returned from Copenhagen, where our mission was to inform the Danish government and the Danish public of the desire by many Americans for aggressive action. We appealed for a cessation of this reckless and uncivilized practice. We met with the Minister of Fisheries and the Minister for Foreign Affairs. We presented positions and statements from conservation organizations, including state governmental agencies, condemning the high seas fishery. We received no encouragement whatsoever.

Thus time is of the essence. For the present, the CASE Committee feels that the enacting into law of these salmon bills could act to postpone, and perhaps even to prevent, the probability of an all-out boycott of Danish products by the American public at large.

The corollary to this legislative action should be its implementation through certification by the Department of Commerce.

Such legislative, and subsequent executive, action by the United States government would clothe with dignity the forceful acts necessary to the conservation of a valuable national resource. Such a course is vastly preferable to an unofficial boycott which should be undertaken by the citizens only as the final persuader.

The Committee on the Atlantic Salmon Emergency strongly recommends that your Subcommittee take favorable action on these bills.

————————

My testimony was followed by intensive questioning by subcommittee members, which gave me an opportunity to enlarge on the statement with supporting evidence of the Danish overexploitation. Wilfred Carter then read a statement for the International Atlantic Salmon Foundation, and David E. Scoll, Vice President of the Federation of Fly Fishermen, did the same for his organization. We felt that we had made constructive and perhaps decisive contributions.

On July 8, 1971, Ambassador Donald L. McKernan, Special Assistant to the Secretary of the Department of State for Fisheries and Wildlife — considered the most experienced and knowledgeable authority on international fisheries affairs in the United States — testified before the same subcommittee that he was generally in agreement with the purposes of H.R. 3304 and particularly in the implementation of internationally approved rules. He recommended specifically "the application with discretion of the principles of an embargo," and stated that "the President should have the authority to determine in individual cases the extent of the action which would be applied to the importation of fish products from those countries not applying the widely accepted conservation rules."

So these bills were broadened and amended accordingly, with the pertinent and most important parts now reading:

> SEC. 8(a). When the Secretary of Commerce determines that nationals of a foreign country, directly or indirectly, are conducting fishing operations in a manner or under circumstances which diminish the effectiveness of an international fishery conservation program, the Secretary of Commerce shall certify such fact to the President. Upon receipt of such certification, the President may direct the Secretary of the Treasury to prohibit the bringing or the importation into the United States of fish products of the offending country for such duration as he determines appropriate and to the extent that such prohibition is sanctioned by the General Agreement on Tariffs and Trade.
>
> (b) Within 60 days following certification by the Secretary of Commerce, the President shall notify the Congress of any action taken by him pursuant to such certification. In the event the President fails to direct the Secretary of the Treasury to

prohibit the importation of fish products of the offending country, or if such prohibition does not cover all fish products of the offending country, the President shall inform the Congress of the reasons therefor.

(c) It shall be unlawful for any person subject to the jurisdiction of the United States knowingly to bring or import into, or cause to be imported into, the United States any fish products prohibited by the Secretary of the Treasury pursuant to this section.

These amendments met with our complete satisfaction. The new wording extended the regulatory measure to all species of fish, not just Atlantic salmon, and it covered sea mammals as well. We knew that broadening the base would make it easier to get the legislation through Congress.

And best of all, this bill as amended was the perfect foil for our use — the best threat to Denmark that could possibly be devised. An embargo of Danish fish products would bring to bear the full weight and power of the government of the United States and would be much more successful than any private-sector boycott.

CASE members lost no time shifting into high gear to secure passage in the Congress. We counted particularly on Trout Unlimited throwing the full support of its 15,000 members behind CASE's leadership. Both Otto Teller and I were vice presidents and members of the executive committee of TU, and President Elliott Donnelley had backed CASE with both his personal and his financial support. TU's Executive Director Pete Van Gytenbeek was already effectively organizing our councils and chapters in the overall salmon effort. We also were fortunate in having Stephen G. ("Salty") Saltzman, an active and persuasive lobbyist, as TU's Washington representative.

Believing that there is no substitute for personal persuasion, I spent a great deal of time wearing down a considerable amount of shoe leather in the halls of Congress. Congressman Silvio Conte of Massachusetts, the ranking member of the powerful Appropriations

Committee of the House and a salmon fisherman, was a great help. Congressman James Cleveland, from my home state of New Hampshire, was also a salmon fisherman and an avid supporter of CASE. They both were happy to set up meetings for me with key House and Senate members and their staffs.

CASE acted as the coordinator of information and effort regarding this legislation for not only the leading Atlantic salmon organizations but also the more broad-based groups.

Pete Van Gytenbeek and Salty Saltzman involved the TU membership in an enthusiastic letter-writing campaign, and letters started pouring in to Congressman Pelly's office. I made a point of being in Washington during the week when the bills would be up before a vote of the full House. Every morning at 8:30 I would meet with the congressman and we would tally the votes for and against. I remember that about 90 percent were in favor, with those opposed being mostly a few American importers of Danish fish products, such as smoked salmon.

The legislation sailed through the House on the afternoon of July 8.

An identical Senate bill, S. 2191, had been cosponsored by Senator Tom McIntyre of New Hampshire. He had a hearing set up on the morning of November 30 before the Senate's Committee on Commerce. Appearances and statements were made by CASE, the International Atlantic Salmon Foundation, and Trout Unlimited. I followed generally the same exercise I had for the House bills, but I paid particular attention to senators who were members of what was referred to as the New England caucus and was successful in securing 100 percent support. In order to avoid hearings and save valuable time in committee work, the House version, H.R. 3304, was adopted and passed by the full Senate on the day of the hearings, November 30, to become Public Law 92–219 on December 23, 1971.

The ensuing letter of December 16 from Salty Saltzman is worth recording:

Congratulations! You have a piece of legislation with which to threaten the Danes and their high seas fishery for the Atlantic salmon....

You and CASE deserve a hearty clap on your respective backs! A word of advice, though: Don't approach the Danish embassy in daylight, and bring cavalry if you approach by night!

Staffers on the Senate Committee are still shaking their heads at the extent and quality of interest your committee turned to this problem. I have it from them that the committee's members were "swamped" with mail and calls. The staff was highly complimentary of the way in which you and your committee approached its work. You gained—and earned!—a constituency.

Standing by for the next set of orders; there's still work to be done, as you point out.

Regards and seasons greetings.

This law has always been referred to as the Pelly Amendment, and because it has been considered the core element of protection for fish and sea mammals of U.S. origin, Pelly's actual wording has been carried over in ensuing years as part of the basic authority contained in maritime laws of the United States government.

Other than fisheries experts, very few people know anything about the Pelly Amendment, and those that do often ask how many times it has been enforced. Actually, the sanctions (embargoes) have never been imposed; they have only been threatened. The threat itself, in the form of certifications, is so powerful that embargoes have not been required. To date, eight foreign countries have been certified under the Pelly Amendment on a total of sixteen occasions:

Country	Year	Cause
Japan	1974	Commercial whaling
USSR	1974	Commercial whaling
Chile	1978	Commercial whaling
Peru	1978	Commercial whaling

Korea	1978	Commercial whaling
USSR	1985	Commercial whaling
Norway	1986	Commercial whaling
Japan	1988	Research whaling
Korea	1989	Driftnetting
Taiwan	1989	Driftnetting
Norway	1990	Research whaling
Japan	1991	Turtle trade
Korea	1991	Driftnetting
Taiwan	1991	Driftnetting
Mexico	1991	Tuna/porpoise
Norway	1992	Research whaling

Sanctions have never been imposed by the President under the Pelly Amendment; certifications and the threat of sanctions have been effective negotiating and diplomatic tools. In every case, presidential decisions regarding the imposition of Pelly sanctions have been based primarily on conservation grounds, which is itself testimony to the effectiveness of the statute as a tool for conservation purposes. Although the Pelly Amendment has never been used for Atlantic salmon, it is comforting to know that it is there should it be needed.

All of us who were a part of the work of the Committee on the Atlantic Salmon Emergency in support of Pelly — in whatever capacity — can be proud that CASE was able to play the decisive role in the passage of this important legislation.

11

Private-Sector Involvement

IMPORTANT EVENTS often begin with a chance encounter. There is one such episode that resulted in perhaps the most important high-level meeting of the whole CASE effort.

In June 1971, my wife and I gave a cocktail party at our house in Manchester-by-the-Sea, Massachusetts. One of the guests turned out to be a salmon fisherman. He was from Washington and mentioned that he had heard about the Danish overexploitation and was wondering how he could help. I said that I was trying to figure out how to get the top people in the Nixon administration interested in the salmon problem. He said, "You might get a hold of my friend Peter Thompson of Easton, Maryland. He knows them all. Call him and mention my name." I did this the next day. Thompson listened carefully, and then said, "How can I help?" My answer was — boldly — that I wanted to meet with Rogers Morton, the Secretary of the Interior. Thompson said, "He's one of my best friends; I'll call you in a few days." Well — I had been in situations like this before, and usually nothing important came of them, even though people were well-intentioned. This time was different. Peter Thompson just happened to be one of those fellows who doesn't mess around. He called back the next day and said, "You have an appointment with Rogers Morton next Tuesday at 10 A.M."

Peter Thompson — who over the years has become a close friend — and I met with Rogers Morton as planned. The secretary had not been involved in Atlantic salmon matters but became very interested. The three of us finally decided that it would be productive to set aside a day for a full discussion of ways and means of stopping the Greenland overkill. On July 2, I received an invitation from him to attend a luncheon on July 15 at the Department of the Interior, the purpose of which was "to promote discussion among the appropriate Executive Departments concerning the steps which may now be taken to study and conserve Atlantic salmon."

In the spirit of the occasion, I had two large Atlantic salmon sent down to Rogers Morton to serve as the main course of an elegant luncheon that took place in the secretary's private dining room at the Interior Building. In attendance were Rogers C. B. Morton, Maurice H. Stans, Ambassador Donald L. McKernan, Nathaniel P. Reed, Robert M. White, Howard Pollock, Wilfred M. Carter, Peter S. Thompson, and me.

At the afternoon meeting, I briefed those in attendance on the current situation, which was followed by a general discussion of the issues involved. At the conclusion of this session, Secretary of Commerce Stans turned to me and said, "It seems quite clear, Mr. Buck, that what you want is a North American policy on Atlantic salmon conservation. Let's meet tomorrow to discuss parameters and set the wheels in motion."

The next morning, I outlined in detail the action program that I had been working on for some time. This was generally endorsed, with minor variations, and consisted of:

> 1) A personal appeal by the President of the United States, direct to the Prime Minister of Denmark, for an agreement by Denmark to an early phasing out of the high-seas fishery for Atlantic salmon, this appeal also to contain.
>
> 2) A request that Denmark receive a delegation from the United States whose mission will be, first, to hold discussions with the Danish government with respect to a desirable means of achieving such a ban on high-seas operations, and, second, to discuss terms of a possible fisheries agreement which might be acceptable to the nations and territories involved, primarily Denmark (for Greenland and The Faroe Islands) and Norway.

Assistant Secretary of the Interior Reed proposed that Canada and the United States should agree to act together to sponsor such a mission and meeting. This concept met with the approval of all those present.

Secretary Stans proposed that a North Atlantic salmon policy be established and subscribed to by the United States and Canada. Again, there appeared to be complete agreement that this was desirable. Ambassador McKernan offered the opinion that such an agreement could be consummated.

Nat Reed was asked to prepare this North Atlantic salmon policy and, after the meeting, asked Wilfred Carter and me to give him our collective suggestions as to the content of such a policy. We accomplished this, using my testimony at the congressional hearing on the Pelly Amendment as the core of the position. I then submitted our suggestion to Reed.

The next step would be for the federal government agencies involved to approve the final draft of the policy and secure Canada's acceptance, after which the recommended actions could be undertaken by the government. These agencies enthusiastically supported the policy.

Here is what Dr. Robert M. White, administrator of the National Oceanic and Atmospheric Administration (NOAA), had to say in an August 16, 1971, letter to me on the subject:

> You are well aware of the various possible approaches to salmon conservation, as well as the problems associated with these options. We are determined to seek the most effective international program for salmon that can be developed. To achieve this goal we plan to meet in the near future with our counterparts and facilitate progress toward the development of a viable salmon conservation program. We know that you are committed to this same end. I hope you will not hesitate to keep us advised of your views.

Another official who had attended the meeting, Howard Pollock, assistant administrator of NOAA, commented in a similar letter: "The Administration is ready to focus attention at the highest levels to the Atlantic salmon problem. One thing is obvious — something must be done, and quickly."

We were well started on the long, arduous road that could lead to achieving the ultimate objective.

This July meeting with Stans and Morton turned out to be the central motivating factor in getting other top members of the Nixon administration involved in the U.S. salmon effort. Secretary of State William Rogers and Russell Train, Administrator of the Council on Environmental Quality, were informed and became fully supportive.

To get the ball rolling, Secretary Morton appointed Nathaniel Reed to be the sole representative of the Department of the Interior, working on a strong new position on the management policies concerning Atlantic salmon. This was a welcome move, since I had known Nat Reed in private life and had also been working with him for several months on the Pelly Amendment. I knew that when Nat made up his mind to go for something, he went. We needed people like that.

From then on, high-level meetings on strategy and tactics took place regularly with Don McKernan at the State Department during the late summer and fall of 1971. My part in all this was to develop and coordinate the involvement of private-sector groups and individuals in the United States and other salmon-producing nations in an all-out move to stop the Danish overkill off Greenland.

THE CASE "UNDERGROUND" IN DENMARK

At this point in the Salmon War, I kept wondering just how well our effort was succeeding in Denmark. I reasoned that the Danes should be willing to listen to our side of the story, because they were always referred to as a fair-minded and friendly people. And who better to give this story to them than their own salmon fishermen? So I arranged for a trip in August.

During the CASE mission to Denmark in April 1971, I had taken pains to lay the groundwork for what I euphemistically began referring to as our "underground." Actually, in time it would come to deserve that appellation.

It all began by my enlisting the aid of Peter Kriendler, who was now one of CASE's special advisers and had been so helpful during our Copenhagen trip. His connections were with the most important people in Denmark. Peter Heering, whom I had met on the same trip, could also be counted on. But I decided to build the underground around Svend Saabye, with whom I was now corresponding regularly and who was eager to help. His closest friends were people with whom he went salmon fishing every year. They were among the leaders of industry in Denmark, mostly as manufacturers and exporters. Thus they also were influential in government circles, for they had to protect their channels of trade, particularly with the United States and members of the fledgling European Economic Community.

In a letter, Svend proposed that he and some of these friends meet with me for several days for a thorough discussion of the background of the Salmon War and possible solutions. The venue he suggested was far from displeasing—the famous Laerdal River in Norway, one of the premier rivers of the North Atlantic for fly-fishing for salmon.

So my wife and I went and met these men and their wives at a lovely inn called Rikheim Gard, adjacent to the river. It was of whitewashed stone set in a spotless and well-tended flower garden surrounded by a manicured evergreen hedge. We had all this to ourselves for five days—no eavesdroppers. Most of the party spoke some English, but I spoke no Danish. Still, we got along fine. I understand now why people find the Danes such good company; they were charmers. The men met and talked all morning, followed by the day's big meal with the ladies—a sumptuous luncheon—and then a nap. Later—for the rest of the day until early nighttime (still in daylight)—we fished for the salmon.

A personal note here may be of particular interest to naturalists and salmon fisherfolk. Of all the salmon rivers I have fished all over the North Atlantic, this was the most turbulent and raging. It was exciting, because the salmon were running these rapids, and that's where they would rise, from alongside or just in front of big boulders.

One fish that I took with a large Black Mary fly, size 1½, weighed twenty-two pounds. The weight itself was not important, but this hen fish had the largest overall fins and tail in proportion to her size of any salmon I have ever taken. Svend Saabye, artist that he was, made a very accurate charcoal sketch of this Laerdal fish on the drawing paper he always packed in his duffel bag for this purpose. The drawing now hangs framed in my office. The tail is 9½ inches broad, the caudal fin 4 inches broad, and the dorsal fin 4½ inches (extended)! I also have in my office a mounted 32½ pound hen salmon from the Restigouche in New Brunswick with a tail span of only 10 inches, a ventral fin of only 3 inches, and a dorsal fin of only 4 inches (extended).

In the case of the Laerdal, salmon need a tremendous tail drive together with a great steering and planing ability of the fins to enable them to navigate these boisterous and violent stretches of rapids, so they are long, taut, and compact. The Restigouche fish is full-bodied, broad, and chunky. The answer here, of course, is that the Restigouche River is generally a big, wide, deep, relatively slow-moving river.

This example offers further convincing proof that over the millennia salmon have taken on the structural characteristics, bodily forms, and appendages necessary for coping with the particular requirements of the natal river in which they will spawn.

As for the business sessions at Rikheim Gard, here is the gist of my memorandum of August 10, 1971, to CASE:

> We covered all aspects of the West Greenland fishery, geopolitical, sociological, and economic. In turn, the Danes pointed out that the public-at-large does not understand, and couldn't care less, about the Atlantic salmon problem. They feel that only rich Americans and Englishmen fish for salmon. They don't know that the species is in danger. This in turn is because the Danish

press and radio-television, if not actually controlled in this socialist country, are certainly subject to governmental pressure, and the government reassures them that there is no scientific proof of danger of extinction. Thus an all-out CASE public relations effort in Denmark would not only fall flat, but it would not be permitted to have an audience in the first place.

These Danes are 100 percent in favor of the boycott principle! They say over and over again that only the threat of economic pressure will change their government's position. They are too highly placed to come out openly and announce this, but they want CASE to be aggressive, and they will use this to persuade their government.

American importers should go back to their Danish exporters, to get them to put pressure on the government. They feel that letters from concerned Americans to government officials are effective, and that this effort should be intensified.

If the threat of the boycott is unproductive, they will understand that there is nothing left but to actually declare a formal boycott. They say that the boycott will produce ill will but it will succeed, because the exporters will make the government come around.

By the end of the week, it was apparent that all of us were working for the same objective — a healthy future for the species. This nucleus of influential Danes was ready to take action domestically to bring about a ban on the Greenland high seas fishery. Most important, these Danes produced a formal statement that would be used to enlist the support of key groups such as trout fishing clubs and exporting concerns. (There were no salmon clubs in Denmark, because the country has no rivers that would support salmon runs.) This statement set forth the following points:

An effort should be made on a purely Danish or possibly Scandinavian basis.

Contacts with CASE will be of importance, but any actual connection with CASE must strongly be advised against.

The above chief point of view — independent Danish initiative — does not mean that the views of CASE should not be stated, and it seems reasonable that the chairman of CASE should get an opportunity to express his views with one of the big Danish newspapers.

It must be added that a Danish committee should be set up, which could, of course, strongly repudiate a boycott.

The task of the committee must be to create interest for the preservation of the Atlantic salmon and to bring about a Danish prohibition in strict regulation of high seas net fishing.

We couldn't have asked for more, and from then on we in CASE respected and supported their position — they could do more for the salmon by their own private efforts than we could by trying to work with them officially.

And they did carry out their mandate as expressed in the above statement. A committee of Danes was soon organized, including several of those who had been with us at Rikheim Gard as well as representatives of the leading trout fishing clubs in Denmark. The committee made its feelings known to the Danish fisheries minister. They also arranged for me to be interviewed in the United States on a program that was beamed all over Denmark. There was no question in my mind that this group had considerable influence — probably decisive — in getting the prime minister to eventually come down on the side of a ban on high seas fishing for salmon.

While at the Laerdal, I had discussed with Svend plans that Lee Wulff and I had made for a trip to Copenhagen in November to meet with angling associations and individuals. Lee Wulff would be the speaker, talking about the art of fly-fishing and how important the salmon were as a source of recreation. My role was to be in the background, present only to answer any questions that might come up about the CASE movement. But because of the impression I had gathered of the "climate" in Denmark, it seemed appropriate to stay clear at this particular time. Things were going so well that it might be counterproductive to press our point any further. I discussed this with Svend Saabye, and he agreed. So I told Lee that our trip was off.

NORWAY

My wife and I went from the Laerdal to stay at the American embassy in Oslo with a friend, Philip K. Crowe, the U.S. Ambassador to Norway and a salmon fisherman who knew the Danish background very well. Before his current assignment, he had been the U.S. Ambassador to Denmark. Philip wanted to be brought up-to-date and also to help promote the CASE effort. This he would continue to do throughout his tour of duty.

The Norwegian salmon situation was very serious. Before 1950, about 800 tons of salmon had been taken both commercially (including driftnetting and fixed nets) and by the rod in territorial waters. Considerable money had been spent in recent years, with some 150 new fish ladders having been built, all of which had added about 500 miles of new salmon water. The result of all this was an aggressive buildup of the commercial catch. Between 1950 and 1960, the total take increased to 2,000 metric tons and has stayed about the same. Angling had represented only about 15 percent of the total and had suffered at the hands of commercial fishing. Preliminary indications were that the 1971 angling catch would be disastrously low. For instance, on the great Vosso River, the 1969 catch was 72, the 1970 catch was 102, and so far in 1971 it was 19!

The official Norwegian position was that high seas fishing is unscientific, but Norway let its own fishermen operate because Danish boats were working close off the Norwegian coast. Thus, the overall situation in the northern European sector was chaotic. Sweden now had boats on the high seas for salmon (off the Lofotens), as did West Germany, Denmark, and Norway. England was apathetic about doing anything to stop high seas operations.

All this led me to the conclusion that the United States would have to go it alone to protect our restoration effort — North Atlantic salmon policy with respect to salmon of North American origin. We would, of course, be helped immeasurably if Canada would go along with us in facing up to the Danes.

Phil Crowe was very enthusiastic about the work of CASE. Unofficially, he was strongly in favor of exerting great economic pressure on the Danes, and his only fear was that CASE would not go far enough. Philip was working continually to try to get all the Scandinavians he knew to understand the inequity of the high seas fishery. He arranged a large Sunday luncheon to which he invited a number of prominent Norwegians, including several top public officials, shipping magnates, and owners of salmon lodges. After lunch, I showed the sound film *High Seas Fishing Off Greenland*, answered questions, and spoke about the salmon problem. The party went off in good style, and the showing of the film apparently accomplished its purpose — to provide a factual background and to support the story that Philip was telling wherever he went.

And so we went back to the United States wiser and full of confidence that the Americans were on the right — and necessary — track. We could win out, if only we didn't drop the ball.

PRIVATE-SECTOR INVOLVEMENT IN THE UNITED STATES

Early in September, I set to work on the next step in the CASE campaign, which was to get our private-sector organizations to agree on a formal recommendation to the U.S. government to implement the U.S. position being developed under the leadership of Nat Reed of Interior and Don McKernan of State. Here the previous coordinating work that CASE had done proved fruitful. We now had a solid constituency of leading salmon organizations in the United States that supported the action program that CASE had previously recommended to the administration.

I set up a full-day meeting for September 27, 1971, of the top officials of these groups at The 21 Club in New York City. The invitation read:

> CASE has promoted a plan calling for the U.S. and Canada to approach Denmark proposing a short-term fisheries agreement (not a long-term formal treaty) which would liquidate the high seas fishery. A furthering of this ambitious, complicated, and difficult effort requires the cooperation and support of leading conservation organizations in the U.S. and Canada interested in the Atlantic salmon.

RESOLUTION OF SEPTEMBER 27, 1971 WITH RESPECT TO
A NORTH ATLANTIC SALMON POLICY
BY
CERTAIN CONSERVATION ORGANIZATIONS AND INDIVIDUALS

WHEREAS, the Atlantic Salmon (Salmo salar) is a valuable natural resource, providing recreation and food for our citizens; and,

WHEREAS, the propagation, management, and harvesting of this species provides employment directly and indirectly to large numbers of persons in the United States and Canada; and,

WHEREAS, governments, private industry, conservation organizations and individuals in both the United States and Canada have invested, and plan to continue investing, millions of dollars both in the restoration, the propagation and management of Atlantic salmon stocks of North America; and,

WHEREAS, Atlantic salmon of North American origin leave the river of birth and descend to the ocean to use the Davis Strait off West Greenland and as a principal feeding ground, before returning to the natal river to spawn; and,

WHEREAS, a high seas fishery in the Davis Strait, organized and developed principally by Danish nationals during the past decade, is basically unsound from a conservation point of view, taking fish indiscriminately, perhaps from the very North American river runs needing particular protection, and thus precluding scientific control of return to rivers of origin; and,

WHEREAS, a joint cooperative effort on the part of the United States and Canada to persuade the Danes and others to agree to liquidate this high seas fishery holds more promise of success than unilateral action by each country separately; and

WHEREAS, apart from the depletion caused by the high seas fishery, the problems of the two countries surrounding the rebuilding of, and ultimate increase in, stocks of Atlantic salmon of North American origin have many aspects in common, the solving of which could be immeasureably aided by joint deliberations;

NOW, THEREFORE, BE IT RESOLVED, that the undersigned substantial and vitally concerned conservation organizations, assembled in New York City, this 27th day of September, 1971, do herewith urge the United States Government, utilizing in particular the offices of the Department of the Interior, the Department of Commerce, and the Department of State, to propose to our Northern neighbor that the United States and Canada join in an agreement to establish a "North Atlantic Salmon Policy", which policy shall, first, affirm a belief in that scientific management of Atlantic salmon stocks requires that harvesting occur essentially at or near the mouths of rivers or in the rivers themselves and that fishing for salmon on the high seas is contrary to principles of good conservation, and, second, provide that the two countries consult, plan and cooperate in research, management and propagation of Atlantic salmon with the objective of restoring the species to abundance in New England and Canadian waters.

The Committee on the
Atlantic Salmon Emergency
by Richard A. Buck, Chairman

National Wildlife Federation
by Philip A. Douglas
Asst. to Exec. Dir.

[signature] Fisher Institute
by Richard H. Stroud, Exec. Vice Pres.

Federation of Fly Fishermen
by James E. Gifford, Pres.
(cso)

Theodore Gordon Flyfishers, Inc.
by Gardner L. Grant, Pres.

TRout Unlimited
by Ray ___, Vice President

International Atlantic Salmon Foundation
by Francis Goelet, Pres.

Conservation Foundation
by Sydney Howe, President

North American Wildlife Foundation
by C.R. Gutermuth, Secretary

The Wilderness Society
by Stewart M. Brandborg

Wildlife Management Institute
by Daniel A. Poole, President

Friends of the Earth
Geo. Alderson
Legislative Director

The Wildlife Society
Fred W. Evanden
Exec Director

American Forestry Assn
William E. Towell
Exec Vice President

Izaak Walton League of America
by Jack Lorenz
Conservation Director

National Audubon Society
by: Elvis J. Stahr,
President

Sierra Club
by: Michael McCloskey
Executive Director

The response far exceeded my expectations, with fourteen environmental organizations — the leading ones in the United States — participating. The meeting itself can be characterized as having displayed an understanding of the seriousness of the problem and a universal desire to solve it on the part of all present. I had prepared a rough outline of the language that might be used in a resolution to be presented to the U.S. government. We spent the morning discussing the background of the whole Greenland situation and the plans of the U.S. governmental agencies in trying to bring the matter to a successful conclusion. In the afternoon, a final resolution was hammered out that met with the approval of all:

I delivered the resolution to Nat Reed on October 6. He seemed pleased with it and began referring to me as "the watchdog of the Atlantic." Coming from Nat — an action-taker himself — I considered that a big compliment. Next, officials of the Department of the Interior wove such parts of the resolution that they deemed pertinent and desirable into the North American joint policy statement that Interior, Commerce, and State were preparing for use by Canada and the United States. The Canadians welcomed the initiative, and the wording of a common agreement was thrashed out at a meeting in Washington on November 22-23.

Then, on December 24, 1971, President Nixon included in his customary Christmas Eve broadcast to the American people an announcement that the Joint Statement on Atlantic Salmon had been signed by American and Canadian fisheries officials.

On Christmas Day, the Pelly Amendment was signed into Public Law 92-219 at the White House — two big Christmas presents for Salar the salmon!

12

Reaching Agreement

AS THE NEW YEAR 1972 dawned, it was obvious that the CASE public relations effort was kicking up a big storm in Denmark—just what we wanted, and well beyond our expectations. Our strategy was to have the Danish people know just what was going on, understand the injustice of it, and get their government to do something about it.

To keep this whole geopolitical situation in proper perspective, it is important to review the principal factors of cause and effect, namely, the escalation of the high seas driftnet fishery operated by Danish flag vessels out of Bornholm, and the ensuing reduction in home-water catch in the largest salmon-producing nation, Canada.

Danish High Seas Catch

Year	Pounds
1965	80,000
1966	262,400
1967	672,000
1968	1,208,300
1969	2,646,000

Canadian Atlantic Salmon Catch

Year	Angling (Numbers of Fish)	Commercial (Pounds)
1969	122,000	6,300,000
1970	92,000 (off 25%)	4,700,000 (off 25%)
1971	65,000 (off 29%)	3,900,000 (off 17%)

In two years, the Canadian angling catch was off 53 percent, and the commercial catch was off 37 percent.

The chaotic political climate in Denmark played right into our hands. I had met with our Ambassador to Denmark, Guilford Dudley, during my trips to Copenhagen, and he and his staff were very supportive of our effort. The regional fisheries attaché, A. Hauge, made a point of sending me pertinent clippings from the leading Danish newspapers, "loosely translated," as he put it, into English from the Danish. Here in his own words is what he had to say about the overall situation in Denmark:

> Fisheries Minister Christian Thomsen protects the Danish salmon fishery and export interests and rejects the United States protests against the exploitation off West Greenland.... Thomsen of course was interested in the Bornholm (Danish) trawlers which had been fishing on the salmon in the North Atlantic for several years.
>
> Prime Minister Jens Otto Krag's minority government also had a Greenland Minister, Knud Hertling, who had chosen to protect the local Greenlanders' interests. Thus he agreed with critics of the "high-seas" operations, believing there was reason to implement a "total preservation" of the salmon outside Greenland's 12-mile fisheries limit, thus preserving the possibilities of future catches for the local "inshore" native fishermen.
>
> The Prime Minister had been urged to clarify the government's position in this salmon feud between the two ministers by responding to the question of whether statements by Thomsen or Hertling represented the government's position.

An excerpt from the newspaper, the *Politiken*, of December 28, 1971, shows that CASE's work with the American importers of Danish foods had begun to have the desired effect:

> There is danger that the new flare-up in the salmon war will cost Denmark several million kroner as a result of a decline in the sales of Danish products in the United States.

According to Arne Christiansen, Folketing [the Parliament] member and Agricultural Council information director, there is considerable risk that the Danish sales of canned meat will be affected should Denmark not immediately react to the criticism of the Danish salmon fishery in the North Atlantic by certain circles in the United States.... Mr. Christiansen is of the opinion that several U.S. buyers hesitate to buy Danish products because of these reports, and, recently, the sale of Danish ham has been affected.

By far the leading newspaper in Denmark was the *Berlingske Tidende*, whose editor, Terkel Terkelsen, was very powerful and very close to top government officials. We never met, yet he and I developed an extensive correspondence. Although he was very careful in his expressions at first, and naturally inclined toward Danish interests, he was fair-minded in presenting the U.S. point of view. He was also a close personal friend of Svend Saabye, and he ultimately came to realize that it would be in the best interests of Denmark to stop the high seas fishery. Here's an excerpt from the *Berlingske Tidende* of December 28, 1971:

> The strongest declaration yet [the U.S.-Canadian Joint Statement on Atlantic Salmon] has stated that Canada and the U.S. were extremely concerned over the failure among North Atlantic fisheries nations to agree to a ban against salmon fishing. President Nixon signed the bill which authorizes him to stop an established export of fisheries products from Denmark to the U.S. valued at 150 million kroner annually.... The salmon feud thus has shifted from private protectionistic organizations and sports fishermen associations to a government plan even though the private campaign has played a large part in the flare-up.
>
> The joint declaration from Ottawa and Washington fails to mention any specific nation but it is clearly directed toward Denmark and is the culmination of attacks on the Danish fishery which began to grow in strength in recent years. The declaration refers to failing international negotiations and shows how much emphasis the two countries attach to Denmark's unwillingness to join the request for a ban, thereby leaving it without effect.

Hauge also sent me a translation of an editorial of December 29, 1971, entitled "Cold War on Salmon," also from the *Berlingske Tidende*.

> There is reason to take the salmon war a bit more seriously than Denmark has been previously inclined to do. The mere fact that the Fisheries Minister and the Greenland Minister are in direct opposition indicates the possibility of several viewpoints in the matter. The two posts were previously held by one minister, and the problems may well have caused inner conflicts of conscience, which have resulted in only very limited arrangements that are entirely incapable of reaching a cease-fire in the salmon war.
>
> During the American campaign against the Danish salmon fishery...a small group of determined individuals has within a short time been able to move the Congress to implement a bill that in reality is directed toward Denmark. This has been possible because of public feeling, which is founded on a late-awakened U.S. interest for nature conservation, after the Americans for several generations have succeeded in destroying a continent.... Added to this fact, the support from many millions of sports fishermen...and the fast passage [of the bill] through the complicated machinery of the Congress are clear indications that there exists a public opinion behind the bill.

Perhaps the most interesting, and certainly the most accurate, account of what was going on in Denmark at the highest levels of government came in a letter of January 3, 1972, from Svend Saabye. Here are some of his more important points:

> The salmon war has been escalated. We have a new government, and it will be some time before the political situation can be defined as far as Atlantic salmon are concerned. Terkel Terkelsen and I had a meeting with Minister for Economics Ivar Norgaard, who was well informed on the salmon problem and particularly concerned about the dangers to Danish trade with the U.S. He told us, in confidence, that the salmon war would be solved in connection with other commercial and fishing problems.

The new Minister for Greenland wants the salmon protected with only Greenlanders permitted to fish along the coastline. So the opposition parties in the Danish parliament are asking: "Are we going to have a minister crisis?" The Prime Minister answered this by commenting that there will be no crisis — the question will be handled before the next meeting of ICNAF in May 1972.

But today the Danish radio told us that the fishermen from Bornholm are demanding that the Minister for Greenland abdicate. So the war is going on, but something will have to happen now. Yet it always is difficult to give up strategical positions.

Back home, CASE had been continuing its extensive public relation's program whenever and wherever possible. Early in December 1971, I was interviewed by the Washington correspondent of *Berlingske Tidende*, and this received full-page treatment in that paper. Next, shortly before Christmas, a film crew from the Danish national television interviewed me near my home in Hancock, New Hampshire, standing on a bridge over the Cold River, a tributary of the Connecticut. In this stream, the U.S. Fish and Wildlife Service was stocking young Atlantic salmon fry. I naturally pointed out the futility of stocking if the future fish were to be decimated by the Greenland fishery. The program went out over the Danish network several days after Christmas. All this had apparently been arranged by the committee that had been organized by our Rikheim Gard "underground."

Other CASE members also appeared on many national, regional, and local programs. On January 20, 1972, we held a CASE press conference in New York City that was attended by over forty-five correspondents, including representatives of such newspapers as the *New York Times*, *New York Daily News*, and *Washington Post*. At this meeting we showed the movie *High Seas Fishing Off Greenland*.

Our posture in these interviews was one of an appeal to the newly elected Danish government to stop the high seas fishery and join the salmon-producing countries in a conservation and restoration program. We did not threaten a private-sector boycott per se, but pointed out that there might be no alternative to implementation of the new law (the Pelly Amendment) in the event Denmark and Norway did not agree within the next few months to stop high seas operations for Atlantic salmon.

Needless to say, there was considerable tension throughout the entire Atlantic salmon community. There was no doubt that, the Americans — meaning the White House, the governmental agencies involved, the Congress, the private-sector organizations, and interested individuals in the general public — were ready for a showdown. The Danish ranks were still in complete disarray and seemingly ready to capitulate. It came suddenly.

THE CAPITULATION

Early in January 1972, Prime Minister Krag announced in the Folketing that, due to "pressure from private interests in America [read CASE] and the threat of an embargo [read the Pelly Amendment]," Denmark was seeking a meeting with the United States. The State Department confirmed this on January 7, noting that "the U.S. intends to consult fully with the Canadians on the meeting and to coordinate the positions of the two governments on any results thereof, in keeping with the spirit of the Christmas Eve statement."

On January 28, 1972, CASE participated in a preliminary planning meeting held by the Department of State. The formal bilateral discussions with Denmark took place in Washington on February 3–5. Ambassador Donald L. McKernan, Assistant Secretary of the Interior Nathaniel P. Reed, and John S. Gottschalk, Special Assistant to the Director of the National Marine Fisheries Service, headed the U.S. delegation at these meetings.

Nat Reed shared with me some of the interesting incidents that took place during those hectic days. He wrote:

> Just before the negotiations commenced, I was summoned to a meeting at the Council on Environmental Quality where Russ

Train had been fully briefed. In the midst of the meeting, in walked Dr. K. [Henry Kissinger] in person. He sat down in a blue funk and, after listening, remarked that we were about to break up the NATO alliance. My dander came up and I stoutly defended our position. I remember saying that neither Canada nor Denmark were going to defect from NATO because of salmon conservation. When he became Secretary of State, Kissinger enjoyed calling me "the secretary of the fishes" in a very German tone of voice. . . .

Another little known fact — during the negotiations with the Danes, Kissinger would be personally briefed at noon and again at the day's conclusion. After day two, when there had been no forward motion, he said to me, "Congratulations." He obviously knew something I did not know. It became obvious toward the end of the week that the Danes were receiving a series of new positions and alternate back-up positions. I nicknamed them A, A-1, B-1, B-2, etc., much to the amusement of the State Department aides.

It also became common knowledge that the Danish messages were being furnished to the U.S. delegation at about the same time they were being received by the Danes. So much for secrecy.

High drama. Exhausting but worthwhile. I remain furious that the U.S./Danish negotiations were bilateral. The British and the Canadians pulled out. The Brits had traded for herring and ground fish rights; the Canadians had some never discussed problems which they could not solve internally so we went to the table alone.

The fact that Canada at the last moment failed to take part in the final negotiations in support of the American position was particularly disappointing, especially in view of that nation's commitment under the U.S.-Canadian joint statement on Atlantic salmon.

It was about this time that John Olin, head of Olin Industries and an avid salmon fisherman, became involved. He had a close association with President Nixon, so Nat Reed kept Olin advised of progress, knowing that developments would be relayed to the president.

Finally, the U.S.-Danish negotiations were successful. The two delegations formulated recommendations to their two governments. The two governments agreed to the recommendations, and on February 22, 1972, the Department of State issued a press release, from which the following is excerpted:

ATLANTIC SALMON AGREEMENT
The high seas fishery by Danish flag vessels will be gradually phased out over a four year period, 1972 through 1975. In 1972, the maximum *high seas* catch will be 800 metric tons; 600 tons in 1973; 550 tons in 1974; and 500 tons in 1975, with the complete ban in effect in 1976.

In addition, the *inshore* salmon catch by local Greenland fishermen will be stabilized at 1,100 metric tons while looking to their special interests.

The agreement thus serves the interests of the countries of origin of the Atlantic salmon, such as the United States, which undertake heavy expenditures to protect the salmon runs in the streams of origin, and of Denmark in the local Greenland fishery considering the special importance to the Greenland economy of the salmon fishery.

The recommendations of the February 3–5 meeting have been reviewed and approved by the two governments. In addition, they have been consulting other governments directly concerned, such as Canada and Norway. Denmark and the United States will seek to have the essentials of their agreement incorporated in the conservation regulations of the International Commission for Northwest Atlantic Fisheries (ICNAF) at its annual meeting in May. ICNAF has already adopted a ban on high seas salmon fishing effective for twelve nations, and interim measures on other aspects of the salmon fishery in the Northwest Atlantic.

The two sides agreed to cooperate in measures for the conservation of Atlantic salmon. Future meetings to review the status of the salmon stocks will be held at the request of either government. The U.S. will also seek to ensure that further appropriate conservation measures are undertaken within North American inshore waters. In a joint statement on Atlantic salmon issued on December 24, 1971, the United States and Canada pledged to cooperate closely on the conservation of Atlantic salmon.

Finally, the United States had won the big battle, but not the final victory. There was still much to do. We in CASE issued a position statement, which included the following principal points:

On February 22, 1972, the United States Department of State announced that agreement had been reached with Denmark in curtailing the salmon fishery off West Greenland.

This agreement is an important breakthrough in salmon conservation because it calls for the ultimate elimination of the high seas fishery. This should remove the danger of the potential development of a multi-nation high seas fishery....

No negotiated agreement can ever be completely satisfactory to both sides, and CASE has two principal concerns with respect to this agreement:

First, CASE would have preferred a phase-out period of no more than two years, rather than four—and a steeper reduction in the first year, and we feel that the inshore stabilization has been fixed at too high a figure. It may well be that Atlantic salmon stocks cannot stand four more years of overexploitation at a rate that would be only gradually reduced. The steep reduction in the 1971 Canadian catch is an indication of how second generation stocks can be affected by the high-seas take in previous years. It takes at least five to six years to produce an adult salmon. So what effect will the West Greenland steeply escalated harvest for the period 1965–1971 have on the stocks of 1972–1977? Thus the privilege of the right "to review the status of salmon stocks" is a most important part of this agreement; it may well have to be invoked—and soon. And we would expect that Denmark would act in good faith once again, and cooperate in any necessary reduction.

Secondly, this agreement is an informal understanding between two governments, no more, no less. As such, it could be abrogated by either party at any time. Most particularly, it is possible that a new government in Denmark might not go along with a former position. Our committee believes that the government of Denmark is acting in good faith. Yet even people of good faith have the habit of entering together into contracts, and we therefore feel that this agreement should be formalized...at the annual meeting of the International Commission for Northwest Atlantic Fisheries (ICNAF) in May 1972.

Norway, which fishes for Atlantic salmon off West Greenland, in the past has announced that she...will permit her nationals to fish for salmon as long as others do. CASE therefore expects that Norway, in view of the Danish agreement with the United States, will shortly announce that she will either terminate or phase out her fishery under conditions no less stringent than those of the Danish-U.S. agreement. We further expect that, in order to show good faith and consistency, she also will support an incorporation of the essentials of this agreement into conservation...proposals at the May 1972 meeting of ICNAF....

It has been reported that Swedish owned vessels have operated in the high-seas salmon fishery off West Greenland in 1971. Sweden is not a member of ICNAF, yet we would expect her, also, to make the decision to give up this fishery. To do otherwise would subject her to possible retaliatory measures under the new United States "Atlantic Salmon Law," Public Law 92-219 [the Pelly Amendment].

All salmon-producing nations, on both sides of the Atlantic, can now treat this agreement as an added incentive to correct abuses within their own territorial waters. Using the Danish high-seas fishery as an excuse for refusing to face up to domestic problems is no longer a valid argument.... Driftnetting within territorial waters, in principle essentially no different from high-seas driftnetting, should be liquidated, with just remuneration paid to those fishermen adversely affected.

CASE's objective remains the same as when originally announced—"to bring about an increase in world stocks of Atlantic salmon." Now, for the first time, we see a ray of light penetrating the darkness which has enshrouded the hopes of those fighting to save the species. With the light comes the dawn — renewed courage and determination to restore to abundance the Fish-King—"The Leaper"—in the rivers he once knew.

AMBASSADOR McKERNAN EXPLAINS
THE U.S. RATIONALE

It had been a great disappointment to all of us to find that the Canadian posture and positions throughout the final negotiating process left much to be desired, at both the governmental and the private-sector levels. As noted, the GOC had pulled out of the negotiations with the Danes at the last moment.

As to the private-sector involvement, just after the news became public information, Wilfred Carter, the Canadian Executive Director of the International Atlantic Salmon Foundation, wrote a letter to me on March 6, 1972, criticizing CASE's public announcement that "this agreement is an important breakthrough for salmon conservation," and then proceeded to tear the agreement apart from his point of view.

Wilf sent a copy of his letter to Donald McKernan. Don, who had masterminded the formal U.S. negotiation strategy and tactics, and who was considered to be without peer as to knowledge, experience, and ability within the international fraternity of fisheries negotiators, wasted no time in writing a sharp and detailed response to Wilf.

For had we pushed the Danes further by attempting to get them to do away with the inshore native Greenlandic fishery — or even cut it back substantially — we would have lost the support of The Minister for Greenland, and his two controlling votes in the Folketing would have defeated the whole Danish-U.S. Agreement, and probably brought down Prime Minister Krag and the minority government to boot.

Don's letter of March 20, 1972, to Wilfred Carter was a masterpiece, rational and philosophic. It was lengthy, so here are only the most pertinent parts of the letter:

> I have received a copy of your letter of March 6, 1972, to Richard Buck concerning the recent agreement reached between this government and the government of Denmark. I interpret your remarks as being critical of the agreement and, since I must

assume a major share of responsibility for the agreement, I want to comment on the points made in your letter.

Your first point maintains categorically that the phase-out of the high seas fishery does not represent the biggest and probably final battle of the Atlantic salmon war. I believe your categorical statement is far more incorrect than the one made by Dick Buck. I am inclined to agree with his statement. Those of us who have been involved with high seas salmon fishing for the past twenty years recognize from our experience on the Pacific Coast as well as recent experience on the Atlantic Coast that the big danger is in the potential development of a multi-nation high seas fishery. No one can deny that if the Danes are permitted to continue high seas fishing, as the regulation passed by ICNAF in 1971 permits (which, incidentally, was approved by Canada), other nations are going to see the economic benefits gained by Denmark, withdraw from the ICNAF ban, and begin fishing. The phase-out, even though extending over a longer period than any of us wanted, quite obviously will discourage newcomers from entering the high seas fishery. I must state unequivocally that I believe the major objective in any negotiations with high seas fishing nations is the elimination of the high seas fishery. The agreement between the United States and the Danes has accomplished that although perhaps not as quickly as many of us would have liked.

With regard to your second point, I find it difficult to believe, indeed, that Canada will not consider the agreement a substantial advance, which I presume could be interpreted as a victory. It certainly is true that the agreement is a compromise between two sovereign nations, both of whom present substantial, reliable and convincing evidence to support their view. I would again remind you of the actions taken by nations including the United States and Canada in ICNAF over the past four years which have been far less satisfactory; far less acceptable to both sides; and entailed far greater risks to the resources than the compromise agreement reached between the United States and Denmark.

I am surprised at your comments on the inshore fishery.... If you had had an opportunity to see the agreement you would have noted that the Danes were willing to accept the principle that the arrangement was open to review to take into account "the need for conservation of the species," and there was a clear understanding among the Danish government and the Greenland representative that, if conservation requirements dictated, the Greenlanders would feel a responsibility to further reduce their fishery so as to accommodate conservation needs. This seemed to me at the time, and still does, a reasonable approach. In the meantime, the catch by Greenland residents understood to be by their small boat fishery would continue at the average level of the past eight or nine years. Furthermore, the local fishery is confined within their 12 mile limit. I conclude that we have gained two important concessions from Denmark with respect to this point.

First, they have agreed to control and limit the fishery by native Greenlanders even within the territorial seas of Greenland and, secondly, they have agreed to adjust the catch according to the needs of conservation of the salmon resources. I find little to criticize in the Danish position and I defend this aspect of the agreement as being reasonable from both points of view....

The assumption you have made in your third point, that the high seas fishery is the only cause of the decline of salmon in North American rivers, is one I simply cannot accept. It is one that the scientists of Canada and the United States as well as other countries have not accepted either. My negotiations with Denmark were based upon the premise that there are other factors involved in the present condition of the salmon stocks of North America both in Canada as well as in the United States. This, of course, led me to the conclusion that a substantial reduction in the offshore fisheries starting immediately, coupled with corrective measures which must be taken by the United States and Canada, will over the long period lead to a rehabilitation of these runs....

I realize I have been argumentative in this letter and I have meant to be so. Furthermore, I recognize that I am defending my own action. I don't intend to apologize for that but my experience leads me to conclude that the agreement reached with the Danes was not only the best that could be obtained but, in the long run, is so much superior to what we have had and leads to results which are so much better than do-ing nothing that I believe, as Dick Buck has stated in his letter, we have made important steps towards arresting the decline. With appropriate domestic action in North America, we can bring about rehabilitation of the Atlantic salmon.

As a diplomat, Don McKernan quite rightly chose not to take the political gamble of pushing the Danes to the wall on the native inshore fishery. It must be be remembered that cutting back or closing down this inshore fishery was never included in the final understanding. It was Don's decision that we must not risk losing the whole ball game. We had achieved our mission — bringing the west Greenland high seas fishery to an end.

13

The Fate of the Salmon Hangs in the Balance

THE OLD ADAGE "It isn't over 'til it's over" accurately describes the international situation after the U.S.-Danish understanding had been reached in Washington during the February 3–15, 1972, meetings. The U.S.-Danish agreement was not announced until February 22 by the United States, and this delay was caused by the following reasons.

Even though Canada did not join the United States at the negotiating table, the United States wished to extend the customary diplomatic courtesy of discussing with Canada the definitive points of the document before making an official announcement of the agreement. The government of Canada wanted to take the matter under advisement. Finally, according to a U.S. Department of State telegram, because "the Canadians have been slow in reacting to the Americans," the United States announced the details of the agreement on February 22, 1972.

The agreement was to have been made public in Denmark and the United States at the same time. But, according to unofficial sources in Washington, the U.S. statement was released without discussions with the Danish government because the Americans were of the opinion that the Danish Fisheries Ministry, during its obvious feud with the Greenland Ministry, had begun to leak details of the agreement to the press before the time agreed on.

During all this confusion, tensions did not subside, because the general public knew nothing of the agreement. The politicians were busy arguing the pros and cons of the opposing views, with the Fisheries Minister supporting his Bornholm constituency and the Minister for Greenland protecting the inshore Greenlanders and thus opposing the high seas operations.

On February 23, the Danish Foreign Minister finally announced the signing of the agreement, with the Foreign Ministry emphasizing that during the negotiations, the Danish government had stressed the following three points:

1. Even if no scientific evidence exists on the connection between the salmon catch off Greenland and the decrease in salmon catch in American rivers, such a connection is possible. According to recent information from the United States, a considerable decrease in the salmon stock has taken place in the salmon rivers that the Americans maintain at high costs.

2. The government is extremely concerned about nature conservation, particularly animal species that are threatened. The salmon fishery's use of driftnets has proved risky to the guillemots (birds), which represent an important source of income to the Greenlanders.

3. The government cannot ignore public opinion in the United States and other countries, and which is also held by Danish interests. The Pelly Amendment could threaten the export of fish and fisheries products to the United States, which is Denmark's third largest buyer of fish.

It is important for the future record to get a feeling of what actually went on behind the scenes in these final days of the Salmon War. And no one expresses it better than Svend Saabye, in his somewhat broken yet picturesque English. He was in the thick of things and related events to me in a letter dated March 26, 1972:

> On the 16th of March Terkel Terkelsen and I attended the meeting in the Danish Folketing. For three hours the debate was going on like a Danish vessel in high seas waves. All that you could read in the newspapers in the last two years was used, from Bing Crosby to all about the 100,000 American millionaires — but I am happy to tell you, that the account given by the Prime Minister was fair, and so was the word of the new Minister for

Fisheries, who is in a miserable situation with the fishermen from Bornholm.

Now with an agreement between our governments, I hope very much that not anything will disturb the peace. We are sorry we cannot celebrate the event together, but from the bottom of our hearts we congratulate you on the result of all your work and fair fight.

The matter was and still is so mixed — the mind and feelings of the Danish people and the Danish newspapers are still influenced by the statement given by the retired Minister of Fisheries and his department, with the result that the situation could have lasted for years if it had been handled publicly. Now your Danish friends are happy that you and your CASE committee trusted us to try private pressure as a way to influence the question. I hope very much that you will believe me when I tell you that this is not the usual way that the Danish politic can be influenced — the situation was ripe.

NORWAY SUPPORTS U.S.-DANISH PROPOSAL

Denmark and the United States agreed to seek to have the essentials of their agreement incorporated into the conservation regulations of ICNAF at its annual meeting in May and had been consulting the other governments concerned. On April 12, the State Department sent me a copy of a telegram announcing that Norway would support the U.S.-Danish proposal for the ICNAF area. This meant that Norway would recommend a phase-out and total ban by 1976 on high seas operations off its coast. This was welcome news, because Norway was a key player in ICNAF.

CANADA BANS DRIFTNETTING

As a result of the U.S.-Danish accord, new positions and actions were coming thick and fast. On April 26, the Canadian House of Commons gave Fisheries Minister Davis unanimous backing for his stand that all Atlantic nations should ban commercial salmon fishing on the high seas. Then, in early May, Minister Davis announced a crash program banning all commercial fishing for salmon in the province of New Brunswick, including driftnetting within

Canadian territorial waters in Miramichi Bay and off Port aux Basques, at the southern tip of Newfoundland.

The area affected by the federal ban accounted for about 40 percent of Canada's Atlantic salmon commercial fishery. It affected over nine hundred fishermen and called for government compensation to those adversely affected — amounting to about $2.3 million for 1972, with reduced amounts in ensuing years. The length of the ban was not specified but was estimated to last at least for a full reproductive life cycle of the salmon, some five to six years. (*Note*: In fact, the ban was never lifted and exists to this day.)

Thus Canada at one stroke removed a principal argument for Denmark to continue high seas operations off west Greenland, since the Danes had always claimed — with considerable justification — that Canadian driftnetting, even though operating within Canadian territorial waters, was no different in principle from high seas netting.

The call by Canadian Minister Davis for a total ban on high seas fishing was not at all popular in Denmark and caused considerable commotion in the Folketing. This led Prime Minister Krag to send a telegram to the Danish delegation to the upcoming ICNAF meeting to the effect that Denmark was not bound by the agreement with the United States until the agreement had been confirmed by legislation in the Folketing, which would not meet until October 1972. So any conservation proposal adopted at ICNAF to approve the U.S.-Danish agreement might be overturned by the Folketing. More troubles?

ICNAF ADOPTS THE U.S.-DANISH AGREEMENT

The International Commission for Northwest Atlantic Fisheries held its 1972 annual meeting in Washington, the week of May 28. I was present as a member of the official United States delegation.

After opening statements and preliminaries had been run through, the Atlantic salmon question came up. Canada was defeated on an early motion for an amendment that called for a total ban on high seas fishing in the northwest Atlantic effective after March 31, 1973. This motion was overwhelmingly defeated. Only Canada, the USSR, and Iceland voted in favor of it.

Next, the four powers — the United States, Denmark, the United Kingdom, and Norway — cosponsored a proposal with the following principal requirements:

A. That, begining in 1976, a complete ban would be in effect on the taking of Atlantic salmon on the high seas in the Northwest Atlantic Ocean. In intervening years, the fishery would be phased out, with the total catch not to exceed the following amounts (in metric tons):

	1972	1973	1974	1975
Denmark	800	600	550	500
Norway	300	225	210	195
Other contracting governments	10	10	5	5
Total	1,110	835	765	700

That the Greenlandic inshore fishery, within the territorial limits of Denmark, would be limited to 1,100 metric tons annually (in excess of 1,200 metric tons were taken in 1971).

B. That, at the request of any contracting government, a review of the status of the salmon stocks may take place within five years.

C. That catches differing from the amounts pursuant to the above in any year would be followed by an adjustment the following year.

D. That contracting governments having coastlines adjacent to the Convention Area take appropriate action to ensure the application of conservation measures within the 12-mile zones which would correspond in effect to the measures taken by Denmark (i.e., using the catch levels of 1969 as a base).

Otherwise, this proposal amounted to a verbatim reiteration of the U.S.-Danish agreement of February 22, 1972.

Of the fifteen member nations of ICNAF, the following voted for the proposal: Denmark, Federal Republic of Germany, France, Iceland, Italy, Japan, Norway, Poland, Portugal, Rumania, the United Kingdom, and the United States. Canada voted against the proposal. Spain and the Soviet Union abstained.

Several comments are in order with respect to the voting action. A two-thirds majority was required to carry the proposal — ten votes. With only a few more no votes or abstentions, it would have been all over. The cosponsors of the proposal could easily have lost, due to the obstinancy of countries such as Portugal, Spain, Rumania, and Iceland.

According to the ICNAF protocol, this proposal would become effective if it was ratified by the member governments. Member governments had six months in which to register objections, and the protocol provided for extending this period under certain conditions. Thus, this June ICNAF proposal was not necessarily binding, because any one or more of the ICNAF nations could refuse to ratify it and render the conservation proposal ineffective.

The emergency was considered so critical, however, that the commission also approved a resolution to the effect that member governments should notify ICNAF of their acceptance of the proposal before August 1, 1972. This would bind Denmark and Norway to implement the 1972 restrictions during the year's fishing season, beginning in August. So, by this stratagem, everything was buttoned up.

————————

It was felt by many of the delegates that Canada, meaning Minister Jack Davis (the Canadian delegation was under instructions from Ottawa throughout), acted irresponsibly in voting against the proposal. Canada also acted irrationally, because had the proposal been defeated, we would have had nothing — meaning a return to the status quo of 1971 and an extension of the hold-the-line freeze at the maximum high seas take of 1,200 tons. Davis took the risk, and luckily the vote saved him. From his point of view, he was now a hero back home — and in an election year, too!

After their walkout just before negotiations began on the U.S.-Danish agreement, the Canadians were not held in very high regard by the nations involved. They lost even more stature at this ICNAF meeting.

Throughout, Don McKernan had stressed the fact that we were very lucky to get what we did, and that it would be a breach of faith to press for more. I had come to agree with him completely, now that I knew from personal observation and experience what the situation in Denmark was like. We still had to secure the approval of the Folketing. Not only was the agreement unpopular with the powerful fishing lobby, but considerable money had to be raised to compensate the owners and employees of the high seas fishing fleet. In front of a number of us, McKernan roundly criticized the Canadian position and Canada's lack of understanding of how touch-and-go the whole question was. He chose as his particular target the Canadians Wilfred Carter, Executive Director of the International Atlantic Salmon Foundation, and Jack Fenety, President of the Miramichi Salmon Association. Both organizations received the major part of their funding from sources in the United States, but Carter and Fenety were formally listed as advisors to the Canadian delegation, and, at the ICNAF meeting, they both sat with the Canadian delegation. This was understandable but the result was that Carter and Fenety were tagged as representing Canada and therefore as supportive of the Canadian position, which was a completely unrealistic one — and politically motivated.

One collateral yet important result of this meeting was that it served to bring ICNAF itself under close scrutiny with respect to whether this treaty was a viable mechanism for conserving Atlantic salmon stocks. We had come to the conclusion at least three years earlier that the answer was definitely in the negative.

Feeling that the present was an appropriate time to sow some seeds for the future, CASE, in a position statement of June 10, 1972, announced that "a permanent multilateral international treaty is the only type of mechanism that can act to protect and increase world stocks of Atlantic salmon. We will work towards this." Thus CASE became the first private-sector organization to come out formally for an Atlantic salmon treaty.

RESOLUTION

Now the scene shifted back to Copenhagen and the bitter skirmish in the Folketing—the political pressure from the powerful Danish high seas commercial fishing constituency against the Minister for Greenland's stout defense of the interests of his flock of native fisherman in small boats off west Greenland.

The official position of the United States during all this was stated in a letter of September 25, 1972, from Don McKernan to me: "while the Danish government is not in a legal position at the present time to accept the ICNAF proposal, we still expect them to honor the bilateral agreement between the United States and Denmark."

In late May, Prime Minister Krag had told a special Folketing committee investigating the legal question that he would request specific legislation to implement the recommendations anticipated — and subsequently made — at the ICNAF meeting. Such a bill was presented to the Folketing on October 4, with the government of Denmark contending that it had legal authority to impose quotas and even a ban on salmon fishing by its nationals. Opponents of the ICNAF proposal disputed the government's contention. There would be several readings of the bill, plus the customary interim delays, so final action was not expected before December.

As it stood in late November, the Minister for Greenland, with two votes in the Folketing, held the power to unseat the minority government, and he was on our side!

It was not until late December that I received an airmail letter from Terkel Terkelsen that stated, "on Friday, December 4, the

Folketing passed the salmon law as outlined in the American-Danish agreement . . . it was touch-and-go in the Parliament."

It was finally over — we were victorious in the Salmon War! With our mission accomplished, CASE was disbanded in early 1973.

14

Reflections on the Salmon War

IN THE UNITED STATES, the tide was running strong for the preservation of any of God's creatures, particularly when a beleaguered species represented a resource of exceptional aesthetic, recreational, nutritional, and economic importance. So the roster of those actively supporting the CASE movement to save the Atlantic salmon included not only sport fishermen but also persons of other callings, such as priests, businesspeople, students, bird lovers, and, yes, even a number of housewives who did not wish to see this gourmet fish disappear from the dinner table. These people spoke from a sense of moral outrage, and their voice was heard by governments.

Our own government, through the Departments of State, Interior, and Commerce as well as important committees of the House and Senate, had formally and consistently responded to the CASE plea for opposition to high seas fishing for Atlantic salmon. The citizenry and the government were able to coordinate their efforts toward a common goal. This fortuitous concord of purpose and action enabled the United States to become the leader — the rallying point — among nations willing to promote sound management of Atlantic salmon stocks.

The name CASE became known and respected throughout the Atlantic salmon community of nations. We were referred to as the people who had turned the thing around. We moved governments, and because we made the Danes move, this inspired others along similar lines. Witness the 1972 action by the government of Canada to end driftnetting in its own waters and to ban commercial netting entirely off New Brunswick and Nova Scotia. We were mentioned and quoted often, not only in the Danish parliament but also in European embassies. As a result of this, and because much of the diplomatic action took place in Europe, CASE had as high a standing in European countries as it had in the United States.

It is important to emphasize that other conservation groups gave continuing support to the job at hand, particularly Trout Unlimited (U.S.), the Sport Fishing Institute (U.S.), the Connecticut River Watershed Council (U.S.), the Atlantic Salmon Association (Canadian), the International Atlantic Salmon Foundation (Canadian-U.S.), and the Atlantic Salmon Trust (British). Many of the national broad-based conservation organizations lent their names in support of the common cause.

But as the late Arnold Gingrich put it in his book *The Joys of Trout*: "CASE came to be considered as the single most responsible factor in bringing about the agreement for phasing out the Danish high-seas salmon fishing." Noted salmon historian Anthony Netboy had this to say in his book *The Salmon — Their Fight for Survival*: "CASE became the most effective spokesman for the groups attempting to curtail or eliminate the slaughter of Atlantic salmon."

People have asked a number of times what it took for CASE to succeed in this leading role. To begin with, CASE developed a personality all its own. We were a happy concord of quite special people, and there was a mutual respect among those most active in the work. Specifically, it appears that the CASE formula for success can be reduced to six basic qualities. Three of these are necessary to the mounting of any important campaign, so they are mentioned first, with little comment:

1. Dedication. One has to believe that a thing simply has to be done, and commit oneself to this end.

2. Knowledge. One has to know the subject, and keep doing the homework; this, along with experience, is what leads to the ability to make sound decisions.

3. Persistence. I am always reminded of the newsreel pictures of Winston Churchill, in the middle of the London Blitz, giving the victory signal and saying slowly: "Never give up — never — never — NEVER."

4. Perception. One must have the ability to look far down the road with a clarity and objectivity of purpose. Also necessary is an ability to ferret out the weaknesses of the particular situation or of the opposition, develop the options, figure the reactions, then make the choice.

5. Imagination. One has to make dramatic and innovative moves to throw the opposition off guard. The CASE mission to Denmark is perhaps the best example of this. It was a brainstorm, and the more I developed the concept, the better it looked. Why not request, and somehow secure, a meeting with the foreign minister, if not the prime minister? Despite the initial reluctance of the Danish officials to meet with me, and the State Department's misgivings, the plan worked. It not only furthered the cause, but also brought about the acceptance of CASE as one of the few big players in this whole affair. The concept of making a film such as CASE's *High Seas Fishing Off Greenland* also fits this category of imaginative approaches, because it turned out that a film actually showing salmon and seabirds hanging in the nets gave real substance to our appeal. Also, getting Bing Crosby on a radio program broadcast to the Danish people is another example. It was dramatic, and the result (banning his records) was very newsworthy.

6. Teamwork. To me, the ability of the CASE team to work together was the principal and overriding reason for our success. I attribute most of this to the fact that each person was secure in his own talent. Thus we were not plagued with the internal jealousies that seem to inhibit the administration of most charitable organizations. Individuals who work on a voluntary basis sometimes consider themselves a notch above ordinary mortals and therefore worthy of special attention. Not so with our team. Bing Crosby went out of his way to help. Ted Williams — a household word and, incidentally, one of the best salmon fishermen extant — was very effective in appealing to people about saving the resource. Curt Gowdy, the sportscaster, was in his element as the master of ceremonies at CASE meetings such as the big Waldorf affair. Lee Wulff was without peer in his knowledge of the salmon's ways and could advise us about the best way to manage the resource. Marshall Field had a business acumen that got to the nub of a problem quickly, then analyzed the options accurately. And he also kept us on a sound track organizationally. David Scoll, our treasurer, attended to the administrative problems. All a team of this caliber needed was a quarterback to design the campaigns, call the signals, and direct the operations. This was my particular contribution.

Although all these people were salmon fishermen — and thus easily dedicated to the cause — we shouldn't forget that luck played a part in making such a group available at that particular time. Where could one find such a bunch of luminaries today — and ones who would give, voluntarily, so much time and effort?

One final generalization is a personal one. If a person wants to be successful in directing an ad hoc conservation effort, he might as well accept the fact that along the way he may have to step on some people's toes. And he is usually in a hurry to get things done within the time frame set for the particular project. So if he makes it a rule always to come down on the side of the resource, after it's all over, he should be excused for hurting the feelings of a few people who, with the best of intentions, offered what they perceived as — and what in fact may have been under different circumstances — constructive suggestions.

PART

IV

CHAOS IN THE NORTH ATLANTIC

15

RASA—Successor to CASE

WHEN THE PRINCIPALS of CASE decided to terminate that organization, we knew that we had put together a winning team, so we resolved to simply roll the whole thing over into a permanent tax-exempt Atlantic salmon organization operating with a broad range of powers.

CASE had been a group of individuals formed on an ad hoc basis to bring about an end to the high seas fishery off Greenland. This fishery would be phased out by 1976, so we could now direct our minds and energies to the long-term future of Atlantic salmon conservation and restoration.

Restoration of Atlantic Salmon in America, Inc. (RASA) was organized on April 4, 1973, as a corporation operating under the laws of the state of New Hampshire. We received notice of tax-exempt status as a publicly supported foundation under Section 501(c)(3) of the Internal Revenue Code on July 27, 1973. The incorporators were Robert A. Bryan, John C. Calhoun, Marshall Field, Lee Wulff, and me. We also became the original directors. Marshall Field and Lee Wulff were already well known in the salmon community because of their leading roles with CASE. Bob Bryan had been an early supporter of CASE and was well started on what was to become his lifelong career and devotion—improving the way of life of the native inhabitants of the Maritime Provinces of Canada, particularly those on the north shore of the St. Lawrence River. Along the way he had developed a passion for salmon fishing and a desire to help restore the species to abundance in Canada and the United States. John Calhoun was a conservationist and President of the Connecticut River Watershed Council, whose executive director,

Christopher Percy, had become active not only in supporting CASE's objectives and programs but also in assisting CASE with fund-raising and the many other administrative details attendant on building the membership of a young organization.

We named a coordinating committee of individuals active in salmon conservation work, and our special advisers included those who had been especially supportive of our previous work — people like Bing Crosby, Curt Gowdy, Roderick Haig-Brown, Peter Kriendler, and Ted Williams.

RASA's objective was — and still is — to restore Atlantic salmon in abundance to the rivers of New England and to protect these stocks not only within territorial waters of the United States but as far offshore as the stocks may range in the ocean. We knew that the road to a successful restoration of Atlantic salmon would be long and arduous. We recognized that we would have to enlarge the scope of our operations in order to secure broader commitment by governmental agencies, industry, conservation groups, and individuals.

First, and most important, we had to continue, under the mantle inherited from CASE, our involvement in the hard-won international agreement to phase out the west Greenland high seas fishery. We also decided to extend our commitment and influence to domestic matters pertaining to the restoration. Of particular importance were programs and projects of regional significance whose success or failure might affect the abundance of stocks of U.S. origin. We would have to become involved in securing a number of grants for projects to expedite the return of salmon to our rivers and for which federal or state funds would not be available. We would also need to undertake extensive public information and educational programs. We commenced some of this work in 1973, and, in the years that followed, we became the leading salmon organization in the United States, coordinating the work of private-sector groups in support of salmon conservation programs.

First, RASA awarded a grant to the commonwealth of Massachusetts for Atlantic salmon release tanks, generally referred to as "stock-out ponds," to be used on the Tarkill Brook tributary of the Connecticut River near Springfield. Here young salmon, before migrating to sea, received an "imprint" from Connecticut River water. This new concept, used successfully in Sweden, was designed to direct adult salmon back from the ocean to the particular river, and even the actual stream, in which the young fish were stocked.

Next, we made a joint grant with the U.S. Bureau of Sport Fisheries and Wildlife for the completion of design parameters for fish ladder facilities to permit migrating salmon and shad to bypass the dams on the Merrimack River at Lowell and Lawrence, Massachusetts. Project Lola was the key that opened the door to the Merrimack restoration.

During 1973, RASA coordinated its efforts closely with those of the Department of the Interior to break the bureaucratic bottleneck holding up construction of fishways on the Connecticut River. On September 21, Assistant Secretary Nat Reed, under authority of the Federal Power Act, requested the Federal Power Commission to require licensees of the dams to construct the facilities. As a direct result of this pressure, the Connecticut River program got under way.

Congress passed the Interior Appropriations Bill, which included $600,000 for a new federal Atlantic salmon fish hatchery in Bethel, Vermont. Congressman James C. Cleveland paid tribute to RASA, announcing that "its work had been indispensable" to the success of this project, which would help replenish juvenile stocks then in short supply.

We held meetings with top Corps of Engineers officials and influenced the Corps to change its long-standing negative position with respect to the whole Connecticut River restoration program. For years, the Corps had claimed that excessive water pollution would render the river unacceptable to migrating salmon. In a letter of April 24, 1973, to RASA, the Corps stated that it now "concurs with you that such runs can be reestablished." Thus, no longer could pollution per se be used by the power companies as a reason for delaying restoration actions.

And it was in this year that RASA became the first salmon organization to announce and undertake an educational program designed to interest secondary-school students in Atlantic salmon conservation. Under the direction of Andrew V. Stout, RASA's Director of Educational Programs, students were made aware of the fascinating lifestyle of this species and the problems in restoring it to abundance, both inriver and on the high seas. Andy Stout conducted over forty seminars at boarding schools and high schools and with other interested groups.

Thus, throughout this first year of our existence, RASA held many conferences, attended many meetings, filled many speaking engagements. The large number of newspaper and magazine articles inspired by our action and information programs engendered a wider public knowledge of the exciting challenge of bringing the great Atlantic salmon back to rivers in which it had once flourished.

RASA had landed on its feet, running.

16

Denmark Violates the ICNAF Agreement

IT PROBABLY had been too much to expect that Denmark, with its long history of taking whatever it wanted from the ocean, would live up to the ICNAF agreement of 1972. But the trouble this time was to come from the inshore fishery by native Greenlanders rather than from the big offshore trawlers from Denmark, which were, by the same agreement, phasing out high seas driftnetting.

The ICNAF agreement had set a quota for the inshore fishery of 1,100 metric tons, some 350,000 salmon. Having agreed to this quota, Denmark promptly proceeded to permit the Greenlanders to take 1,320 tons in 1972 and 1,574 tons in 1973, exceeding the limit by 43 percent. Greenland, of course, was Danish, administered by a governor from Denmark. The Danish excuse was that the coastline of Greenland is so long and communications so inefficient that policing the fishery was very difficult.

On top of this, the Danish government had the audacity to request that ICNAF, at its 1974 annual meeting, sanction these violations by revising the limit upward to 1,400 tons, an increase of some 27 percent in a limit that they had not honored in the first place. The Danes claimed that an upward revision of the salmon quota was of great economic importance to the native Greenlanders, particularly because of the recent failure of the cod fishery.

Such reasoning was so unsound as not to be worthy of consideration. How could the failure of one kind of fishery justify the overexploitation of a different species?

Denmark also claimed that an upward revision of the quota would not endanger the species. But the International Council for Exploration of the Seas (ICES), in the summary report of its working party on Atlantic salmon, dated March 11–15, 1974, found otherwise. This highly respected scientific organization found that return migrations of Atlantic salmon from Greenland to the three largest river systems in Canada (the St. John, the Restigouche, and the Miramichi) had declined in recent years. The report pointed out that "the greatest danger to be faced from the West Greenland fishery is the possible reduction in long-term recruitment" — that is, not enough escapement of stocks upriver to spawn and renew the life cycle.

In a special news release dated April 25, 1974, RASA had this to say:

> The United States, Canada and other nations (but not Denmark) are pouring millions of dollars, and effort, into fish hatcheries, fishways and pollution control to aid in the restoration of Atlantic salmon, the most valuable and sporting fish that swims. Yet the Greenland fishery, offshore and inshore, takes perhaps as much as 40% of all the salmon that go from these countries to Greenland to feed and grow before returning to their natal rivers to spawn. The starting point for conservation is long overdue. . . .
>
> The pattern emerging now in the inshore fishery parallels the Danish escalation which commenced ten years ago in the high seas fishery. Will history be allowed to repeat itself, once again threatening to exhaust stocks of salmon? Or will ICNAF this June take forceful action to halt this build-up before it is too late?

In my official capacity as adviser to the U.S. commissioners of ICNAF, I proceeded to alert the proper U.S. authorities to the intention of the government of Denmark to propose a review of the status of the salmon stocks with a view to increasing the quota. This brought our old comrades in arms Nat Reed, Assistant Secretary of the Interior; Dave Wallace, Associate Administrator of the National Oceanic and Atmospheric Administration (NOAA); and John Dingell, Chairman of the Subcommittee on Fisheries and Wildlife and the Environment, into the picture; also, the Secretary of Commerce, Frederick B. Dent, as well as Stuart Blow, Acting Coordinator of Ocean Affairs, U.S. Department of State. We set wheels in motion that would ensure that all the governmental agencies involved would act together to support a solid U.S. rejection of the upcoming Danish proposal.

Still looking ahead to the ICNAF meeting, I was concerned not with how the Atlantic salmon–producing nations would vote but with the difficulty of securing a sufficient number of other nations to produce the necessary two-thirds majority of the votes against the Danish proposal. I took the precaution of writing to the ministers of fisheries of Norway, Spain, Portugal, France, and Italy — five nations all on the fence, historically, with respect to Atlantic salmon measures — pointing out that "violations of this type (i.e., exceeding the quota for two years) have to be treated as a test of the ability of ICNAF to enforce its regulations."

It is of interest at this point to refer to a letter I received from my friend Ambassador Philip Crowe. In a report on an official visit to Greenland on May 7–12, 1974, he pointed out that he had paid special attention to the position of the Greenlanders. Here are some pertinent extracts from his letter:

> It was common gossip that the fishing [in 1974] was the best in years and there is no question to me that prompt action to stop fishing by Knud Hertling, the Minister for Greenland, would have prevented most of the overcatch. Instead of acting, however, the Minister temporized and by the time he got around to issuing the stop orders, the damage had been done. This may have been good internal politics, but it was poor international relations.

The Greenlanders have fished from time immemorial and see no reason why, when they now rely on the salmon catch to make up for the cod losses, they should not be allowed to continue to do so. They are also a simple people who can not be expected to understand the value of conserving today to profit tomorrow. In the whole population of 48,000 persons — spread along 25,000 miles of coastline — only one Greenlander has passed his medical examination to become a doctor and only three have become lawyers.

As a guest of the Governor and of the Royal Danish Navy I sailed on the frigate *White Bear* to some of the larger fishing towns as well as the smaller hamlets along the southwest coast and talked with the mayors and simple fishermen. They were polite as all Greenlanders are but there was no mistaking their bitterness. They had it firmly in their minds that the United States was primarily responsible for the Danish decision to limit their salmon catch and that the reason for this stand on our part was due entirely to pressure from the sport fishermen led by Bing Crosby. My explanation that my country was only one of 15 nations involved in the salmon problem and that our joint purpose was to protect the species from destruction made no headway whatsoever.

Nor did my argument, that Atlantic salmon stocks have been in a definite and provable decline since commercial fishing began, impress them. Reports such as that of the Joint Working Party on Atlantic Salmon, which showed clearly that returns from three of the major river systems in Canada have declined appreciably, would be met with total disbelief.

The precautions that we had taken paid off at the June 1974 meeting of ICNAF. The Danish proposal to increase the inshore Atlantic salmon quota to 1,400 tons was rejected, with only two nations, Denmark and Japan, voting for: five nations — Canada, France, Iceland, the United Kingdom and the United States — voted against; the rest abstained, with Italy and Rumania absent.

Denmark did, however, succeed in pulling off a fast one, which ensured for Greenland a small increase in the inshore quota.

Denmark stated flatly that the Greenlanders would fish up to a limit of 1,191 tons, this being the estimated level of annual catches during the 1964–1971 period. Denmark used the flimsy excuse that, at the time of signing the original ICNAF agreement, the estimate of 1,100 tons as the inshore catch was far too low; a subsequent investigation revealed 1,191 tons to be a more proper estimate. Who could prove them wrong? There was nothing for the other ICNAF commissioners to do but accept this as a fait accompli. But this cheap trick simply added insult to injury and didn't sit well with the other ICNAF members. Why hadn't Denmark brought this matter up a year ago, at the 1973 ICNAF meeting, rather than wait until they had already substantially violated the agreed-upon figure of 1,100 tons?

Commenting on the fact that the overexploitation amounted to an estimated 40 percent of the total salmon stocks feeding off West Greenland, David Wallace, ranking U.S. commissioner of ICNAF, said, "Denmark's exceeding the 1973 quota has to be considered a violation of the 1972 ICNAF agreement, and a repetition of this would be a matter of the gravest concern to the United States."

What would be done in the event of a violation by Denmark next year, which would be the third straight year? What action might satisfy the "gravest concern" of the United States? The United States would have no alternative but to implement the Pelly Amendment, under the Fishermen's Protective Act of 1967. This law permits the President to prohibit the importation of fish products from any foreign country whose nationals "are conducting fishing operations in a manner or under circumstances which diminish the effectiveness of an international fishery conservation program."

In 1972, Denmark's total exports to the United States were valued at about $367 million. Of this, some $44 million, almost 12 percent, was in fish products, so an embargo on these products could have an important effect on Denmark's balance-of-trade figures. Thus, it would be in Denmark's interest to comply with the inshore salmon quota. The Danish officials knew this, for the threat of Pelly was always on their minds.

RASA's official and announced position, however, for the balance of 1974 was "to give the Danes full opportunity to comply with their own self-imposed quota of 1,191 tons." We commented:

> One can sympathize with the plight of the Greenlanders, whose fishery is in trouble due to a steep fall-off in the cod catch, in conjunction with an increase in population. But the failure of one fishery is no excuse for the overexploitation of a different one.
>
> And yet one has to sympathize even more with the plight of those Canadian commercial fishermen who have been forced by their own government to stop all driftnetting in inshore waters, and netting at the mouths of rivers in New Brunswick and parts of Quebec. These fish were produced in Canadian rivers and the fishery had been in existence for generations.

In the face of the firm rebuff they received from ICNAF in 1973, the Danes did pull themselves together and brought the Greenland inshore fishery under control during 1974 and 1975, staying within quotas. The Danes also confirmed that they would cease high seas operations for salmon after 1975, as required by the 1972 Danish-U.S. and ICNAF agreements. So far, so good.

CANADA ALSO ESCALATES

A little-recognized fact was that Canada itself also was in violation of the ICNAF Agreement of 1972. This stipulated — as has the original Danish-U.S. Agreement — that "contracting governments having coastlines adjacent to the Convention Area take appropriate measures within the 12-mile zones which would correspond in effect to the measures taken by Denmark." Canada's coastline was of course "adjacent." But, instead of cutting back on their inshore catch of salmon, Canada had proceeded to escalate their take during these years, especially off the coast of Newfoundland.

No one was more apprehensive about this than Jack Fenety, the energetic President of the Miramichi Salmon Association in

New Brunswick. He sensed the implications of it. Jack worked tirelessly to get his government to act responsibly, but to little avail.

Why Denmark did not pay any attention to all this, and use the Canadian escalation as an excuse for their malfeasance, is beyond comprehension. Probably too concerned about their own infringement of the Agreement.

THE DEMISE OF ICNAF

The International Commission for Northwest Atlantic Fisheries met in Montreal in June 1976 under circumstances that were unique in its twenty-six-year history. The United States had just passed into law the Fishery and Management Act of 1976, which (among other provisions, which are discussed in the next chapter) established a two-hundred-mile fishery conservation zone beyond the three-mile limit (in fisheries parlance, the "territorial sea"). This U.S. action caused other nations to follow suit, which spelled the end of ICNAF as a viable international mechanism for maintaining a maximum sustained catch for fisheries of the signatory nations.

The government of the United States served its notice of intention to withdraw from ICNAF on December 31, 1976. Other nations were taking similar actions. Thus, ICNAF was forced to self-destruct.

17

Breaking New Boundaries

WITH THE DEMISE of ICNAF in 1976, salmon on feeding migrations were without protection in the northwest Atlantic Ocean, that is, outside the inshore territorial limits — usually three or twelve miles — claimed by nations bordering the sea.

In 1972, RASA had been the first salmon organization to call for a multilateral convention to protect salmon in the ocean. But 1976 was not the time to introduce the draft of such a treaty. The situation with respect to highly valuable fish resources other than the salmon was so chaotic that governments could not keep abreast of the problems at hand.

During the late 1960s and early 1970s, there had been a rapid buildup in fishing efforts on the U.S. and Canadian continental shelf by fishing fleets from such nations as the USSR, West Germany, Poland, Japan, Norway, Spain, and others — perhaps twenty nations in all. Working from large and small vessels, including trawlers referred to as "distant oceangoing vessels," foreigners caught and processed at sea thousands of tons of ground fish, including haddock, cod, herring, flounder, and other fish living on or near the ocean floor. Haddock, the most sought-after species, was almost wiped out because the spawning stock was included in the harvest. It was the same story with other species. As a whole, this group declined by nearly 70 percent between 1963 and 1974!

All this had a disastrous effect on U.S. commercial fishermen. During the same period, their total tonnage suffered a reduction of about 50 percent.

William W. Warner, in his important and interesting book *Distant Water — The Fate of the North Atlantic Fisherman*, gives us a vivid portrayal of the manner in which the Soviet Union came to dominate fishing in the northwest Atlantic through a community concept that came to be referred to as "floating cities":

> By 1974, in what some experts have called the most rapid and successful development of a specialized fleet in the history of merchant shipping, the U.S.S.R. had by far the world's largest fishing fleet. Within its ranks were 2,800 side trawlers and other smaller fishing vessels of all kinds, 103 factory or mother ships, and 710 factory trawlers. The latter, as always, were the heart of the fleet, accounting for seventy percent of its tonnage and approximately two thirds of its catch. Sustaining this armada, moreover, was a large train of fleet support vessels.... They included not only the giant factory ships, but also refrigerated fish carriers for offloading at sea, oceangoing tugs with well-equipped repair shops, research and scouting ships, food and fresh-water supply ships, tankers, and, ultimately, combined tanker-fish carriers. All were considered necessary because the Soviet government wanted its fishing fleet to be completely self-sufficient at sea.

Note: See the photograph on page 160 by William W. Warner of the Norwegian fish meal factory mother ship the Norglobal, said to be the largest of its kind in the world, capable of producing three hundred tons of fish meal a day. Here it is seen on the Grand Banks in the summer of 1977, with a typical Norwegian purse seiner alongside, offloading a catch of capelin. The purse seiners were the boats most likely to take an Atlantic salmon by-catch while the salmon were feeding on capelin. The Norwegians were using capelin for fish meal, and the Soviets used it not only for human consumption but also for cat food! All this precipitated the "capelin crash" that began in 1978. The worldwide annual catch dropped from 4 million tons to 2.5 million tons in three years.

A RUSSIAN MOTHER SHIP

It was my good fortune to be able to visit a Russian mother ship in St. John's, Newfoundland, in the summer of 1970. This vessel served as the nerve center for a fleet of Russian trawlers and was

The Norwegian fishmeal factory mother-ship, the Norglobal. Photograph courtesy of William W. Warner.

in harbor for refueling. As a member of the U.S. delegation to ICNAF, I was invited to a reception on board. This was the chance of a lifetime for a glimpse at how the Russians comported themselves with foreigners during the period of the cold war. We were immediately impressed by the friendliness and decorum of the crew members, all in naval uniform, who acted as our guides.

The ship included a substantial hospital floor, which attended to the emergency medical and surgical needs of the whole fleet. We were taken below to inspect these facilities, and it was obvious that the hospital and operating room equipment were kept at the peak of cleanliness and efficiency. The wards and private rooms were spotless. Nurses were very much in evidence, and we noticed that considerable attention was given to the rehabilitation needs of the patients.

Otherwise, the ship contained all manner of supplies for the needs of not only the trawlers but also the fishermen. There were dormitory facilities because the ship often acted as an occasional respite spot and as a way-station for sailors who were being replaced after months at sea. There was a large entertainment room, complete with up-to-date motion picture facilities.

After the tour, we were entertained royally with drinks and hors d'oeuvres. Caviar, smoked salmon, and other delicacies were in profusion, as well as libations such as the national drink, vodka. All was laid out on a long table in the officers' saloon.

We left disabused of the then current notion that Russians were an uncouth and rough lot. Undoubtedly, this show of friendliness and modernity was part and parcel of the Kremlin's public relations policy. Yet it seemed genuine, and it probably accomplished its purpose — to let the world know that the Russians could be human after all.

NATIONS FACE UP TO THE CRISIS

What was to be done about this wholesale intrusion by foreign vessels upon the traditional fishing grounds of U.S. and Canadian fishermen? The limits of the "Territorial Seas," as they were designated, differed widely among nations. At that particular time, in the 1970s, there were twenty-nine nations that adhered to a three-mile Territorial Sea limit, including the United States, Canada, France, the United Kingdom, Japan, and Taiwan. Some forty nations claimed twelve nautical miles as their Territorial Sea limits, including the USSR and mainland China. Fourteen states, including Israel, Italy, Spain, and the Republic of South Africa, maintained a six-mile limit. In addition, almost thirty states laid claim to an "Exclusive Fishing Zone" contiguous to the Territorial Sea and extending twelve miles from the coast. The United States, Canada, the United Kingdom, and France were among these.

All in all, this made for a completely confusing picture. So the United States government turned to the speediest and most effective means of bringing an end to this overkill — an extension of fisheries jurisdiction beyond the three-mile Territorial Sea.

Senator Warren G. Magnuson of Washington took the lead on March 5, 1975, introducing S. 961, (the so-called two-hundred-mile-limit bill), and Congressman Gerry Studds of Massachusetts followed with a comparable version in the House of Representatives. After many hearings, compromises, and adjustments in the Senate-House Conference Committee, the final version of the Fishery Conservation and Management Act of 1976 was signed into law by President Ford, to become effective January 1, 1977.

RASA was very active in support of these bills, working in Washington with the Senate and House committees concerned. The act directed that immediate action be taken "to conserve and manage the fishery resources of the coast of the United States and to do so through the establishment of a fishery conservation zone which shall extend seaward of 200 nautical miles on the baseline from which the territorial sea is measured."

Specifically, the United States would exercise exclusive fishery management authority over:

1. All fish found within the fishery conservation zone;

2. All anadromous species that spawn in U.S. water, throughout their migratory range beyond the zone, except when

they are in another nation's territorial sea or fishery conservation zone that the United States recognizes; and

3. All U.S. continental shelf fishery resources that extend beyond the zone, such as coral, crab, lobster, clams, abalone, and sponges.

Eight regional fishery management councils were the basic tool for managing and conserving U.S. fisheries within the two-hundred-mile zone. Members of the council were state officials and private-sector groups and individuals. The duties and responsibilities of each council were to develop fishery management plans and amendments and to review and revise assessments of optimum yield and allowable foreign fishing.

The new law creating the two-hundred-mile fisheries zone meant that the Coast Guard and National Marine Fisheries Service would have — potentially, at least — about two million square miles of ocean to patrol.

It is important to note that Canada also extended its fisheries jurisdiction to two hundred miles, and the other North Atlantic nations followed suit, although some claimed other limits.

These were landmark legislative acts by the two nations. In one fell swoop, the Americans and Canadians had forced the flotillas of foreign fishing fleets to depart the coastal and continental shelf waters of the North Atlantic continent — unless specifically permitted to conduct fishing operations therein.

18

The Law of the Sea

THEY WERE ALL THERE, a huge assembly representing approximately 150 nations, regardless of whether their countries had any frontage on salt water: big nations, little nations, third-world emerging nations. This was the Third United Nations Conference on the Law of the Sea (LOS Conference), held in Geneva from March through May 1975.

The objective? To attempt to hammer out—after a number of earlier sessions that had begun in 1958—a single negotiating text that would be the final accord binding all the nations of the world to one international constitution covering all conflicts throughout the oceanic waters of the world.

It became obvious early on that the great majority of nations were not all that concerned about their interests in finfish or sea mammals. They wanted to participate in what promised to be the biggest international grab bag in history; they wanted a share in the mining rights to the untold mineral riches of the seabed—and not just oil. Scientific research had shown that miles beneath the surface of the sea lay thick beds of metal nodules, the remnants of volcanic eruptions millions of years ago. These nodules of copper, manganese, nickel, and cobalt were worth billions of dollars.

Although the fish did have their day in court, they were a secondary concern. Considering that over 60 percent of the protein consumed by humans comes from fish or fish products, this was unbelievable. The little attention that was given to fisheries concerned almost exclusively the problems affecting the big players, those nations that took an estimated mind-boggling total of 62 million tons of marine fish and mammals annually. Small wonder that little time was left to address the overexploitation of anadromous fish and, in particular, the catch of some 2,000 tons of Atlantic salmon taken in the West Greenland fishery.

This session came and went without solving the many conflicting views of the negotiators regarding the items on the agenda. At the New York session from May 23 to July 25, 1977, however, an informal composite negotiating text on anadromous fish was approved, and this would become the text adopted in the final treaty.

Over the ensuing five years, various sessions of the Third Law of the Sea Conference were held to bring together what had turned out to be sharply opposing points of view that had little to do with fisheries matters. At the United Nations, the third-world countries had organized themselves into an effective voting bloc, known as the Group of 77. It was their purpose at the Law of the Sea Conferences to, first, secure the right to mine the ocean beds (even though some of these countries were landlocked), and, second, to secure the right to relieve the industrial nations of their deep-sea mining technology. They almost succeeded at the final conference in 1982. The Reagan administration, however, stating that the impasse on seabed mining issues could not be resolved in terms acceptable to the United States, exerted strong pressure on its allies among the industrial nations and secured support in resisting approval of the treaty.

The Law of the Sea Treaty was adopted, however, at the United Nations in New York City on April 30, 1982. Although the third-world nations approved this wide-ranging treaty, the United States was part of an isolated group that rejected the code. The vote, ending eight years of diplomatic bargaining, was 130 to 4, with those voting against being the United States, Turkey, Venezuela, and Israel. Seventeen nations, comprising a combination from the European Economic Community and the Soviet bloc, abstained.

Following are the main provisions of the Law of the Sea Treaty:

Territorial Sea. Each nation's sovereign territory extends twelve miles beyond its coast. In this zone, however, all foreign vessels must be allowed the right of innocent passage, that is, passage that does not threaten the nation's security.

Free Passage. Beyone twelve miles, all ships and planes, military and commercial, can move freely. Submarines can travel underwater.

Exclusive Economic Zone. Every coastal nation has exclusive rights to the fish and other marine life in the waters extending two hundred miles beyond its shores. When nations are separated by a body of water of less than four hundred miles, they must establish dividing lines for the zones.

Straits. More than a hundred straits or choke points that are twenty-four miles wide or less do not become territorial waters. All ships and planes have a right of "transit passage" through the straits, such as Gibraltar and Hormuz.

Continental Shelf. The most critical economic portion of the treaty deals with the continental shelf extending from a nation's shore and under the seas. Each nation is given exclusive rights to the oil, gas, and any other resource in the shelf for 350 miles beyond the coast.

Seabed Mining. The nodules of copper, nickel, cobalt, and zinc lying on the Pacific Ocean floor under the high seas are "the common heritage of mankind." To mine these metals, a complex global authority is established, but priority contracts will be awarded to four groups of companies led by American mining concerns, a French consortium, and ventures controlled by Japan, the Soviet Union, and India. The treaty fixes a production ceiling to support present prices of the metals and ensure that they are not reduced by seabed yields. Private mining concerns must sell their technical knowledge to the global enterprise. The whole arrangement can be amended by agreement among three-fourths of the treaty signers.

Disputes. Arguments involving nations or individuals over the convention must be settled by a new International Tribunal for the Law of the Sea, arbitration, or the International Court of Justice at The Hague.

Here are the treaty provisions regarding anadromous fish:

THIRD UN CONFERENCE ON THE LAW OF THE SEA
COMPOSITE SINGLE NEGOTIATION TEXT
PART I

Article 66
Anadromous Stocks

1. States in whose rivers anadromous stocks originate shall have the primary interest in and responsibility for such stocks.

2. The State of origin of anadromous stocks shall ensure their conservation by the establishment of appropriate regulatory measures for fishing in all waters landwards of the outer limits of its exclusive economic zone and for fishing provided for in subparagraph (b) of paragraph 3. The State of origin may, after consultation with other States fishing these stocks, establish total allowable catches for stocks originating in its rivers.

3. (a) Fisheries for anadromous stocks shall be conducted only in the waters landwards of the outer limits of exclusive economic zones, except in cases where this provision would result in economic dislocation for a State other than the State of origin.

   (b) The State of origin shall cooperate in minimizing economic dislocation in such other States fishing these stocks, taking into account the normal catch and the mode of operations of such States, and all the areas in which such fishing has occurred.

   (c) States referred to in subparagraph (b), participating by purpose, shall be given special consideration by the State of origin in the harvesting of stocks originating in its rivers.

   (d) Enforcement of regulations regarding anadromous stocks beyond the exclusive economic zone shall be by agreement between the State of origin and the other States concerned.

4. In cases where anadromous stocks migrate into or through the waters landwards of the outer limits of the exclusive

economic zone of a State other than the State of origin, such State shall cooperate with the State of origin with regard to the conservation and management of such stocks.

5. The State of origin of anadromous stocks and other States fishing these stocks shall make arrangements for the implementation of the provisions of this article, where appropriate, through regional organizations.

REFLECTIONS

The United States did *not* become a signatory to the Law of the Sea Treaty and to this day has not done so. The Reagan administration, in essence, rejected the socialistic nature of a supranational organization having the right to throttle the free-enterprise system.

Even though the United States did not sign the treaty, the United States does make it a point, as a matter of principle, to take the Law of the Sea Treaty into consideration whenever there is a possibility of conflict as far as fisheries practice and management are concerned.

Regarding anadromous fish like the salmon, there is a great deal of ambiguity in the requirement that "the State of origin shall cooperate in minimizing economic dislocation in such other States fishing these stocks." User states like Denmark can argue that commercial fishing of stocks of foreign origin is necessary for the economic well-being of the Greenland fishermen. Producing states like Canada, the United States, and the United Kingdom, for instance, could point out that overexploitation to the point of endangering the resource is not justified. And the catch off Greenland was escalated so sharply in the late 1960s and early 1970s that a compelling case could be made that the resource was being endangered.

In effect, the text on anadromous stocks was shoved through without due regard to the original intent. With respect to the LOS Conference in Geneva during the spring of 1975, a special report to the U.S. Senate of August 1975, printed for the use of the Senate Committee on Foreign Relations by Senator Claiborne Pell and others, states in its conclusion:

We should note here our reservations regarding the advisability of including in any such interim arrangements (or in an eventual Law of the Sea Treaty) any clauses granting special legal status to those nations which fish for anadromous species outside of the 200-mile economic zone, on the basis that these countries will experience some form of "economic dislocation." It is particularly disturbing that the single text provides that the determination of "economic dislocation" will be made by those nations which now fish for anadromous species in the high seas, a practice which is questionable from both a management and conservation point of view.

Then, later on, in the LOS Appendix, there is a Summary of Delegation Report (U.S.) on the Geneva session of the Law of the Sea Conference, March 17–May 9, 1975, which appends the following comments:

The text establishes the special interest of the State of origin in anadromous species, gives the State of origin exclusive conservation authority in its own economic zone and beyond the economic zone, and requires other States through whose waters anadromous fish migrate to cooperate with the State of origin. At the same time, the State of origin must by agreement cooperate in minimizing economic dislocation in States that have fished these resources beyond the economic zone; *this clause is intended to apply only to traditional fishing.* [Emphasis added.]

This information, brought to light here perhaps for the first time, is relevant even today. Now it can be generally known and understood that it may have been the original intent of the 1975 U.S. delegation to the LOS Conference to apply the test of economic dislocation only to "traditional" fisheries, such as the Greenland fishery.

The Greenland fishery was certainly a "traditional" fishery, as is clearly indicated by the fact that in 1960 — the first year that the International Council for Exploration of the Sea (ICES) reported on the world catch of Atlantic salmon — only 60 tons of salmon, some

16,500 fish, were taken off Greenland. At the time, Greenland had a population of somewhat less than 50,000 inhabitants. So this was a very small fishery indeed, and obviously operated for local consumption only, not commercial profit.

What went wrong back in 1975? Why didn't the United States and other producing nations hold out for the inclusion of the "traditional fishing" yardstick?

Down through the years since the LOS Treaty was signed in 1982, too little attention has been paid to the stipulation that states of origin have "the primary interest in and responsibility for such stocks." *Webster's New Unabridged Dictionary* defines *responsibility* as "the condition of being responsible, answerable, accountable, or liable." These are powerful words, for if a salmon-producing nation is to be held "accountable" in the ocean for the stocks it has produced, it is only rational and reasonable that it be given primary consideration in establishing the conditions under which the stocks may be exploited.

Finally, we in RASA, since our beginnings in 1973 up to the present, have adhered to one basic principle: Necessary and urgent conservation measures transcend the luxury of commercial or recreational exploitation, and "economic dislocation" can never be an acceptable justification for the depletion of an abundance of wild, renewable stocks of fish, particularly by harvesting-only nations that contribute nothing in the way of production or conservation of the resource.

One final point: It is important to note that Atlantic salmon organizations and interested individuals were not encouraged by the United States government to participate as advisers on Atlantic salmon at the various LOS meetings. They were not even invited to attend as observers. Thus, neither I nor any of my colleagues in the United States were present at the meetings, which was not only disappointing but a continuing source of irritation.

I did request observer status at LOS from Ambassador-at-Large T. Vincent Learson, who was in charge of the makeup of the U.S. delegation. He informed me in a letter dated January 8, 1975, that the U.S. delegation would consist of either governmental officials or members of the Public Advisory Committee on the Law of the Sea. Further, he wrote that, "due to budgetary and other restraints in the size of the U.S. delegation, only those individuals who are required for the negotiating process will be accredited. As in the past, our delegation will include individuals with expertise in all pertinent aspects of fisheries matters. They will take into account your substantive comment in the letter on anadromous species."

This letter seemed to be just the usual bureaucratic run-around. I never heard from any member of the U.S. delegation regarding RASA's recommendations.

Early on, I also wrote to Ambassador Elliott L. Richardson, the head of the U.S. delegation at LOS, asking for his assistance in securing observer status for RASA. Interestingly enough, he was, and still is, a member of RASA. Yet my letter was never answered, and I am sure that he never saw it. I was so disgusted with the whole performance that I never pressed the matter further.

Was the inattention paid to Atlantic salmon just an oversight, was it a calculated effort on the part of some bureaucrat to sidetrack the whole issue? And where were the champions from those two largest producers of the species, Canada and the United Kingdom? The answers to these questions are shrouded in mystery.

What concerned me particularly about all this was that although Ambassador Don McKernan was busy with matters of top-level importance, he should have had someone at hand whose sole concern was with Atlantic salmon. Otherwise, the U.S. position on salmon would get lost in the fray. It appears that this is exactly what happened. And we are still living with the LOS ambiguity today.

19

River Harvest

OF ALL THE PRESSURES on salmon throughout the North Atlantic Ocean, the most serious has always been excessive netting in the ocean, both legal and illegal. During the decade 1967–1977, for instance, the Newfoundland commercial catch increased from 50 to 80 percent of the total Canadian commercial catch. The driftnet catch off Ireland more than quadrupled in the same period. There was also the birth of a substantial, illegal driftnet fishery for salmon off Scotland and the doubling of the driftnet fishery off the Northumbrian coast of England.

Governments were loath to take up such problems, which seemed inconsequential alongside the many other pressures demanding their attention. So it was up to private-sector groups on both sides of the Atlantic to come up with recommendations for setting up uniform standards for productive management and harvest.

As noted previously, in 1965, one of the proposals made by the Hunter Commission in Great Britain had been that of "no headlands" fishing for salmon. During the next decade, CASE came to support this theory strongly and used it on May 24, 1971, as the basis of testimony on the proposed Pelly Amendment before a committee of the U.S. Congress.

The Hunter Commission proposals never did catch fire; perhaps they were too revolutionary at that time, challenging long-established patterns of harvest. The concept languished for some six years. Then in 1977, RASA reaffirmed support for and refined the application of this principle and decided to promote its acceptance throughout the community of Atlantic salmon nations.

Over the years, we in RASA had become more and more dissatisfied with the term "No Headlands" as applied to the inshore fixed net fisheries. It was not only negative but also clumsy and confusing. We needed a catchy and descriptive slogan. No matter how rational the objective — in this case, saving a wild species in crisis — an affirmative and constructive appeal is fundamental when the validity and justification of an ingrained and traditional means of livelihood are called into question.

Finally, I came up with a solution. We christened the principle "River Harvest." This name was a natural because it relates to the objective, has a positive connotation, and implies constructive remedies for present abuses.

In a major address before the Second International Atlantic Salmon Symposium held in Edinburgh on September 26, 1978, RASA called for a "program for minimizing interception and exploitation of Atlantic salmon in the ocean — River Harvest." Here are several excerpts from that address that highlight the rationale for River Harvest:

> Present regimes for managing salmon are ineffectual, incapable of protecting the species. Clearly, the system is sick.
>
> National and regional considerations of self-interest conflict, causing severe social and economic disruptions. Thus, the most urgent problems affecting management today are political, rather than ones of science. It is in this political arena, then, that *Salar*'s struggle for survival must be engaged.
>
> We must define and activate a relevant and urgent program of change — new directions, new dimensions, new disciplines.
>
> Implementation of the principle of "River Harvest" calls for just such a program of change.
>
> The objective of River Harvest is to minimize international and regional interception and exploitation. Atlantic salmon would be taken, either by commercial nets or by angling, only at the mouths of rivers or in the rivers themselves.
>
> River Harvest offers the best means of control of escapement of salmon upriver for spawning. River Harvest would

be a permanent solution to the long-standing, and previously condoned, practice of one nation's intercepting another nation's stocks.

Endorsement by Atlantic salmon-producing nations of the principle of River Harvest will not come easily, however. Many salmon fisheries, whether driftnetting or fixed engines on headlands, are traditional, inherited from generation to generation. It will be argued that to relocate and limit netting to river areas only would require actual relocation of families, or elimination from the fishery.

Implementation of this discipline also involves economic considerations, and should be undertaken on a phasing-out basis, with just compensation to those adversely affected. The cost of such rescue missions will be relatively small compared with the long-term economic benefits to the very communities whose fishermen now deplete the resource — and their own future well-being to boot.

The role of the private sector here is clear. As was the case with the overexploitation off West Greenland, leaving it to bureaucratic involvement is simply not enough. Fisheries problems are not high on the priority lists of governments, and Atlantic salmon are not high on the priority lists of fisheries problems. Enlightened fisheries ministries therefore understand that only support from the private sector will move governments to undertake innovative programs of political and sociological change necessary to salmon salvation.

The campaign for River Harvest is already under way, but many more conservation groups must be added, on both sides of the Atlantic. Specifically, we not only should endorse the principle, but also formally register our request with our own governments for action now to implement the principle. And, in order to be effective, we have to generate a ground swell of public opinion, education, and action.

In 1978, both the Atlantic Salmon Association in Montreal and the International Atlantic Salmon Foundation followed RASA's lead and adopted endorsing resolutions. The job now was to try to get the North Atlantic salmon-producing nations to agree to the principle and commence implementation.

The first thing to do would be to attempt to open up Canadian consideration of River Harvest through an exchange of correspondence with Canadian Fisheries Minister Romeo LeBlanc. In a letter of November 28, 1977, RASA first drew attention to the November 23, 1971, U.S.-Canadian statement on Atlantic salmon, which had affirmed the belief that harvesting should be limited "to the extent practicable to the country of origin of the salmon." Our letter then reasoned that this mutual understanding between the two countries was the rationale for the government of Canada to adopt and implement River Harvest. The minister's long and evasive reply was to the effect that "the concept of harvesting salmon within the home river areas will doubtless receive further attention in the years to come."

The next exchange started with our letter of April 7, 1978, in which we raised new points favoring Canada's adoption of River Harvest and stressed that "today's problem surrounding U.S. stocks on migration in Canadian waters will become tomorrow's burden unless preventive measures are taken to cope with the situation." LeBlanc's reply of May 25 promised that, in accordance with the request made in my first letter, there would be a "review undertaken by a federal task force which will include study of international factors associated with salmon harvest within the Canadian fishery." So Canada was at least addressing our concerns.

Then on October 5, 1978, RASA again advocated River Harvest, but received no reply. The reason — we later found out — was that LeBlanc had been relieved of his position. He was reappointed, however, as Fisheries Minister two years later, in 1980. So again we went at it.

At that time, due to two back-to-back declines in annual salmon catches, Canada had to adopt strong regulations reducing the salmon quotas and cutting back on open seasons. Our letter of April 4, 1980, to the minister pointed that this would be an ideal time to institute River Harvest, because it would be "a far less

176 · River Harvest

drastic measure than the total closures that are being advocated today." And I reminded him that back in 1978 at the Edinburgh symposium he had had no question about the logic of the concept of River Harvest, for he had stated that to the extent he could be, he was in favor of it.

The minister wrote back that "my Department's Atlantic salmon enhancement program, now in the planning stages, may propose exploring river mouth harvesting on a pilot scale. Implementation of such an approach would be contingent on the approval of the entire program, the feasibility of which will not be known for at least one year." This was encouraging — an indication that perhaps we were getting somewhere.

Yet, sad to say, nothing came of those efforts. So we had to be content with the knowledge that we had at least opened a constructive dialogue with the Canadian government, which would serve us in good stead in the future.

Otherwise, the private-sector groups in the United States and Canada became supportive of the soundness of the River Harvest rationale. In 1982, both the Atlantic Salmon Association and the International Atlantic Salmon Foundation now adopted formal position statements endorsing the concept and recommending that Canada's policy follow the principle of River Harvest.

Since these early years, River Harvest has always been one cornerstone of RASA's proposals for conservation of salmon in the ocean.

RASA COMMENT

River Harvest has yet to be formally adopted as policy by any of the North Atlantic salmon-producing nations. The reasons for this lack of commitment have to do with the fact that fisheries ministers are always compelled to avoid alienating the commercial fishermen. After all is said and done, the tenure of a minister's appointment in all probability depends on maintaining a satisfactory working arrangement with the main body of commercial fishermen. In Canada, fisheries ministers historically have come from Newfoundland, the hub of commercial fishing in the Maritime Provinces and Quebec. And many of these fishermen hold licenses to net salmon.

It must also be remembered that this Canadian salmon fishery is only a part-time occupation, generally from early June through September. It is considered a profitable one, by comparison with the fishery for cod, halibut, and flounder.

In general, this same political situation obtains in the nations bordering the northeast Atlantic Ocean.

These years — 1977 through 1980 — were frustrating for all of us who were committed to conserving and restoring the species. We knew that means other than existing management regimes would have to be sought, and we were eagerly anticipating and planning for the day when the signs would be propitious for offering new solutions.

PART

V

INVENTING THE
SALMON TREATY

20

Towards a Salmon Treaty

IN A WORLD of sovereign states, accepted principles of conservation of species like the Atlantic salmon can be ignored with no risk of retaliation. But when blatant violations of these principles damage neighboring countries and threaten the future of world stocks, it is time for international action.

As we have seen, every major Atlantic salmon-producing nation had permitted not only the excessive legal and illegal ocean netting of stocks originating in their own rivers but also the intercepting of stocks of foreign origin seeking to return to natal rivers to spawn, after grazing on forage fish in the Labrador Sea, the major feeding grounds for both European and North American salmon.

Protection for creatures of the sea grows by accretion, like a coral reef, and each new fisheries treaty extends the global consensus on norms of management. Treaties were in force for other highly migratory species — the whales, the seals, the tuna, and the Pacific salmon — but never had there been any attempt to provide something of lasting value for the Atlantic salmon.

Sensing the need for new directions, new dimensions, and new disciplines in salmon management, our organization, Restoration of Atlantic Salmon in America (RASA), had been the first to call for an international treaty. This was in June 1972, at the time the Danes had agreed to phase out the overkill off Greenland by the end of 1976.

On July 10, 1975, we again issued a formal position statement on the subject, emphasizing the need for controls on ocean netting under "a multilateral convention between the nations whose salmon are known to migrate in substantial numbers to feed off West Greenland and the host nation Denmark." Such an agreement "would provide for the setting up of an International Commission for supervision of reporting of catches of salmon, inspections, the setting of 'grazing fee' quotas, and the arbitration of disputes."

In 1976, the extensions of fisheries jurisdictions, generally to two hundred miles, had brought about the self-destruction of the International Commission for Northwest Atlantic Fisheries (ICNAF). Nations rushed into bilateral agreements, which, as far as the Atlantic salmon were concerned, were a patchwork quilt, lacking any semblance of uniformity. With no provision for inspection and no penalties for infractions, the agreements were probably unenforceable.

Self-serving bilateral agreements were entered into primarily on the basis of political expediency. They addressed only the problems of the two particular governments involved and overlooked those of third parties that might also have a legitimate interest in the fishery in question. Atlantic salmon are not only transnational but often multinational, in some cases visiting the waters of as many as four nations. These interchanges, and the fact that different races intermingle off Greenland and The Faroe Islands, would be reason enough for joint action by all countries concerned.

PLANNING THE TREATY EFFORT

During 1976 and early 1977, I had been corresponding and meeting with Rozanne Ridgway, Deputy Assistant Secretary of State for Oceans and Fisheries Affairs, with respect to my recommendation that the United States undertake to negotiate an international treaty on Atlantic salmon. I had also met and discussed RASA's treaty concept with Assistant Secretary of the Interior Nat Reed and with Dave Wallace, Associate Administrator of the National Oceanic and Atmospheric Administration (NOAA), and they were supportive.

Roz Ridgway was to leave shortly to take up her duties as the newly appointed Ambassador to Finland and was desirous of maintaining the continuity of the Atlantic salmon effort. On May 18, 1977, she held a meeting for the purpose of long-term planning on how best to secure a multilateral Atlantic salmon treaty. We decided that the time was ripe for the effort and that the United States should design and open negotiations on such a treaty. The United States would approach Canada first, in an attempt to secure its cooperation, before approaching the European Economic Community.*

THE SECOND INTERNATIONAL ATLANTIC SALMON SYMPOSIUM

On September 26, 1978, the Second International Atlantic Salmon Symposium took place in Edinburgh, Scotland. In our remarks there, RASA once again urged support for a multilateral treaty. In the closing address, Donald McKernan, the former U.S. Assistant Secretary of State for Oceans and Fisheries Affairs, with whom I coordinated closely, called for a resolution urging the establishment of an international convention for Atlantic salmon that would:

1. Bar fishing for Atlantic salmon beyond twelve miles.

2. Provide for cooperation among all the countries in conservation, regulation, and enforcement measures.

3. Provide a forum for international cooperation in research and the exchange of data on Atlantic salmon.

---

* The European Economic Community (EEC) is an association formed in 1958 to effect a closer economic union among European nations. It is more popularly referred to as the Common Market, or sometimes simply as the Community. By 1974, it consisted of the United Kingdom, Ireland, West Germany, Denmark, Belgium, the Netherlands, Luxemburg, France, and Italy. The European Commission (EC) is the executive arm of the EEC and thus represents the EEC in negotiations and at international forums.

The permanent members of a U.S. team, to be designated formally as the U.S. Negotiating Team on Atlantic Salmon, would be David Wallace, Associate Administrator of NOAA; Larry Snead, Deputy Director of the State Department's Office of Oceans and Fisheries Affairs; and me, Richard Buck, Chairman of RASA. This team would be augmented at formal international meetings by the Assistant Secretary of State for Oceans and Fisheries, or by his deputy, either of whom would be the head of the delegation.

The resolution passed unanimously.

In early 1979, organizations such as the Atlantic Salmon Association and the International Atlantic Salmon Foundation followed RASA's lead in calling for a treaty by giving their approval to the Edinburgh resolution.

Still, this "motherhood" kind of statement came as an anticlimax to those of us in the United States who had been working diligently for several years on developing a draft of an international convention. We felt that we were way ahead of the Atlantic salmon community, for our draft was almost ready.

THE UNITED STATES INTRODUCES THE DRAFT TREATY

In January 1979, the State Department circulated to salmon-producing and -harvesting nations the draft of a proposed treaty, the International Convention on Atlantic Salmon in the North Atlantic Ocean, and offered it for comment. The proposed convention, in its basic principles, followed the general format of the ICNAF convention now in the process of self-destruction.

In the Preamble, the treaty recognized that "primary interest in, and responsibility for" the stocks rests with "the state in whose rivers an anadromous stock of fish originates." It is desirable to promote "conservation...through regional cooperation between the states of origin of these stocks and other states fishing these stocks." The treaty would cover all salmon, not just *Salmo salar*, the Atlantic species.*

* This could offer an opportunity to control the introduction of "exotic" anadromous species, such as the Pacific salmons. Decisions would be made by all nations that might be affected on the basis of the greatest benefit to society, not according to the whim of one nation, province, state, or industry. RASA was responsible for the inclusion of this provision in the draft and, surprisingly, the subject never came up in the ensuing negotiations. It remains to this day in the treaty text. We never know when we may need its protection.

The convention area would consist of all waters of the North Atlantic Ocean, including "territorial seas" and "fisheries jurisdictions," in which Atlantic salmon migrate and feed. Fishing for salmon in the convention area would be prohibited beyond twelve miles from the baseline from which the territorial sea is measured. Fishing within the twelve-mile area would not exceed the average annual catches during 1976–1978, or the annual catch level permitted under ICNAF (i.e., the Greenland inshore quota) for these years, whichever is less.

An international commission would be established to provide a forum for cooperation in the management of salmon resources and scientific information, and to promote research and maintain records and reports. The commission could adopt proposals, by a two-thirds majority vote, to conserve, manage, maintain, or restore stocks.* Such proposals, after being referred back to the contracting governments, would go into force after sixty days for those nations not lodging an objection. If more than a simple majority objected, those nations objecting to the proposal would not be forced to comply with it. The inclusion of this objection provision guaranteed that the sovereignty of nations' territorial seas or limits need not be violated. Lest it be thought that this "out" might render the commission ineffective, recall that ICNAF operated under the same protocol and restriction yet was able to bring the Greenland overexploitation under control. An important advantage of a commission lies in its "fishbowl" atmosphere. Nations have

---

* It was that part of the treaty that permitted proposals to be made for management and harvest inside the twelve-mile territorial seas and two-hundred-mile jurisdictional areas that would cause the greatest debate. Nations had just recently extended their fisheries jurisdictions and were now more jealous than ever of their declared sovereignty within their territorial seas. Yet these nations would have to realize and agree that conservation of Atlantic salmon is a multinational problem, with more at stake than the protection of one's own resource.

to stand up and state their positions, and pressures can be brought to bear.

Each contracting party would enforce the provisions of the treaty within two hundred miles of its coast in accordance with its domestic law.

The draft also contained coverage of such important features as enforcement by flag nations, inspections, penalties, and central reporting of catch figures.

THE COMMITTEE FOR AN ATLANTIC SALMON TREATY

Once the State Department had circulated the draft and opened discussions concerning it with other nations, it was RASA's job to develop support among the private sector. The objective was to open the channels of information and participation respecting the treaty and avoid duplication of effort and confusion of direction. On February 21, 1979, RASA held an informational meeting in Boston at the New England Aquarium, to which the general public was invited. Larry Snead of the State Department explained the terms of the proposed treaty.

At the conclusion of the meeting, officials of the salmon-oriented private-sector groups met, and we organized the ad hoc Committee for an Atlantic Salmon Treaty (CAST), with the objective of "coordinating and expediting the efforts of the private sector in support of an international Atlantic salmon treaty."

CAST was to meet regularly — and specially, as required, — throughout the long four-year negotiating effort. The initial members of CAST were David Egan, Connecticut River Salmon Association; Gardner Grant, Federation of Flyfishermen; Theodore Lyman, Miramichi Salmon Association; Christopher Percy, Connecticut River Watershed Council; Thomas Pero, Trout Unlimited; Andrew Stout, International Atlantic Salmon Foundation; Lee Wulff, RASA; and myself as chairman.

THE OCEAN AFFAIRS ADVISORY
COMMITTEE — U.S. DEPARTMENT OF STATE

On October 24, 1979, Thomas R. Pickering, the Assistant Secretary of State for Oceans and International Environmental and Scientific Affairs, appointed me a member of the Ocean Affairs Advisory Committee of the Department of State. A voluntary appointment without remuneration, its functions were to advise the assistant secretary and his two deputies "on all aspects of ocean affairs, particularly the formation and implementation of international... marine environmental policies... and international fisheries policies." This would give the private sector input at the highest levels of the State Department. It would also give me professional standing in connection with the important assignments the State Department was asking me to undertake.

AN URGENT NEED FOR ACTION

The introduction of a draft treaty and all the resultant activity were set against a backdrop of severe declines in the commercial and angling catches of salmon. The working group of the International Council for Exploration of the Seas (ICES) had estimated that in 1978, the total worldwide landings of Atlantic salmon had dropped 30 percent from the 1973–1977 average. Canada's decline in 1978 exceeded this overall average — off over 36 percent from 1977.

There was little doubt in most peoples' minds: The Greenland escalation, which had reached its peak of about 750,000 salmon in 1971 and 1972 before the high seas phase-out took effect, was the principal cause of this critical situation. This overkill had obviously caused a severe drop in the regenerative capacity of the stocks and was now taking its preordained toll.

There was now clear evidence that the 1979 figures would show a catastrophic loss in Canada, with reported declines from 1978 in the 50 to 70 percent range. Back-to-back losses of this magnitude foretold another future drop in reproduction in the years

1984 and 1985, coinciding with the salmon's five- to six-year life cycle.

TESTING THE WATERS

In accordance with the original plans of our U.S. negotiating team, the United States, during the latter part of 1979 and early 1980, would be holding informal preliminary discussions with the fisheries ministers of those nations we hoped would ultimately become signatories to a mutually agreed-upon convention.

We held the first of these talks with Canada on July 23, 1979, in Washington. Ambassador John Negroponte, who had succeeded Roz Ridgway, represented the United States. After outlining the treaty, the United States stated that it sought to create a multilateral forum to discuss the problems of Atlantic salmon on a systematic basis and cautioned against too specific an approach to objectives at this point, lest broader objectives be excluded. The United States viewed the creation of a commission as an important rallying point for Atlantic salmon protection and as a means of highlighting the issues. The United States also indicated that specific management objectives might change over time, and that it was necessary to lay the basis for future cooperation.

Canada commented in general on the treaty and then made three particular points: First, Canada would like the United States to join it in asking the European Commission to get Greenland to cut back on the quota of 1,191 tons. Second, Canada was reluctant to enter into any international agreement that might regulate its catch. Third, Canada was particularly cool to the idea of a commission that might have the power of regulation in the early years of the agreement. John Negroponte's rejoinder to all this was that the United States was "committed to no turning back on the plans for a commission."

Shortly after this meeting with Canada, I called John and recommended that, inasmuch as Canada had rejected the United States' concept of a commission, we should consider approaching the European Commission and Norway to seek support for our objective. He enthusiastically endorsed this proposal, and we planned the trip for the week of November 4.

CANADA INTRODUCES A DRAFT TREATY

On October 9, 1979, the government of Canada, not content to work from the U.S. draft, circulated to interested nations its own proposed draft of an Atlantic salmon convention. This apparent "red herring" was obviously a rebuff to the United States, but the whole thrust and content of the Canadian draft were also of considerable concern.

On November 28, in answer to the November 23 written request of Larry Snead of the State Department, our private-sector Committee for an Atlantic Salmon Treaty (CAST) presented reactions to and recommendations on this Canadian draft. We made the following principal comments, and a recommendation:

> The convention proposed by Canada is almost totally lacking in substance as being of basic and lasting value as a mechanism for bringing under control the overexploitation and interceptions that are so widespread today throughout all waters of the North Atlantic Ocean....
>
> The Canadian proposal has nothing in common with the American draft.... Because the Canadian version will, we believe, be unacceptable to the U.S., there is no point in our reviewing and commenting on it, paragraph by paragraph, and sentence by sentence. Rather we will state below the two principal reasons for rejecting the whole proposal:
>
> 1. Canada would limit the Convention Area to the Northwest Atlantic. This, of course, would exclude coverage of the Northeastern Atlantic, meaning the waters off Iceland, Norway, The Faroe Islands, Ireland, the UK, France, and Spain. All of these nations have Atlantic salmon waters.
>
> This goes against the basic premise of the United States position, which is that the waters of all nations whose stocks migrate to Greenland in substantial numbers should be covered, simply because what happens on one side of the Atlantic affects the other side.

2. It is in that part of the Canadian draft that calls for an "international organization whose object shall be to contribute through consultation and cooperation" that the whole Canadian proposal breaks down. "Consultation and cooperation" — that's all! There is no provision for, or reference to, the right of the members of the "organization" to vote on proposals for regulating the management and harvest within the territorial waters of the signatories, which is where the great majority of damaging actions take place.

The fact that the Canadians desire to use the name "Council" rather than "Commission" is indicative of their whole approach. A council can, in the last analysis, only deliberate and discuss; a commission provides a mechanism for bringing management and regulation into effect. . . .

There is another important consideration in favor of returning to the American draft. It is the understanding of CAST that the American concept and approach met in general with the approval of Denmark, the UK, Ireland, and the EC during the November State Department mission to those countries and jurisdictions. It is therefore our opinion that these potential signatories would not support a convention of the type proposed by Canada.

Our recommendation is that the Canadian draft be rejected in toto by the United States, and that the United States once again invite the Canadians to work from the United States draft.

A MEETING WITH CANADIAN FISHERIES MINISTER McGRATH

RASA had a significant number of members who were Canadian citizens. They were fully supportive of our State Department's views and impatient over their government's reluctance to approve the American concept of a salmon treaty. Several of them wrote or telephoned me and suggested that I meet with top Canadian officials. This would be a sensitive issue because of my involvement as a member of the U.S. Negotiating Team, so I bounced the whole idea off John Negroponte. Surprisingly, he was all for it and set up a meeting with Fisheries Minister McGrath in Ottawa on October 11.

My principal thrust throughout the meeting was on the multilateral aspects of the Atlantic salmon problem, which the United States believed could best be handled by an overall commission patterned after ICNAF. The minister listened carefully, but several times he expressed his feeling that Canada simply was not going to allow other nations to propose regulations within Canadian waters. He used expressions such as "these fish were spawned and raised in our rivers and sea, and should be under our control." At the end of the meeting, he said that he did not believe that the United States would be able to conclude a treaty calling for a commission of the type described in the draft.

I left the meeting with a feeling that McGrath was a tough administrator and negotiator, and that he meant what he had said. After all, he was elected from Newfoundland and did not want to report back to his constituents that he was willing to give a commission the authority to make recommendations respecting salmon in Canadian waters.

At least the meeting brought into sharper focus the polarity existing between the United States and Canada on the whole subject.

THE EUROPEAN MISSION

During the week of November 4, a U.S. interagency team headed by John Negroponte visited Brussels, Copenhagen, London, and Dublin for informal discussions with fisheries officials of the European Commission. Our delegation also consisted of Larry Snead from the State Department; David Wallace, Associate Administrator, NOAA; Galen Buterbaugh, Associate Director, Fisheries, Department of the Interior; Marshall Field, a director of RASA; and myself.

At each of these meetings, the United States announced that it had three primary considerations in developing the position on

Atlantic salmon that was reflected in the U.S. draft. The first concern was for conservation of stocks, which in recent years had shown a sharp decline in abundance in both North America and Europe. Second was the absence of effective and adequate international control measures for Atlantic salmon stocks, particularly in light of the demise of ICNAF in 1978 and the imminent expiration of the Canada-EEC salmon arrangement in December 1979. Third was the U.S. view that the Atlantic salmon problem required a long-term institution for multinational coordination and cooperation rather than ad hoc bilateral arrangements.

Negroponte always pointed out that the natural intermingling of European and North American salmon off Greenland required cooperation between the states of origin and the host states that provide forage grounds for the salmon.

The United States delegation always made it a practice to describe the principal provisions of the U.S. draft convention, emphasizing that the convention area should include both eastern and western portions of the North Atlantic and advocating the establishment of a strong commission, patterned after ICNAF, that could make management proposals.

We stressed the need for Greenland's support of an international conservation program and also that the United States favored a flexible quota for Greenland. In good years, as the number of fish are increased through enhancement, Greenland's quota should be increased. In years when the fish are less abundant, Greenland's quota should be less. Thus Greenland would share in both the benefits and obligations of effective conservation.

At these meetings we always drew attention to the fact that, although there appeared to be differences in view between Canada and the United States on the Atlantic salmon issue, it was essential that the salmon treaty have Canadian support and participation. The U.S. delegation said that it planned to visit Ottawa again, soon after this European trip, to report results to the Canadians.

At our first meeting, in London on November 5, Julian Kelsey, the United Kingdom Fisheries Secretary, expressed informal support of the U.S. approach. He recommended inclusion of the northeast Atlantic area but questioned the need to include states of the Baltic region; they have their own separate salmon treaty, and Baltic Atlantic salmon are not known to migrate to the Atlantic Ocean in great numbers.

The U.S. delegation next met in Copenhagen on November 7 with a Danish delegation headed by Henrik Netterstrom and including Jonathan Motzfeldt, Chairman of the Greenland Local Parliament, and Arni Olafsson of The Faroe Islands (the waters off these islands are feeding grounds for Atlantic salmon, principally of Norwegian and United Kingdom origin). The Danes, speaking for their territory of Greenland, emphasized the importance of the subsistence salmon fishery to Greenland and the unacceptability of Canada's refusal to consider a northwest Atlantic commission. They favored a northwest Atlantic treaty only, which would include as member states the United States, Canada, and the EEC. They were opposed to the inclusion of Baltic states. The Danes also expressed a preference for consensus voting, "if indeed [as they put it] voting is necessary at all." They were opposed to fixing quotas in the agreement itself, preferring that these be agreed upon annually and based not only on science but also on the economic needs of Greenland.

Motzfeldt said that Greenland could not agree to any decrease in the quota for 1980 and emphasized that Denmark felt that the ICNAF arrangement had been unfair to Greenland. He said that native Greenlanders fish salmon out to forty miles off the coast; thus the U.S. proposal to restrict catches to within twelve miles was a problem. He concurred with a flexible-quota concept.

The U.S. delegation met November 9 in Brussels with the delegation of the European Commission representing the European Economic Community, led by Raymond Simonnet, Director, Resource Division. There were no representatives from the Community states. The EC representative reported that the Commission generally supported the U.S. initiative but that, inasmuch as the EC represented both salmon-originating and salmon-host states, it recognized an important obligation to increase and manage the stocks. The EC strongly preferred that such a matter be handled through an international agreement rather than an EC determination. It was concerned about the Canadian position, feeling that any treaty must satisfy both the producing and the harvesting-only states.*

Greenland, the EC believed, was a special case because it provided the major feeding grounds for both European and American salmon. The EC also questioned the need for inclusion of the Baltic region, but commented that Norway and Iceland should be included.

The European Commission closed the meeting by saying that it would probably be in a position to participate in a United States working group meeting in the spring of 1980.

Finally, in Dublin on November 12, the Irish delegation reacted favorably to the U.S. salmon proposal and indicated their strong support for an international conservation program. They supported the proposed ban on fishing salmon beyond twelve miles. The Irish reported that their commercial salmon fishery was tightly controlled through seasonal restrictions, fishing gear, vessel size limits, and licensing, but that the interception of Irish fish in the area off Greenland was a serious problem. The Irish definitely wanted the treaty area to include the eastern as well as the western North Atlantic Ocean but would exclude the Baltic region. In addition to the United States, Canada, and the EEC, the Irish envisioned Norway, Iceland, The Faroe Islands, and possibly the USSR and Sweden as potential treaty members.

---

* As a result of this meeting, we gathered that the EC and Canada were beginning to have strained relations on the salmon question. At different times during our conference, EC personnel commented critically on Canada's violation of the bilateral salmon fisheries agreement with the EEC and the fact that Canada had exceeded the agreed-upon quota by some three hundred tons. All this seemed to spell roadblocks down the road.

As we left Europe, our delegation was unanimous in agreeing that the general European reaction to the U.S. salmon initiative was very supportive.

THE UNITED STATES MEETS AGAIN WITH CANADA

The U.S. negotiating team wanted to let the Canadians know what we had learned from our trip to the European capitals and to get their reaction. John Negroponte led a delegation to Ottawa on December 18, 1979, for this purpose. This would be another informal meeting, preliminary to the opening of the formal multilateral talks planned for 1980. The Canadian side was represented by Anthony Campbell, Director-General, Directorate, Fisheries and Oceans, and Robert Applebaum, Associate Director.

After reporting on the reactions of the EC, the Danes, the British, and the Irish to the text of the U.S. draft, we had a general discussion concerning the differences between the U.S. and Canadian points of view. It soon became obvious once again that the hang-up on the part of Canada centered on the view that our proposed commission would intrude in Canada's domestic salmon management and give nonproducing states an unwarranted voice in what was essentially Canadian business. We acknowledged the Canadian difficulty but pointed out that perhaps it could be overcome by changing our proposed voting mechanism from two-thirds to unanimity and adding an "objection" procedure, thereby offering complete protection of sovereignty. Still, Canada did not seem impressed by this concession. In this regard, it is worthwhile to report one particular part of the dialogue between Tony Campbell and John Negroponte:

> *Campbell:* The Canadian-U.S. cooperative thrust is an important element of our thinking. The Canadian prerequisites, however, are that:
>   1. There must be no multilateral management of the Canadian resource.

2. There must be no increase in the Greenland take.

3. And Canada is not prepared to go forward to a formal working group meeting unless there is a Canada-U.S. proposal on the table.

Negroponte: It might be difficult to come up with what you want. Can our positions with respect to management be reconciled? What part of management are you trying to protect? What is the inadequacy of the U.S. proposal? Let us strengthen the decision-making process rather than rely so much on an objection principle. What about a "consensus" type of decision-making? Is any of this so difficult?

Later on in this meeting, I had an opportunity to suggest that consideration might be given to setting up two or more commissions, presumably a North American Commission and a West Greenland Commission, each with its own decision-making authority. The Canadians apparently believed that this idea had some merit, because on January 2, 1980, in a telephone discussion with Morris D. Busby, Acting Deputy Assistant Secretary for Oceans and Fisheries Affairs, Bob Applebaum stated that the Canadians would like to discuss my suggestion. Perhaps we were on to something here.

ATTEMPTING TO RECONCILE THE U.S. AND CANADIAN POSITIONS

Still another meeting with Canada — preliminary to the initial working group meeting of all interested nations — was held in Washington on February 25–26, 1980. Morris Busby headed the U.S. delegation, and Tony Campbell represented the Minister of External Affairs of Canada. Following are the highlights of the discussions on major issues:

Convention Area Coverage. The consensus was that the convention area should include the northeast as well as the northwest Atlantic Ocean and adjacent seas, except for the Baltic Sea, which would be excluded.

Conservation Measures. The consensus was that the U.S. proposal for a ban on fishing salmon beyond twelve miles should be retained in the treaty so long as the total Greenland catch did not exceed an agreed-upon limit. There was agreement that panel membership should be limited to those countries having fisheries jurisdiction or fish in the panel region. The North American panel would have the United States and Canada as members; the West Greenland panel would include the United States, Canada, the EEC and possibly Norway and Iceland; and the Northeast panel would include the EEC and possibly Norway and The Faroe Islands. It was agreed that all the panels would have the same operating and voting arrangements.

Convention Structure. The United States proposed the creation of a single umbrella commission for the convention area, having discrete panels for the consideration of salmon conservation and management issues in specific geographic areas of concern (e.g., North America, West Greenland, and the Northeast Atlantic). Canada expressed the view that the panels might be called commissions and that they should operate independently and be able to adopt autonomous proposals, which could be discussed but not vetoed in the overview body.

Voting. The consensus was that voting in the panels should be by unanimity.

Membership in the Constituent Bodies. It was felt that the treaty should be limited to those countries that have fisheries jurisdiction or produce salmon that are caught in the convention area. Generally, it was felt that the United States, Canada, the EEC, Norway, Iceland, and Denmark (for The Faroe Islands) were potential members.

Quotas. The government of Canada stated that commission quotas on Canadian-origin salmon in the Canadian zone were unacceptable. The United States proposed that commission quotas be limited to salmon interceptions (e.g., Canadian catch of U.S. fish, Greenland catch of U.S., Canadian, and European fish) and that the commission provide a forum for review and discussion of domestic salmon programs and the impacts of such programs, all in support of the commission's international objectives. This was agreeable to Canada, so long as the United States would support Canada in seeking an initial quota for Greenland that would not exceed 1,191 metric tons a year for a five-year period. The United States commented that it favored a flexible-quota concept for all interceptions, whereby quotas would move up or down depending on stock conditions and other relevant factors. The United States also made the point that, although Canada's quota position in Greenland did not present a problem to the United States, it would probably be unacceptable to the European Commission.

Enforcement. Both sides felt that a provision obligating the members to enforce provisions of the treaty, including management measures binding on them, would be satisfactory.

It was felt that considerable progress was made at this meeting, and plans were made to meet in Ottawa in April in an attempt to harmonize a common salmon treaty text.

THE FINAL PRELIMINARY MEETING WITH CANADA

On April 8–9, 1980, we met in Ottawa, again with Morris Busby as head of the delegation for the United States and Bob Applebaum speaking for Canada. Here is the pertinent part of the dialogue between the two representatives:

> *Applebaum* (in his opening remarks) :
> 1. We are far apart, for we are missing the essential elements of a satisfactory treaty. In no way do we agree to an overall commission. Canadian flexibility on this does not exist. For instance, the EEC should have no say in the management of our fish. The EEC does not intercept our fish, and has never been interested in discussing the management of our stocks. The U.S. has tended to create a problem.
> 2. This is an intercepting fishery, and we would like to minimize the interception of U.S. salmon. There is a legitimate

interest of the U.S. in this interception, but it is not in the interest of the U.S. to be involved in the management of Canadian stocks.

3. We want the U.S. on the Canadian side in a reduction of the Greenland quota. But Canada does not need the U.S. to help negotiate a flexible quota. Canada can negotiate a separate flexible quota for Greenland directly with the EEC and get some valuable side effects.

Busby: It is not the U.S. intention to give the EEC a voice in the management of Canadian salmon. There is a difference in purpose between us. Our purpose is a restoration of North Atlantic stocks. If you try to restore stocks, there is an interrelationship, all because of the Greenland connection. You can't just deal with Greenland alone. We need to think very seriously about a freeze on all stocks of salmon, if we are seriously looking at restoration. And we have modified considerably our earlier ideas about a single commission. On your third point, we are prepared to support an initial freeze for some years on the Greenland quota.

Applebaum: Our concept is that this is not supposed to be be-all and end-all of all issues. Our concept is that the treaty is limited to interceptions, not management of all salmon fisheries.

Busby: The United States has come completely away from management by one commission, from what we originally proposed. We are banking on the fact that, since we all would be on a Greenland Panel, the real negotiations will occur in this Greenland Panel.

Applebaum: The word "commission" is misleading. A commission manages, adopts regulations.

Busby: We do want an umbrella organization of some sort. We have moved management powers and formations out into the panels. It is necessary to have a commission, and we have in mind that the commission review in a free-wheeling session in which everyone has an opportunity to express whether or not stocks are being enhanced.

Thus ended a seemingly interminable round of preliminary discussions with the potential signatories to the treaty. They had, however, served the United States — and the other potential participants — very well. The discussions had clearly evidenced Canada's lack of interest in joint treaty action with the United States and the EEC. As Applebaum had indicated, Canada was interested in "valuable side effects" and would have preferred to continue making ad hoc bilateral agreements, using the rich Grand Banks and other fishing grounds as bait.

One comforting thought was that the European Commission appeared to be on the same wavelength as the United States. We both seemed committed to a mission that would encompass all the Atlantic salmon nations and their satellites in an outreaching program that would make possible the restoration of stocks to their former abundance.

Thus we now had a good idea of who the principal players were, where they were coming from, and what their principal purposes and hang-ups respecting the proposed convention were. We were ready and eager to get on with it.

21

Getting Down to Business

ONE CLEAR MESSAGE stood out as a result of the preliminary meetings: Of the producing nations only Canada had a real conflict with the essential nature of the treaty concept.

The proponents of a broad and strong treaty, such as the United States and the EEC, would hold that the overarching objective of a treaty should be to build a bridge of security for the salmon throughout its range in the North Atlantic Ocean. These nations were supporting a coherent and rational ideology that could serve the international purpose for many years to come. It was obvious that the Canadians preferred to limit their interests solely to controlling the Greenland interceptory fishery. Their vision so far had not been broad. They did not understand — or at least were not sympathetic to — the necessity of sharing the burdens as well as the benefits of multinational accord and cooperation.

This reaction on Canada's part was, in a sense, understandable. After all, in this game of geopolitics, Canada held the biggest share of the marbles. These marbles took the form of the largest concentration — approximately 41 percent at that time — of salmon in the North Atlantic Ocean. The remaining 59 percent was split principally among the United Kingdom, Norway, and Ireland, with Iceland, France, Spain, and the United States well down on the list. This situation, plus the fact that Canada controlled the fishing on the Grand Banks of Newfoundland — perhaps the most productive of all feeding grounds — put the Canadians in a prime bargaining position to protect their salmon through bilateral agreements covering other nations' fishing rights in Canadian waters.

How could we drive home the point that Atlantic salmon in the ocean are interdependent, and that what happens on one side of the Atlantic has its indirect, but certain, effect on stocks on the other side? It is this truism that makes it necessary for all salmon-producing and harvesting-only nations to be included under one treaty.

I came up with the concept of The Wishbone Syndrome of Atlantic Salmon Exploitation.

To illustrate this point, visualize a map of the North Atlantic Ocean, and then imagine a wishbone superimposed, with Greenland as the apex or sternum. Labrador, Newfoundland, Nova Scotia, and New England waters then become the left-hand "migration bone," and the waters of Ireland, Scotland, England, France, and Spain the right-hand "migration bone." These are the routes followed by the salmon returning to home rivers. Greenland, for the foreseeable future, will continue to insist on taking a quota of Atlantic salmon annually, in return for permitting these fish to feed on the rich capelin and shrimp abounding in its waters. So if Canada, for instance, permits the "migration bone" to be cracked or broken through overfishing, fewer Canadian and U.S. salmon and their progeny would be entering the Greenland feeding pool, and Greenland would be filling a greater percentage of its quota from European stocks. Thus, the European Community nations should have a chance to comment on the impact of Canada's management measures on the number of fish available off Greenland. The opposite also applies. If, for instance, Ireland overexploits, Greenland then fills its quota in larger measure from the Canadian and U.S. components, so the United States and Canada should be able to offer comments regarding the impact of Irish domestic management programs on the available salmon off Greenland. This "Greenland connection" is indeed convincing proof that all salmon in the North Atlantic Ocean require the protective and regulatory mantle of a multinational management mechanism.

John Negroponte liked the wishbone syndrome concept. It made sense, and that was its appeal. We all began using it regularly, particularly at negotiating meetings. It soon received wide acceptance. The leading English country magazine, *The Field*, popularized it. Feature writers — such as Nelson Bryant of the *New York Times* — picked it up from a RASA special press release and wrote pieces about it. It still crops up every now and then in today's salmon world.

Whether or not it helped accomplish our purpose — who knows? At any rate, it added a new dimension to our story, making for a better understanding of the need for a broad outreach under the proposed treaty.

THE FIRST WORKING GROUP MEETING
The First Working Group Meeting of the consultative parties was held in Washington, D.C., April 29–30, 1980. It was a tripartite meeting, with only Canada, the European Economic Community, and the United States participating.*

The U.S. delegation had nine members, with Morris Busby as the Head of Delegation. Mogens Marcusson headed the three-person delegation of the European Commission of the European Economic Community. Sitting in were twelve representatives of its member states, including Einar Lemke from the Ministry for Greenland in Copenhagen. Tony Campbell, representing the Minister for External Affairs of the Government of Canada, and Robert Applebaum, of the Department of Fisheries and Oceans, backed up by a sizable staff, represented Canada.

The meeting opened with a luncheon at the Cosmos Club, hosted by RASA. Ambassador Thomas Pickering, the Assistant

* Our formal salmon meetings followed the protocol in general use at international meetings of governments. Nations actively negotiating on potential conventions (i.e., treaties) were usually referred to as "The Consultative Parties." Each nation appointed a Head of Delegation who spoke for his or her government. Other members of the delegation could not speak unless given permission to do so by the chairman of the meeting, in answer to a request made by a head of delegation.

Secretary of State for Fisheries and Oceans, welcomed the delegates. Tony Campbell, in his response, graciously complimented the United States on pioneering the treaty concept, including, in a more lighthearted vein, a suggestion that from now on I should be referred to as "The Godfather of the salmon treaty."

The amiable introductory phase of this first formal meeting was not to last for long, however. As we got down to business, it became apparent that we were in for a rough time. After Morris Busby's opening appeal, which centered on the hope that Canada and the United States might now enjoy "real, solid, cooperation," we were taken aback by Bob Applebaum's initial response. Here are excerpts:

> *Applebaum*: We have real doubts about the need for a treaty. We feel that a bilateral is sufficient. We do sense an obligation to consult with the United States about the intercepting of U.S. stocks. There are three elements of consideration here: first, intercepting fisheries are a problem of management, second, there are socioeconomic factors which prevent the avoidance of interceptions, and, third, we do agree that interceptions could erode or eliminate the state of origin's stocks. Yet an all-embracing treaty is unnecessary; we rather could contribute to the efforts of the state of origin. Thus the intercepting states have a responsibility to consult with the state of origin.
>
> *Marcusson*: Bilaterals tend to attach the salmon issue to questions not of the same nature. We need to address the salmon issue in an exclusive context, and so we endorse the principle of the usefulness of a convention. The convention area should be the entire North Atlantic, with management decisions to be divided between more than one body.

So there we had it, early on — Canada on one side and the EEC on the other.

After these opening remarks, the meeting moved to take up the whole agenda. The United States and Canada each tabled a composite text indicating areas of agreement and disagreement, based on their preliminary bilateral consultations in response to the

U.S. initiative in early 1979 to establish a convention. The European Commission also tabled a separate convention text for discussion.

Following are the highlights of the substantive issues covered during the two-day session:

Convention Area Coverage. The consensus was that the convention area should include both the northwest and the northeast Atlantic Ocean and adjacent seas, except for the Baltic Sea, which would be excluded. This convention area would include all waters from the coast (i.e., maritime waters). Fresh waters, including rivers, would be excluded.

Conservation Measures. The U.S. proposal to ban salmon fishing beyond twelve miles of shore was supported by Canada and agreed to generally, so long as an exception could be made to permit Greenland and possibly The Faroe Islands to fish beyond twelve miles (e.g., thirty to sixty miles). Under such exceptions, other conservation measures would apply (e.g., quotas and area and time restrictions).

Convention Structure. Canada and the EC shared the view that there should be a general council to serve as the main administrative body and separate commissions under the general council; such commissions would be autonomous. The United States and Canada agreed that there should be three primary constituent bodies (either panels or commissions): one for North America, one for Greenland, and one for the North East Atlantic. The EC, however, proposed two such bodies (the North East and North West Atlantic) separated by a line drawn south from the tip of Greenland. Both the United States and Canada argued for the three-body approach on the basis that no European fish migrate to or within the two-hundred-mile fisheries jurisdictions of the United States and Canada. Thus a separate panel or commission to discuss bilateral relations between the United States and Canada made sense. In short, neither wanted the EEC to have a vote on measures in an area where no EEC fish existed. This issue was left unresolved.

Voting. Both the United States and Canada proposed that voting in the panels (or commissions) should be on the basis of unanimity, with the overview body being unable to override proposals adopted by the panels. This issue remained unresolved.

Membership in the Constituent Bodies. The United States and Canada saw membership in the North American panel limited to themselves; the Greenland panel to the United States, Canada, and the EEC; and the northeast panel to the EEC, Norway, Denmark (for The Faroe Islands), and possibly Iceland. The EC proposed limiting membership in the northwest panel (or commission) to the United States, Canada, and the EEC; and the northeast panel to the EEC and possibly Iceland, Norway, Sweden, Denmark (for the Faroe Islands), and the USSR.

At the close of the meeting, the United States agreed to prepare a revised draft composite text for use at the next meeting of the working group, which would be in Brussels.

All the delegations expressed their interest in seeking a multilateral mechanism to deal with salmon conservation in the Atlantic Ocean, and the view was that the meeting had been successful in moving that objective forward.

RASA COMMENT
At the conclusion of this meeting, there was considerable discussion within the U.S. delegation about the general softening of Canada's whole attitude toward the proposed treaty. Something must have happened between the first and second days of the meeting. Perhaps they were impressed by the apparent determination and enthusiasm evident within the EC and U.S. delegations respecting the whole concept. Or perhaps they had telephoned Ottawa for approval of a more cooperative approach. In this connection, we had always known that Canadian fisheries ministers held their negotiators to a very tight rein. There was always a bottom line that did not give representatives much leeway.

THE SECOND WORKING GROUP MEETING
In Brussels, November 6–7, 1980, the consultative parties — the EEC, the United States, Canada, and Norway — after considerable

discussion, finally agreed on the most important point in contention, the structure of the proposed convention. There would be three commissions, the North American, the Greenland, and the North East Atlantic. Each commission could propose regulatory measures for management and harvest in waters under its jurisdiction. There was also agreement on an overall council that would act as the forum for discussions affecting all commissions, compile reports, and facilitate the exchange of scientific information.

Otherwise, there was a general rehash of the points discussed at the Washington meeting. Canada's offer to host the next meeting and prepare a final composite negotiating draft was accepted.

THE THIRD WORKING GROUP MEETING

In Ottawa, January 28–29, 1981, the United States, the EEC, Canada, and Norway were represented. Iceland, The Faroe Islands, and Sweden had been invited to attend and were welcomed by the chairman.

This Ottawa meeting was attended by no less than forty-three accredited representatives of the consultative parties, giving an indication of the increased importance the North Atlantic nations now attached to the efforts to establish an Atlantic salmon convention.

The negotiations were opened with the EC commenting on the draft that it had prepared and circulated to the consultative parties. Here are the highlights of the discussions that ensued:

The Convention Area. Bob Applebaum stated that Canada did not wish to delineate a convention area, preferring instead to have "this Convention apply only to salmon stocks which migrate between areas under national fisheries jurisdictions in the North Atlantic Ocean." Morris Busby replied, "The U.S. supports the convention area concept, rather than get hung up on a listing of interception areas. The convention should cover all areas." Mogens Marcusson, speaking for the EC, agreed with the U.S. position.

Convention Measures. The head of the Faroese delegation

described the salmon fishery there, pointing out that it consisted of about forty boats that could take up to a thousand tons of salmon yearly. They wanted to be allowed to fish outside twelve miles, because the fish could be found as far out as two hundred miles. Smorgrav of Norway objected to any exceptions to the twelve-mile limit. Busby said, "We believe in the general principle of no fishing beyond twelve miles," but "an exception could be made in the case of West Greenland and perhaps for The Faroe Islands."

Sweden, Iceland, and Norway expressed an interest in being members of the Greenland and northeast Atlantic commissions. The U.S. position on this was that it would be acceptable for these nations to participate but not to vote. Marcusson for the EC indicated that these nations had no real interest in these regions because their salmon did not migrate to Greenland or to the northeast Atlantic in any substantial numbers, as indicated by the fact that only some .003 percent of tags returned from fish caught indicated an origin from these states.

At the end of this meeting, Bob Applebaum made the following statement: "It is difficult for us to take these steps. They are going further than those which we were ready to take when we began discussing the proposed convention."

RASA COMMENT

My notes show that, at the end of this Ottawa meeting, we were disturbed by Canada's sudden return to a negative approach to the whole treaty concept as it now stood. We had also learned, in confidence at the time, from Greenland Minister Motzfeldt that Greenland wanted an increase in the salmon quota, from 1,191 tons to 1,700 tons; or perhaps they would settle for 1,400 tons. In order to get approval for this, Greenland was willing to set the fishing season back and enlarge the mesh size of their nets. Their rationale was that since the salmon grow substantially in weight during August and September, near the end of the Greenland fishing season, they could get an increased tonnage by taking the same number of fish later in the season. Increasing the mesh size would mean more mean more smaller fish escaping through the gill nets. Thus, the Greenland argument was that, although more tonnage would be taken, there would be no increase in the numbers taken.

We couldn't see anything but trouble over these new developments, even though we had made definite progress on the treaty text in Brussels. Although we should have been encouraged, we left with the sneaky feeling that we were not home free by any means.

THE FOURTH WORKING GROUP MEETING

This fourth meeting of the consultative parties in Oslo on May 19–21, 1981, developed into a discussion of conservation measures that might be in force prior to the ratification of a convention. These were referred to as interim measures, and were of particular interest to the Scandinavian nations and their territories, in particular The Faroe Islands and Greenland, both of which were represented in international forums by Denmark. Oslo offered a convenient venue for their purpose. This was reflected in the size of the delegations; there were now some sixty representatives, which resulted in things getting out of hand every now and then.

After introductory remarks by the chairman, Mogens Marcusson, head of the delegation for the European Commission, asked for a discussion of the Faroese problem. He pointed out that the Faroese catch of Atlantic salmon, which had been less than fifty tons annually until 1979, had accelerated greatly, to a present range of seven hundred to eight hundred tons. He stated that "the magnitude of this fishery has become a great issue, and some conclusion is urgent. It is suggested that there be a freeze at the average tonnage over the last five years, because the consequences to the salmon are unknown as to this level of seven hundred to eight hundred tons."

At this point the chairman of the meeting stated that the consultation on the Faroes should be called off. But the negotiators were persistent and continued their dialogue. Marcusson pointed out that the states of origin had expressed deep concern over this situation, and he hoped that the Faroese representative would take this message home. He then explained that "there will be fait accompli for this fishing until mid-1982, because licenses are given in August of 1981, so conclusive talks should be had before the end of August." The Faroese representative's reply was to the effect that he would convey the message.

Robert Applebaum (Canada) interjected here that he had heard that 150 tons of the Faroese catch came from Danish vessels, implying that the EEC was responsible for that part. Marcusson's reply was that unless there was a fisheries agreement in force, the EC put no limit on catch in Faroese waters, and there was no agreement between the EC and the Faroese. He remarked that "apparently the Faroese are giving fishing rights to Denmark, and so this is a job for the coastal states of origin of the fish." The Faroese representative commented that since there are close constitutional rights between Denmark and the Faroe Islands, it was natural to cooperate.

Applebaum then asked the question, "Will the EC meet on the West Greenland problem?" Marcusson answered that there should be a preparatory meeting on the West Greenland and other interim conservation measures before the final diplomatic conference. There then ensued a discussion between Applebaum and Marcusson on how a West Greenland quota would be handled under the proposed convention. On this point. Applebaum stated that there should be a fixed quota for West Greenland for an interim period of five years, with the status quo remaining—no increase in numbers of salmon allowed, but an increase in tonnage accomplished by increasing the mesh size of the nets.

Marcusson replied, "The interim agreement includes the 1983 catch. Thus the EC wants three years. So leave it at that, and the convention then resolves this. There is no need for double coverage, anyway."

Applebaum countered, "We believe the whole convention depends, as far as Canada is concerned, on a five-year period. This is a very important point to Canada."

At this point, the United States was recognized and joined the discussion. The United States was now represented by Theodore G. Kronmiller, newly appointed Deputy Assistant Secretary of State for Oceans and Fisheries Affairs. His comments were brief and very much to the point: "This whole issue is not a bilateral one, because the United States, for example, does have fish in the area, and these fish are affected. Therefore we are reticent to rely on a bilateral agreement."

The balance of this meeting then concerned itself with general discussions, largely of administrative matters of no primary importance.

Thus, although little progress was made in Oslo in advancing the treaty toward a final diplomatic conference, the meeting did serve to further accentuate the polarity of purpose and objective between Canada on the one hand and the EEC and the Americans on the other.

REFLECTIONS

The following comments, although not pertinent to the negotiations, may be of passing interest to the reader.

The State Department often trains its promising career diplomats in oceans and fisheries work, probably because there are no more complicated or exacting problems to deal with than those involving transboundary questions, the geopolitics of fisheries agreements, and maritime law. It just so happened that two of our top diplomats of recent years got some of their early training through their involvement in negotiations on the Atlantic salmon treaty: Rozanne Ridgway and Thomas Pickering. Both went on to enjoy illustrious careers, and so I touch on these careers briefly:

Rozanne L. Ridgway In 1977, the Office of Oceans and Fisheries Affairs took on new personnel who lacked knowledge and experience on Atlantic salmon and was not set up to maintain a separate section for this purpose. The Director, Roz Ridgway, asked me to indoctrinate these officials in the long and complicated history of the restoration effort in the United States and the international problems arising out of this commitment. She was very appreciative of RASA's involvement, and was especially helpful in our salmon effort. Highly intelligent and analytical, she was always ready to take appropriate action.

After her tour of duty as Assistant Secretary for Oceans and Fisheries Affairs, Roz spent several years as Ambassador to Finland. She retained her interest in the Atlantic salmon and attempted to get the Finnish government interested in a restoration program for salmon. We corresponded about the possibility of patterning such an effort after the U.S. experience in New England, but the interest in Finland simply wasn't there. Although nothing came of these efforts, they undoubtedly helped the overall international cause, because the Finns later became strong supporters of the salmon treaty effort.

Roz Ridgway was next promoted to become Ambassador to West Germany, a key position in the Reagan Administration. From there she was brought back to the United States to become Secretary of State George Shultz's right arm, in a central assignment, as Assistant Secretary of State for the Bureau of European and Canadian Affairs.

Thomas R. Pickering Although I did not know Tom Pickering well, I worked with him often enough to come to respect him greatly. He inspired confidence in his judgment. He was quiet — not one to seek the limelight — but went about his business with foresight, determination, and efficiency. As Assistant Secretary of State for Fisheries and Oceans Affairs, he helped us with a multitude of problems — from securing funding for the State Department for the treaty effort to his major commitment, negotiating with other nations, at which he was highly skilled. He was considerate of his associates; when he left for a more important assignment, he was thoughtful enough to send me a letter of commendation for my assistance to the department.

Subsequently, Pickering served as the U.S. ambassador to several nations, including El Salvador and Israel. But it was in his work as the U.S. Ambassador to the United Nations (1989–1992), preceding and during the Gulf War, that he achieved prominence, for he served with great distinction. He is universally given credit for having welded the leading nations into the United Nations force that accepted the challenge thrown down by Saddam Hussein. Thus he served in the tradition of Adlai Stevenson, Jeanne Kirkpatrick, and Daniel Moynihan.

On January 26, 1993, President Clinton made the first ambassadorial announcement of his presidency, and it was that of Tom Pickering as Ambassador to Russia, certainly one of the most sensitive posts of all in early 1993.

22

The Canadian Recalcitrance

THE CONSULTATIVE PARTIES negotiating the proposed Atlantic salmon treaty met in Geneva on August 12–13, 1981, for a Fifth Working Group Meeting.

CANADA BOYCOTTS THE MEETING

At the last minute, Canada decided not to participate in the negotiations because of a disagreement with the European Commission over a technical point in connection with the Greenland quota for the 1981 catch. There had been provisional agreement on an increase in the quota from 1,191 tons to 1,270 tons, provided, among other things, that the mesh size of the gill nets be increased and that the opening of the season be delayed until August 25.

The agreement had not been ratified by the EC, however, and it announced that it proposed to proceed with a self-imposed quota of 1,270 tons for 1981, but that the mesh size would not be increased until November 1, 1981, since it was too late for the fishermen to accomplish the changeover by August 25. The Canadians took the position that the increase in quota was not justified without the increase in mesh size. The final bargaining came down to an argument over a compromise figure of 1,256 tons.

The United States sought to mediate the dispute, pointing out to the EC, to no avail, that any increase to 1,270 tons prior to the Geneva meeting could jeopardize the success of this round of negotiations and agreement on a treaty in the future. The Canadians had reported to the United States that the technical differences were politically important and that if the EC refused to accommodate, Canada would boycott the meeting.

This is just what happened. Canada did not officially attend, finally sending an observer to the talks who provided a written explanation for the boycott but did not participate in the meeting.

THE TURNING POINT

The purpose of the Canadian boycott was not clear. Was it simply a protest against unilateral action by the EC in raising the quota? Or did it have a deeper connotation — an expression by Canada of a basic lack of interest in the whole treaty concept? Canada must have realized that the boycott might damage the chances for a treaty. Was Canada ready to accept the responsibility for this?

Far from being deterred from proceeding by the defection, however, the delegates were extremely critical of Canada's action and were determined that this incident not be allowed to interrupt the business at hand.

Something happened at Geneva — something spontaneous and unexpected. The treaty-making process had weathered a political storm, and a new feeling of confidence pervaded the sessions. Gone was the negativism that had often surfaced during earlier meetings, to be replaced by a sense of urgency and enthusiasm. A resolve seemed to emerge, based, no doubt, on the sober realization that failure to act constructively and forcefully would result in a loss of impetus and jeopardize the successful conclusion of two years of progress toward multilateral agreement.

Functions of the Council. One substantive issue that had always caused considerable concern had been the difference of approach between Canada on the one hand and the EEC and the United States on the other with respect to giving the umbrella-like council the right to make recommendations to individual parties and to the three regional commissions (North American, West Greenland, and North East Atlantic). Canada had taken the position that, although no violation of fisheries jurisdictions would be involved in this approach, recommendations of such a nature would impinge on its concept of national sovereignty. The United States had, unsuccessfully, made a number of attempts to reconcile this difference through treaty language that might be acceptable to all concerned.

Now, no doubt impelled by the enthusiasm developed in Geneva, the EC took the initiative in proposing that the U.S.-EC position be accepted, thus returning to the concept of stronger powers for the council. Any recommendations in the interest of the world resource could be made to any party or any commission. The United States indicated its preference for this EC approach, and this became the consensus of the meeting.

Canada, even though not participating in the meeting, is reported to have communicated in discussions in the back corridors its opposition to such authority for the council.

The Greenland Plebiscite. In February 1982, the Greenlanders would hold a plebiscite to decide whether they wished a greater measure of self-government from Denmark, including withdrawal from the European Economic Community. This was a political problem, and the EEC was at first reluctant to hold the diplomatic conference and conclude the treaty prior to February, for fear that any discussions with respect to the Greenland catch quota might influence the Greenlanders' vote.

The possible complications arising from this situation had been on the minds of those negotiating the salmon treaty. But should action on the Atlantic salmon treaty be held hostage to a plebiscite of this nature? Any delay would result in a loss of impetus and reduce the chances of a treaty in the foreseeable future. The negotiators understood that the only sensible choice was to conclude the treaty on as equitable a basis as possible for Greenland — one that would not likely be adversely affected by the outcome of the plebiscite.

The Faroe Islands Escalation. Somewhat the same situation existed with The Faroe Islands, a province of Denmark. The Faroese had gained a large measure of self-government in 1948. In 1972, Denmark joined the EEC; in 1975, however, the Danish parliament decided that The Faroe Islands should remain outside the EEC.

Fishing was the mainstay of the Faroese economy, and apparently it was felt that it would be inadvisable for the mother country to speak for the fishermen.

A storm of protest had arisen over the sudden escalation of the Faroese salmon fishery from about 50 tons in the 1970s to some 1,200 tons planned for the 1981–1982 season, which would run from the fall to the following spring. The opinion had been expressed that the Faroese might want to delay action on the treaty in order to secure concessions advantageous to the continuance of this unilateral action. Here again, there appeared to be a consensus that this situation was no reason to hold up plans for convening the full diplomatic conference.

Solid Achievements. Out of the previous working group meetings a complicated draft text had been developed, which presented the differing positions of the seven negotiating parties consisting of the EEC, The Faroe Islands, Norway, Sweden, Iceland, Canada, and the United States. Near the end of the Geneva meeting, however, many issues had been resolved to the point where it was possible to agree on a majority of important provisions. As a result of this progress, it was now possible to prepare a final negotiating text. This in itself was a considerable accomplishment.

The Working Group negotiators had now gone as far as they could. The few remaining substantive issues were political in nature and could be resolved only at a Full Diplomatic Conference, after which the treaty would be opened for signature by all participants. The Geneva session ended with unanimous approval (Canada not participating) for convening such a conference in Brussels in November 1981.

THE DILEMMA

Despite this new spirit of Geneva, the members of our U.S. negotiating team realized that the whole matter of achieving a satisfactory treaty hung in the balance. We still had to face the fact that the Canadians had left the negotiating table.

In this connection, I wrote a letter on October 5, 1981, to the Canadian Secretary of State for External Affairs, the Honorable Mark MacGuigan, urging Canadian participation in the development of a North Atlantic salmon convention. His Deputy Director R. J. Rochon answered on October 30, 1981, stating that "the government of Canada shares your desire for the establishment of an organization which will contribute to the conservation and restoration of Atlantic salmon." Then, after presenting his government's problems with the negotiating text as developed, he concluded with the following sobering paragraph: "Any decision as to Canada's presence at future North Atlantic salmon convention meetings will be based on an analysis of Canada's interest as well as on an evaluation of the likelihood of developing a multilateral convention dealing with the problem of salmon interception on a more effective basis than might otherwise be possible through a series of bilateral arrangements."

We knew that we wanted and needed Canada in the treaty, but we had decided to take the risk of proceeding with the negotiations in order to convince Canada that it was in its own best interest as well as everyone else's best interests that Canada be a signatory. Our ace in the hole, of course, in the event that Canada did not join, would be the threat of invoking the law that we had worked so hard to secure, the Pelly Amendment, which empowers the President to embargo the importation of fish products from any nation "conducting fishing operations in a manner or under circumstances which diminish the effectiveness of an international fishery conservation program."

No one wanted to have to go that route. So what could we do to persuade Canada to come along with us?

CAST SWINGS INTO ACTION
During all the previous treaty negotiations, the Committee for an Atlantic Salmon Treaty had been supporting the American treaty effort, and we now decided that it was time for more definitive action.

After all, most of us had been down this road before, stopping the Danish overkill in the early 1970s. We had experience with ad hoc situations. We decided on a three-part program that would involve CAST members in (1) keeping U.S. governmental agencies informed about the tense situation in case we should need their help, (2) writing letters from our organizations to Canadian officials, and (3) securing greater involvement of Canadian private-sector salmon organizations in bringing pressure on their own government.

To kick off this program, CAST held an organizational meeting in New York City on September 24, 1981. Sixteen top officials of Atlantic salmon organizations attended. Ted Kronmiller, Head of the U.S. Negotiating Team, briefed the assembly on the current situation. The publicity engendered by this meeting enabled us to broaden our efforts to keep our own senators and congresssmen informed and involved. A great many letters urging that Canada return to the working group meetings as a consultative party were sent to members of the Canadian parliament and to Romeo LeBlanc, the Canadian Fisheries Minister (see Appendix 2 for responses to the CAST initiative).

THE ATLANTIC SALMON ASSOCIATION
PROMOTES CANADIAN PARTICIPATION
Of all the private-sector groups in Canada, the Atlantic Salmon Association (ASA) appeared the most interested in bringing pressure on the government to return to the negotiating table. Michael Price, the Executive Director, telephoned me asking if I would go to Montreal and meet with a number of the directors to bring them up-to-date on the actual situation and also advise on how they could best coordinate their actions with ours. On October 1, at an all-day meeting in Montreal, I recommended that ASA act to involve the members of parliament. As a result of this meeting, Michael Price sent a letter to all the members of parliament on October 2, 1981. (see Appendix 3). This was more than we could have hoped for, and it evoked a fine response. Price reported that by far the great

majority replied that they would recommend that Canada take a more flexible approach and return to negotiating a treaty. Thus a good dialogue had been started.

As a result of these intensive efforts in the United States and Canada, I felt it appropriate to write to Mark MacGuigan, the Canadian Secretary of State for External Affairs. I explained that the working group negotiators, principally the United States and the EC, had already made two major concessions:

> First, because of Canada's objection to a single commission mechanism patterned after ICNAF, we agreed to go to a regional basis of dealing with management problems. Second, because of Canada's objection to a system of majority voting in commissions, the negotiators agreed to go to unanimity as the basis of voting in the Commissions.
>
> So it is our sincere hope that the government of Canada will adopt a more flexible approach to the matter of the council's functions, giving that body the power to discuss and make recommendations to the commissions.
>
> Canada and the United States should act together to their common interest, for the problems of the salmon in the Atlantic Ocean are long-term, interrelated, and involving all the producers and users. Patchwork to mend a hole here and there will not work. The whole fabric has to be interwoven.

This letter may have played a part in the next development. Canada requested an early informal meeting of the Working Group negotiators, which took place in Washington on November 25. It was apparent that Canada had had a complete change in direction — and one for the better. Deputy Director Rochon — MacGuigan's close assistant — sent this reply to my letter a week after the Washington meeting:

> I am writing in reply to your letter of November 16 to the Secretary of State for External Affairs. Dr. MacGuigan has asked me to assure you of his keen interest in the development of

permanent multilateral arrangements for the conservation and restoration of Atlantic salmon. I shall also bring your letter to the attention of the various officials, in this and other Departments, who are involved in efforts to develop an Atlantic Salmon Convention. Your comments will be of assistance to them in considering this matter.

We were pleased to have had an opportunity to exchange views with you last week in Washington, in the course of the informal Canada/USA talks on Atlantic salmon. I trust that you share our satisfaction with the compromise text worked out at that meeting, and I hope that the few remaining problems can be settled quickly in order to pave the way for an early diplomatic conference. In particular, it would certainly facilitate progress if the United States could agree that the compromise achieved in Washington will stand the test of time, i.e., that the agreed approach will be maintained even if, despite joint Canada/USA efforts, a diplomatic conference cannot take place prior to the Greenland referendum in February.

For our part we believe that the good will and desire of all sides involved will allow us to bring our work to a successful, acceptable conclusion. Thank you for your letter and your interest in helping to achieve success.

Shortly after this, MacGuigan announced to the press that Canada would "be an active participant in the negotiations for the development of a North Atlantic salmon convention."

The Canadians were finally beginning to understand that the end result of their unilateral boycott action might be the scuttling of the whole treaty, with certain condemnation for Canada by all concerned. Or perhaps the government of Canada had come to realize that the other parties were committed to proceeding to a treaty without Canada, and that Canada could only lose in such an event. Certainly Canada had been influenced by the pressure exerted on members of parliament and on Minister LeBlanc and Minister MacGuigan by individuals and conservation organizations in both Canada and the United States, led by the Atlantic Salmon Association in Montreal and our own RASA in the United States.

THE DIPLOMATIC CONFERENCE TIMETABLE
It is characteristic of long, drawn-out negotiations that by the time one important problem is solved, an unexpected one has cropped up. Canada, by boycotting the Geneva meeting in August, had upset the timetable of the treaty-making process, which had envisioned the Full Diplomatic Conference being held in November, at which time the treaty would finally be signed. Instead, the fall of 1981 had been used up in exhaustive bilateral efforts to ensure Canada's return to the negotiating table. This unfortunate delay threw the earliest possible date for the diplomatic conference into January 1982 at the earliest.

Through diplomatic channels, discussions were held as to a proper venue and date for the conference, and the United States was fortunate in getting Norway to agree to hold it in Oslo on January 4, 1982.

23

The RASA Coup and the Full Diplomatic Conference

ON DECEMBER 23, 1981, Norway formally reneged on its agreement to hold the conference in Oslo on January 4. The reasons for Norway's abandoning its commitment were said to be connected with regional fisheries problems among the Scandinavian countries.

This was a real shocker. As Ted Kronmiller, Larry Snead, and I sat down on Monday, December 28, for a final three-day effort to save the full diplomatic conference, this was the situation:

1. It was obvious by now that the United States was the only nation sufficiently dedicated and committed to making every effort to convene the conference and thus secure the treaty. The United States had to carry the ball. The major salmon producers and users had regional and domestic problems that made it very convenient not to force the issue.

2. We were convinced — and others shared this view — that unless the conference was convened before the Greenland plebiscite in February, the whole treaty-making process would deteriorate, with heavy odds that the whole effort would fall apart.

3. The EC, acting for the Common Market, had said that it would participate in a conference only if it was held before January 20, 1982. The EC believed that any later date might be construed as an attempt to influence the February Greenland plebiscite on the matter of greater self-government for Greenland and withdrawal from the Common Market.

4. The EC had indicated that it would not host the conference, for the same reason. And it would not permit the conference to be held in any of its member nations' cities.

5. The above factor eliminated Belgium, Norway, Denmark, France, the United Kingdom, and the Republic of Ireland as host nations. Therefore, only Sweden, Spain, Iceland, Canada, and the United States were left.

Neither Sweden nor Spain seemed a logical choice, since neither was heavily represented in the salmon catches of the Greenland or Faroese fisheries, control of which was central to any treaty effort. The United States was a logical and desirable choice and would have liked to act as host, but it was not possible, administratively, to set the meeting up before February 2, past the January 20 deadline. A full diplomatic conference in the United States follows a certain protocol, and adequate facilities and special staff requirements had to be scheduled far in advance; they were simply not available on such short notice. Canada would be a logical choice for host but had been lukewarm to this suggestion made right after Christmas by Larry Snead to Bob Applebaum, chief Canadian negotiator.

Kronmiller, Snead, and I agreed that, for political reasons (principally of good relations), Canada should be asked again to act as host. Early Wednesday morning, December 30, Snead put in a call to Applebaum, whose office said that he was unavailable until Monday, January 4. Snead then tried to reach Tony Campbell, the other Canadian official who had been involved, but he was also unavailable until January 4. The three of us concurred that if Canada had had any interest at all in acting as host, the United States would have been so informed before everyone took off for the holidays. We therefore felt free to proceed elsewhere, time being of the essence.

When Norway had first bowed out, I had suggested to Ted Kronmiller that careful consideration be given to Iceland, which had always seemed to me a logical choice. I now explained in detail Iceland's peculiar advantages as a locus for the conference. First, it was committed to its Atlantic salmon program, as strongly as any of the consultative parties. Second, it was recognized as having one of the most effective salmon management programs in any of the

North Atlantic nations. Third, and most important, its whole approach to the political aspects of the treaty concept was neutral; it is geographically and politically isolated from the strains that trouble the European nations on the one side and the United States and Canada on the other side of the Atlantic Ocean.

We now unanimously agreed to invite Iceland to be host. Kronmiller knew that I had close connections with the fisheries people in Iceland; for several years I had gone salmon fishing there and had met a number of times with Thor Gudjonsson, the Chief of Freshwater Fisheries. Thor was very close to the foreign minister and highly regarded in the international scientific salmon fraternity; his judgment always commanded respect.

Kronmiller suggested that I make the initial approach, and he would follow it up to make it official if I was able to raise any interest. From the State Department, I telephoned Thor Gudjonsson, explaining the situation at great length (that Iceland deserved such recognition, that it would be a feather in their cap, and so on). It worked! Some three hours later, Gudmundeir Eirikssen of the Foreign Office called Kronmiller to say that the Foreign Ministry had approved.

Iceland then formally invited the consultative parties to a full diplomatic conference to commence Monday, January 18, 1982. The United States immediately registered its approval through diplomatic channels to all consultative parties.

So there we were. The nice thing about it was that the United States had done it alone — no doubt about it. Government (the State Department) and the private sector (RASA) had worked together in a determined, logical, and imaginative way to arrange a means to a possibly successful end.

And then came a disturbing new development on January 8. Larry Snead called from the State Department to inform me that Iceland might have to cancel its agreement to host the conference now scheduled to open January 18 in Reykjavik. How many times could reversals of this kind happen without wrecking the treaty altogether? What was the reason?

Now it was The Faroe Islands that threatened to drop the bombshell. Just when all of us thought that the timetable had been restored, the Faroese had set in motion a chain of events that threatened the convening of the conference. The Faroese were in the midst of negotiating a bilateral agreement with the EC covering the 1982 Faroese Atlantic salmon catch. They had now said that unless the pertinent issue of the amount of tonnage that they could take was resolved at their next meeting on January 14, for domestic political reasons they could not go to Iceland.

The Scandinavian bloc was so closely knit that Norway then announced that it would not go without The Faroe Islands. This caused the EC to falter and say that it would not attend without Norway and the Faroe Islands.

It could be argued that the treaty could be concluded without The Faroe Islands or Norway. These two countries could become signatories later, provided their regional differences were resolved. But no treaty could be effective without the EEC, due, first, to "the Greenland Connection" and the fact that the EEC also needed to protect the interests of the two major salmon producers, the United Kingdom and the Republic of Ireland.

The clincher was that Iceland now was uneasy. In its formal invitation to the diplomatic conference, Iceland had said that "one or more of the interested parties may find it difficult to partici-pate...and it may prove necessary to cancel the conference." This meant that without Norway and The Faroe Islands, Iceland might not hold the conference for fear of damaging relations with the Scandinavian bloc. We really couldn't blame the Icelanders; Iceland had been settled by Norwegians, and until 1945, it had been a prov-ince of Denmark. Even its language had been derived from the Scandinavian influence.

The issue at stake between the EEC and The Faroe Islands was as follows: The EEC wanted to hold the 1982 salmon catch at 525 tons; the Faroese were holding out for 700 tons, down from their original request of 745 tons—difference of 175 tons, some 38,000 salmon. This was only about one-third the amount of the normal annual run of the Miramichi River in Canada. It was an insignificant amount in the total world picture, and certainly not important enough to wreck the chances of the treaty.

On such short notice, there was not much left that the United States could do. We had made our last important move in suggesting Reykjavik as the venue for the final conference. But it was obvious that we had to make one final effort to keep the long-term treaty from being the prey of a short-term argument over 38,000 fish.

Kronmiller was in Brussels, so on Saturday, January 9, I suggested by telephone that he authorize me to approach Ambassador Borch of Denmark in Washington (The Faroe Islands are a province of Denmark but not a member of the EC, and thus were negotiating their own fisheries agreements). I would urge his government to persuade the Faroese to come to some understanding with the EEC before January 18. Kronmiller thought that this was a worthwhile effort, so I called the ambassador — we had met several times and got along well — and the meeting was arranged for Tuesday, January 12.

On that day, Kronmiller, Snead, and I met with the ambassador and explained the situation in detail. He was very knowledgeable about the whole Atlantic salmon situation, for I had kept him informed off and on during the past two years. He immediately grasped the problem. He said that Denmark wanted the treaty very much, and he would immediately try to get his government to plead with the Faroese to come to an agreement with the EEC. He stressed that the Faroese were difficult to deal with, particularly within a time frame of only a few days.

His effort was successful, however. He telephoned me on January 14 and said that the Faroese had indicated to his Foreign Ministry that they would attend. The ambassador had delivered, and in a letter of January 15, I emphasized that we wished "to commend you for your success in making these important — and we hope final — negotiations possible."

Thus the diplomatic conference was on again in Reykjavik.

Like a yo-yo, the treaty had been pulled back up on the string of control, where it had been dangling, helplessly.

ICELAND — THE LAND, THE PEOPLE, THE SALMON

As the choice for the full diplomatic conference on the salmon treaty, Iceland was an ideal locality for a number of reasons, not the least of which was the fact that it was remote and thus conducive to several days of concentrated work.

Iceland is a land of fire and ice. Even in current times, whole new islands can spring up out of the ocean almost overnight. The island of Surtsey did just that some thirty years ago. Molten lava from live volcanoes can inundate whole towns; hot springs and geysers abound, and the geothermic waters are used to heat homes in cities like Reykjavik. Glaciers cover the center of the island, yet there is little snow in winter. The climate is warmed by the Irminger current, the same offshoot of the Gulf Stream that bathes southern Greenland.

The people — the Icelanders — belie the influences of the fire and the ice. They are friendly, good-natured., and good-looking. They speak their own language, basically Norse, and are very proud of the fact that their national parliament, called the Althing, is the world's oldest.

Because Iceland is near the edge of the Arctic Circle, daylight in midwinter lasts only about three hours. What do the people do during the twenty-one hours of darkness? Iceland is one of the chess centers of the world. It also has the highest literacy rate in the world — 100 percent (the United States is only 97 percent literate). Chess and reading — there's not too much else to do during the long winter nights.

The unusual weather conditions that prevail in Iceland combine to make it an ideal habitat for salmon. Snow and ice from the glaciers melt continuously, tending to keep the salmon-producing rivers at optimum water levels for migrating fish. The air and water temperatures are almost always within acceptable ranges.

These natural conditions are also ideal for aquaculture. Salmon farms are often located at the edge of fjords with thermal spring adjacent, permitting a fully integrated operation: artificial spawning, in-hatchery growth of the progeny to the smolt stage, release into the ocean, with the migrants ultimately returning to the waters of the original release site.

THE FULL DIPLOMATIC CONFERENCE

The delegates to the Full Diplomatic Conference met on January 18–22, 1982, to produce the final act "to elaborate the text of a Convention for the Conservation of Salmon in the North Atlantic Ocean." The conference elected as chairman Gudmundeir Eirikssen (Iceland) and as vice-chairmen Ambassador Janus Paludan (Denmark in respect of The Faroe Islands) and Larry Snead (United States).

On the basis of its deliberations, the conference adopted a Convention for the Conservation of Salmon in the North Atlantic Ocean, with the votes of the following: Canada, Denmark in respect of The Faroe Islands, the European Economic Community, Iceland, Norway, Sweden, and the United States.

FEATURES OF THE TREATY*

The convention applies to salmon stocks that migrate beyond areas of fisheries jurisdictions of coastal states of the Atlantic Ocean north of 36 degrees latitude throughout their migratory range. Fishing of salmon stocks is prohibited beyond twelve nautical miles except off West Greenland, where the fishery extends to forty miles, and off The Faroe Islands, where it goes out to two hundred miles, in each case, the traditional range of the fishery.

The convention established an international organization to be known as the North Atlantic Salmon Conservation Organization

* Copies of the text of the salmon treaty may be secured from The Secretariat, NASCO, 11 Rutland Square, Edinburgh EH1 2AS, Scotland, U.K. Telephone 031-228-2551, Fax 031-228-4384.

(NASCO), whose objective is to "contribute through consultation and cooperation to the conservation, restoration, enhancement, and rational management of salmon stocks subject to this Convention, taking into account the best scientific evidence available to it."

This organization, the operating mechanism of the convention, has its headquarters in Edinburgh.

A Council will act as the forum for exchange of information, recommend scientific research projects, and conduct the administrative affairs of NASCO. Voting is by a three-quarters majority.

Three Commissions are set up, with voting on the basis of unanimity:

1. The North American Commission. Canada and the United States are members. The EEC is not a member but may participate and vote, upon proof satisfactory to the commission that it has salmon in significant numbers in the commission area.

2. The West Greenland Commisson. Canada, the United States, and the EEC are members.

3. The North East Atlantic Commission. The EEC, Iceland, Norway, and the Faroe Islands are members. The United States is not a member but may participate and vote, upon proof satisfactory to the commission that it has salmon in significant numbers in the commission area. (The waters of east Greenland are covered under this commission, and identification tags indicating U.S.-origin salmon have been recovered here from research vessels. The area has not been fished much, however, because of frequent storms and the presence of icebergs.)

The functions of the commissions are to provide a forum for consultation and cooperation among the members; to propose regulatory measures for fishing in areas of fisheries jurisdictions of members, for salmon originating in the rivers of other parties; and to make recommendations to the council concerning the undertaking of scientific research.

The North American Commission has special additional rules, which are advantageous to the United States, as follows:

1. Patterns of salmon fishing cannot be altered in a way that results in the initiation of or increase in catches of salmon originating in the rivers of another party, except with the consent of the latter. (This could act to prevent a sudden escalation by Canada affecting U.S. stocks.)

2. Members will take measures necessary to minimize by-catches of salmon originating in the rivers of the other members. (A substantial and largely unreported percentage of the Canadian and U.S. salmon now netted in Canadian waters is taken in non-salmon fisheries, such as for cod, herring, or capelin.)

3. The commission may request the council for advice on regulatory measures, which the commission may then propose pursuant to the convention.

The depository of the convention was designated as the Council of the European Communities, which would register the convention in accordance with Article 102 of the Charter of the United Nations.

The convention would be open for signature in Reykjavik from March 2, 1982, to August 31, 1982.

REFLECTIONS

After the whole thing was over, it was very rewarding to receive some letters of commendation from governmental officials, especially because it gave me the satisfaction of knowing that the private sector and government can work together to undertake and succeed on difficult missions.

Roz Ridgway, Deputy Assistant Secretary of State for Oceans and Fisheries Affairs, had written to me earlier:

> Thank you for having been such a valued counselor in our negotiations. I feel confident, as I look at the challenges that we have met successfully, that the task could not have been accomplished in a manner consistent with our nation's interest without your willingness to be among those to whom I could turn for advice.

Larry Snead, Director of the Office of Fisheries Affairs, State Department, included the following in a letter of January 26, 1982:

> I recall that it was the result of your urging nearly four years ago that the Department of State initiated the first draft of an Atlantic salmon treaty. It is my firm belief that no one person in the United States, or for that matter abroad, deserved more credit than you, Dick, for the success of this treaty process. Let us continue to work together to see the Atlantic Salmon Convention ratified and implemented.

What was especially pleasing was to hear from some of my Canadian counterparts, with whom it had sometimes been necessary to disagree. Here is what Bob Applebaum, Head of the Canadian delegation to the working group meetings and the full diplomatic conference, had to say:

> There is no doubt that we all owe you personally a great deal of credit for the success of a three year drive to develop an Atlantic Salmon Convention.... It was clear from our side of the border that you were one of the main driving forces behind the Convention in the USA. We also recognized, however, as we drew closer to the conclusion, that you were far from being a one-sided character. Your willingness to be flexible and to compromise, to recognize our very serious concerns, reflected a vision, and a sense of diplomacy, for which you deserve everyone's admiration.

Another Canadian, Walter Carter from Newfoundland, who was chairman of the Atlantic Salmon Board of the government of Canada and a delegate to all the meetings, had this to say:

> I want to write and congratulate you on the success of your endeavours over the past number of years to get agreement on an Atlantic Salmon Convention. I realize that the success we achieved in Iceland in that regard must be attributed to the hard

work and total commitment on the part of a number of people, however, from what I have observed, if there is any one person who deserves a special bouquet, that person would be Dick Buck!

RASA's involvement and accomplishments in the treaty-making process in no way detract from the strong commitment and fine cooperation that characterized the joint efforts of the other U.S.-based salmon conservation organizations. Early on, RASA organized CAST with the objective of coordinating the work of officials of those groups that wished to make a special effort. The most active participants came from members of such organizations as the Connecticut River Salmon Association, Connecticut River Watershed Council, Federation of Fly Fishermen, Restoration of Atlantic Salmon in America, Theodore Gordon Flyfishers, Trout Unlimited, and Woman Flyfishers Club. CAST was the foundation upon which the whole American effort could be built, because our government could be secure in the belief that these leaders in the restoration effort were wholeheartedly behind the effort and approved of the manner in which we were conducting the negotiations. The constituency was solid. In recognition of its particular contributions, CAST received a letter of commendation from Assistant Secretary of State for Ocean Affairs Thomas Pickering.

To sum it all up: By the early 1970s, RASA had become convinced that only in the United States could a treaty effort be mounted, principally because we had none of the ingrained sociological and political strains with respect to management of Atlantic salmon that characterized the other salmon nations. We had no illegal fishing to speak of, no claims of native peoples, no commercial netting of Atlantic salmon, and thus no intercepting of stocks of foreign origin. We could present a unified approach to problems. And we had embarked on a massive undertaking of restoration that had to be protected.

So RASA undertook to provide the leadership and became the pioneer in promoting the treaty concept. We needed government to help, to take action with us; it responded, and the result was principally an American effort all the way. Together we developed the concept, introduced the draft of a treaty, and then for four long years proceeded to control progress in the face of resistance and even a boycott. We kept up the momentum, maintained the visibility, and made the final move that convened the diplomatic conference, and led to the signing of the final act. That we all did the job together is a tribute to the American system. It works, and we can be proud of it.

All along, RASA was engaged in an unprecedented and difficult undertaking. Our watchword was what has since come to be our credo — New Directions, New Dimensions, New Disciplines. We were often disappointed, but never discouraged. And, having started this particular international accord, we had a continuing compulsion to help make it blossom into rational, equitable management of the resource in the future.

24

Ratification of the Treaty

THE CONVENTION on the Conservation of Salmon in the North Atlantic Ocean now had to go through the ratification process, which differs in different countries. In the United States, the treaty must be approved by the Senate, supported by enabling legislation, and signed by the President. In the EEC, its Commission recommends the treaty to the Council of Ministers, which acts after considering the advice of the European Parliament. In Canada, approval by the Cabinet is sufficient.

The treaty would enter into force when four of the parties had ratified. In the normal course of events, all this would indicate ratification perhaps by the end of 1982. Yet there was always the possibility of delays for other reasons, usually of a political nature.

CONSIDERATIONS AFFECTING THE TIMETABLE

On February 23, Greenland held the long-awaited plebiscite and, as we had expected, voted to negotiate changes in its relationship with the European Economic Community. Although the EEC was at the time responsible for the fishery policy of Greenland, Greenland might choose to determine and negotiate its own fishery policy in the future. This would set up a structure similar to that in The Faroe Islands, also a province of Denmark.

We also had to take into account the fact that there was in existence a bilateral overall agreement on fisheries between Canada and the EEC, and part of it dealt with the 1982 and 1983 Atlantic salmon catch levels off Greenland. We understood that the salmon provisions of this agreement might no longer be valid in the event that the North Atlantic Salmon Convention entered into force before the 1983 fishing season. This issue could conceivably affect the timing of ratification by one or more of the parties.

RASA's feelings on this matter were clear, reasonable, and understandable. We viewed with concern any undue delay in ratification. Conditions can change, even governments can change, either of which could alter normal routines. But the importance of implementing the salmon treaty as quickly as possible would not change. Geopolitics could not be allowed to dictate an outcome that was politically expedient rather than one that was good for the salmon.

There was another practical reason that ratification should proceed: to bring about the first meeting of the North Atlantic Salmon Convention Organization (NASCO) at the earliest possible date. There was much to do, and time was beginning to run out for the Atlantic salmon. NASCO was what the treaty was all about — getting all the salmon nations together, for the first time ever, to examine and adopt ways and means of resolving the many problems involved in the management and conservation of salmon, such as interceptions, illegal netting, by-catches, scientific undertakings, and other important issues.

On February 23, 1982, Ted Kronmiller wrote to me, pointing out that there were a number of important areas requiring our attention before this treaty could be ratified and implemented through domestic legislation. He requested that, because of my responsibilities as a member of the Ocean Affairs Advisory Committee of the Department of State, I accept the assignment of advising and assisting the department in its efforts regarding ratification of the North Atlantic Salmon Convention. I, of course, accepted.

TOUCHING ALL BASES

In particular, my new assignment involved lining up support for legislation in the U.S. Congress respecting both ratification and implementation of the treaty. Ted and I first met with Congressman John Breaux, Chairman of the Subcommittee on Fisheries and Wildlife and the Environment. Next, I met with Senator Paul

Laxalt, as the result of an introduction from Ernest Mack, a RASA director (Senator Laxalt was at that time a very close adviser to President Reagan). Then Marshall Field would pave the way with Senator Charles Percy, Chairman of the important Foreign Relations Committee, which would steer senatorial involvement in the "advise and consent" treaty procedure. I already knew Senator Warren Rudman from my home state of New Hampshire and had met Senators Cohen and Mitchell of Maine (which had most of the U.S. Atlantic salmon).

RASA Director Marshall Field also enlisted the help of his friend Jack Hanks in securing appointments for me with members of the White House staff; Hanks had been a member of the Reagan transition team. RASA Director Allen Keyworth's son Jay held the important position of Science Advisor to the President, and he was instrumental in introducing me to key persons in the administration.

Senate hearings on the treaty were scheduled for August. The staff of the Foreign Relations Committee and I agreed that these hearings should proceed without fanfare or coverage by the press, if possible. The reasoning was that we saw Senate "consent" as forthcoming and wanted to prevent any opportunity for raising new issues. We knew that "consent" should be secured before congressional elections in the fall.

TROUBLES

The only roadblock to the treaty's becoming effective in 1982 was Canada's reluctance to ratify. It was our understanding that, in the event that the treaty should come into force by reason of ratification by the United States, the EEC, and Canada, the Atlantic salmon part of a bilateral overall fisheries agreement between Canada and the EEC would expire, with the new treaty taking its place. This bilateral agreement called for a fixed quota on salmon taken off Greenland for the years 1982 and 1983; with the salmon part of the agreement no longer binding, Canada feared an escalation in 1983. So Canada desired a satisfactory assurance, probably a note or formal letter, that the 1983 quota would hold. Such had not yet been forthcoming.

Most of us did not share the Canadian view that the EEC would permit a substantial escalation on the part of Greenland, and, subsequent to the signing of the treaty in Reykjavik in January, an event had occurred that made this all the more unlikely. The Faroese had finally agreed to a reduction in their quota for 1983, down to 750 tons, and it seemed illogical to believe that the EEC would permit another Danish province, Greenland, to increase its take in 1983.

The salmon community had become increasingly dissatisfied with this whole situation and felt that the problem needed to be resolved quickly. There were compelling reasons for this.

First, the Atlantic salmon resource was in trouble all over the North Atlantic, with the world catch continuing its downward trend. To delay the treaty's coming into force until after the 1983 commercial fishing season meant a delay of over two years in the commissions' adoption of regulatory management proposals. It was high time that we made some decisions to help the fish rather than be handcuffed by relatively minor political considerations.

Second, to delay ratifications for over a year would be to take an unjustifiable risk that the treaty might never enter into force. It was conceivable that the loss of momentum and visibility of the treaty could cause the whole effort to die a slow death. Another consideration was that world tensions were at such a point that unforeseen events, even ones not connected with Atlantic salmon interests, could upset four years of building an agreement to cooperate. For instance, the EEC was having severe internal strains, and trade-off decisions might be made that could adversely affect the salmon situation. Another example of the danger in delay had to do with Greenland itself. With the passing of time, Greenland, having opted for a greater measure of self-government, might be more difficult to deal with.

Third, someone had to take the lead in this matter of ratification. If one hung back, all would hang back. Certainly neither Canada nor the EEC would make the initial move. It remained for the United States, which had started the whole thing in the first

SILVER SWIMMER · 239

place, to come forward and then find ways to persuade the others to follow.

Finally, even if the treaty's coming into force at this time should result in Greenland's exceeding its quota in 1983, such an event was insignificant alongside the dangers outlined above. Ten or twenty more tons of salmon were not as important as having the treaty in force.

It was therefore my recommendation to Ted Kronmiller that the United States take action at this time to break this impasse and persuade the EEC and Canada to do whatever was necessary to permit ratification by the two parties. My rationale was that we had a right to do because, after all, our salmon go to Greenland. Also, the fact that the United States had a governing international fisheries agreement with the EEC, covering all species of fish, should not be overlooked. Under it, the United States and the EEC had agreed "to consult" on Atlantic salmon matters.

My recommendation was approved, and Larry Snead called Bob Applebaum to propose that the United States try to help solve the Greenland hang-up. Canada was apparently receptive to the suggestion, for it was decided that the United States would go to Brussels (the EEC's home base) in the event that Canada did not receive satisfactory assurance as to the quota by July 1, 1982.

THE SENATE FOREIGN RELATIONS COMMITTEE

On August 10, 1982, I presented my testimony before the Senate Foreign Relations Committee in favor of the convention (see Appendix 4 for the text of this testimony). Emphasis was placed on four points:

1. The Wishbone Principle of Atlantic Salmon Exploitation was explained to show that the Greenland connection made multilateral agreement and action necessary.

2. The United States now had a growing Atlantic salmon resource to protect.

3. The world salmon resource was in serious trouble, with

240 · Ratification of the Treaty

the world catch having fallen 30 percent in fifteen years, from 10,417 metric tons in the peak year 1967 to 7,301 tons in 1981.

4. The whole treaty process had been a U.S. effort all the way. Americans had originated the concept, introduced the draft treaty, controlled the negotiating process in the face of resistance, and made the final moves that enabled the full diplomatic conference to be convened and the convention adopted. We should complete the job.

U.S. RATIFICATION AT LAST

On September 30, 1982, the Senate, by unanimous vote, resolved "that the Senate advise and consent to the ratification of the Convention for the Conservation of Salmon in the North Atlantic Ocean, signed in March 1982 by the United States, Canada, the European Community, Iceland, and Norway."

The next step in this complex and time-consuming procedure was the passing of enabling legislation to implement the treaty. This administration bill, drafted by the State Department, set forth the duties of the United States Commissioners to NASCO, described functions and responsibilities of various governmental agencies, and authorized the expenditure of funds for carrying out the obligations of the United States government.

Senator Bob Packwood of Oregon was Chairman of the Senate Committee on Commerce, Science and Transportation, and he wrote to let me know that he had every intention of moving this legislation during the lame duck session. He was involved in a similar exercise on the West Coast, as negotiations would soon be proceeding with the Canadians involving salmon interceptions there. He commented that this long process enabled him to appreciate all the time and effort that had been expended on the East Coast effort. He ended by assuring me that this legislation would be expedited to the greatest extent possible.

Senator Packwood made good on his promise, for on December 29, 1982, President Reagan signed into law the enabling legislation covering United States participation in NASCO, thus completing the ratification.

CLEARING THE CANADIAN-EEC ROADBLOCK

We were still plagued by the ongoing inability of Canada and the EEC to resolve their argument over how to wind up the salmon part of their bilateral agreement. Nothing was being done, and the stalemate was preventing their ratification of the treaty.

On June 16, I wrote to Ted Kronmiller, urging that the State Department undertake a rescue mission to Brussels and Denmark, and sent a reminder to him on August 16. Finally, on February 16, 1983, he agreed to make the trip with me.

It wasn't that he was procrastinating, but simply that he, like all the rest of the fisheries people at State, was inundated with other equally important problems. After all, he was the top U.S. negotiator on all fisheries matters. Then, on April 13, Ted urged me to take on the responsibility myself and to accompany Larry Snead of his department for talks with the EC. I agreed to do so.

Our mission was to persuade the EC to give Canada satisfactory assurance that the Greenland quota for 1983 (i.e., 1,253 tons) would be honored in the event Canada ratified the Atlantic Salmon Convention, bringing it into force, which in turn might invalidate a bilateral Canadian-EEC agreement on the 1983 quota.

We met on April 25 in Brussels with Eamon Gallagher, Director-General for Fisheries of the European Commission for the European Economic Community, and his deputy, Mr. Andreasen. After considerable preliminary talk, Gallagher informed us that the day before we had arrived the EC had finally approved and sent to the Council of Ministers a common fisheries policy, in preparation for several years, of which Atlantic salmon was a part. It called for a 1983 Greenland quota of 1,253 tons, mesh size of 140 mm, with the fishing not to begin before August 25. This was the same quota as for 1982, acceptable to both Denmark and Canada. Larry Snead and

I both believed that our mission had been the spur encouraging Gallagher to act.

Gallagher went on to explain that an EC proposal had the effect of bringing the regulation into force, that it was legally enforceable (his exact words), and that the only way the Council of Ministers could disapprove it was by a unanimous vote, which had never occurred. He explained that he expected the Council to approve it June 6 (their next meeting), and it would then become a regulation.

I asked Gallagher if he would be willing to officially inform Canada of these developments, and he agreed. The statement was made officially on April 28 in Edinburgh at a salmon meeting called to make preparations for the first meeting of NASCO, the treaty organization. The pertinent sentence in the statement was "Pending its [the quota regulation referred to above] adoption by the Council, the Commission's proposal has a status which cannot be ignored by Member States of the Community [Denmark].

My guess was that Canada would decide to wait for the Council to approve the proposal on June 6, in which case Canada would have absolutely no excuse for not ratifying right after that date. It was also possible that the Council would not take action on the proposal June 6, in which case the whole matter might drift along until the season actually started on August 25.

Kronmiller and I felt that it was not desirable for the United States to push the matter further. Normally it would be, but our whole relationship with Canada was very sensitive at the time, for reasons having nothing to do with salmon, to which none of us was privy.

REAGAN APPOINTS THE U.S. COMMISSIONERS

With the United States having ratified the treaty, the way was now open for President Reagan to appoint the three U.S. commissioners to NASCO. Public Law 97-389 provided that "the United States shall be represented in the Council and Commissions by three United States Commissioners to be appointed by the President to serve at his pleasure. Of such Commissioners, one shall be an official of the United States Government, and two shall be individuals (not officials of the United States Government) who are knowledgeable and experienced concerning the conservation and management of salmon of U.S. origin."

On July 20, 1983, the White House gave out the following release:

> The President today announced his intention to appoint the following individuals to be United States Commissioners of the North Atlantic Salmon Conservation Organization. These are new positions:
>
> *Richard A. Buck* has been Chairman of Restoration of Atlantic Salmon in America, Inc., since 1973.
>
> *Frank Eberle Carlton, Jr.* has been serving as President of the National Coalition for Marine Conservatory, Inc., since 1973.
>
> *Allen Eric Peterson, Jr.* is Regional Director, Northeast Region, for the National Marine Fisheries Service in Gloucester, Massachusetts.

THE TREATY TAKES EFFECT

Canada had now ratified the North Atlantic Salmon Convention, bringing the new treaty into force. The original signatories were the United States, Canada, Iceland, Denmark in respect of The Faroe Islands, and the European Economic Community, which negotiates and enters into fisheries agreements for its member states, including such salmon-intensive nations as the Republic of Ireland, the United Kingdom, France, and Denmark. Norway and Sweden had yet to ratify.

So the Fish-King got a another chance for survival, and this new hold on life could be a strong one. At last, the Atlantic salmon could be treated as a unique species, highly migratory throughout the North Atlantic Ocean, and meaning different things to different people. No longer hostage to the cod, halibut, and flounder, the salmon and problems of its management and harvest could now be addressed on their own merits, on the basis of the greatest value to humankind.

VI

NASCO — THE EARLY YEARS 1984–1986

25

Early Progress

PERMANENT PROTECTION for salmon in the ocean would not come easily, for it is always easier to slide into a state of disorder than it is to recreate order. So we were in for a long-term proposition.

The new treaty was as good a mechanism as could have been produced for the purpose intended, considering the constraints inherent in any geopolitical situation respecting cross-boundary problems. NASCO's objective was to resolve such issues, and it had been set up as the supporting framework on which to build the sinews of rational management, and the muscles of law and order in the ocean.

One basic objective of the treaty (under Article 7(1)(b)), was to "minimize interceptions" by one treaty member of salmon "originating in the waters of another member." The most desirable and acceptable means of reducing such interceptions would be to produce scientific evidence that clearly points to a need to take specific regulatory actions. What, for instance, was the impact on all home-water stocks of the Greenland and Faroese fisheries? The effect on U.S. stocks of the Canadian interceptions off Newfoundland, Labrador, New Brunswick, and Nova Scotia? Of the Irish fishery on United Kingdom stocks? It might be years before scientific evidence could provide conclusive answers.

So, as had been the case with a similar situation — the high seas overexploitation off Greenland — NASCO would have to adopt pending convincing scientific findings, equitable temporary measures based on reason and prudence, whenever necessary to prevent damaging declines in the abundance of stocks.

A MORATORIUM ON THE OCEAN HARVEST
OF ATLANTIC SALMON

By 1983, the survival of Atlantic salmon as a viable and valuable natural resource was in great danger. The situation had reached a state of emergency requiring immediate action under a program so austere as to preclude normal considerations of private profit or personal pleasure.

At its peak in 1967, the world catch of Atlantic salmon, as reported by the International Council for Exploration of the Seas (ICES), in the home waters of the producing nations had been 10,417 tons, about 2,870,000 fish. By 1982, the world catch had dropped to 6,097 metric tons, some 1,680,000 salmon. This was a fifteen-year falloff of about 42 percent.

The call for such unprecedented and drastic action was dictated by the continued downward trend in the world catch of the species. A growing world population always translates into a need for more food in the form of protein and more opportunities for recreation in the form of angling. Yet just the opposite was happening with the salmon. World Atlantic salmon stocks needed to be restored to at least their former abundance and maintained thereafter at levels that would permit annual sustainable yields.

On November 24, 1983, Restoration of Atlantic Salmon in America (RASA) proposed — in the form of a position statement circulated to governmental agencies and the public — a six-year survival program for Atlantic salmon. This program encompassed a moratorium on the harvest of Atlantic salmon throughout its range in the North Atlantic Ocean and a recommendation that governments adopt strict regulations for inriver management, including complete bans on angling wherever and whenever necessary, that would ensure the restoration of salmon runs to such abundance that available spawning habitats would be substantially utilized.

This emergency regimen for the salmon would be a bitter pill of restraint and self-denial, but one made necessary by humankind's own intemperance and avoidance of responsibility. Here was the rationale for the RASA position:

1. The 1983 salmon season had been a disaster. In Canada, the largest salmon rivers had experienced the poorest season in living memory. Spawning runs were reported to be down 50 to 60 percent in some rivers and as much as 75 percent in others. Newfoundland in particular was paying dearly: In 1980, the commercial catch was 2,103 tons; in 1981, 1,895 tons; in 1982, down to 1,314 tons; and estimated to be about 1,100 tons for 1983 — off almost 50 percent in three years. For the same years, throughout all of Canada, including both commercial and sportfishing, the figures were 2,728 tons in 1980, 2,526 in 1981, and 1,832 in 1982 — off roughly 33 percent in two years.

The most alarming news had come from Greenland. An unofficial private report indicated that in 1983 the Greenlanders would realize only 250 tons of their 1,191-ton quota. This represented the lowest catch in recent history. It didn't take much imagination to foresee what another sixteen years of the same would do to the salmon.

Considering all these factors, it was estimated that the 1983 reported world catch in home waters might go as low as 5,000 metric tons, which would also represent the lowest recorded catch in history.

2. As to the duration of the recommended moratorium, a six-year ocean and inriver program was recommended by RASA in order to overlap the life cycle of the fish, thus protecting ocean-migrating salmon from each year-class and providing maximum escapements upriver for spawning.

3. A moratorium was really not such a revolutionary measure. The government of Canada had declared a moratorium on commercial fishing for Atlantic salmon for the years 1972–1979 in the Province of New Brunswick and parts of the Province of Quebec.

Now, as a result of poor management practices, the ratio of large salmon to grilse in all the Maritime provinces had dwindled. In Newfoundland rivers, for instance, where forty years ago the ratio was about one salmon to four grilse, in 1982 it was about one salmon to a hundred grilse. This was primarily because the ocean gill nets had mesh sizes designed to take only the most valuable fish, the larger ones. The smaller fish that escaped, particularly the grilse, tended to reproduce their own kind. The importance of correcting this imbalance could not be overemphasized, and a moratorium offered the most effective start toward accomplishing this objective.

4. A six-year pause would offer an outstanding opportunity for promoting sea farming of Atlantics. This new aquaculture industry should ultimately relieve the pressure on wild stocks. Governments could undertake programs of this kind designed to reemploy legitimate commercial netters displaced by the moratorium.

5. During the moratorium, concerted efforts could be made to promote the implementation of the River Harvest principle when the fisheries were reopened. This would be the most viable means of continuing the commercial harvest of salmon without intercepting stocks originating in neighboring or foreign rivers.

The above considerations, taken as a whole, offered overwhelming and rational arguments in support of a moratorium on ocean harvest. No alternative even remotely approached the benefits to be derived.

The procedure for securing multilateral approval of the moratorium would be a formal management proposal to that effect by the United States government to NASCO. RASA, along with other U.S. salmon-oriented organizations, had been invited to offer its comments and recommendations concerning the U.S. policy and position at the first meeting of NASCO, to be held in January 1984 in Edinburgh. RASA was the only organization that recommended a six-year moratorium on fishing in the ocean.

INRIVER MANAGEMENT

The United States could not introduce the second part of our proposed six-year survival program, the recommendation calling for regulations for inriver management, because NASCO covers only ocean affairs of salmon. It has no jurisdiction over inriver problems; its authority ends at the beach.

In developing RASA's position for recommending these regulations, we were guided by the following consideration: When one user group, in this case commercial fishermen, is denied access to a fishery as a result of a moratorium in the ocean, this measure must not redound to the benefit of another user group, in this case recreational fishermen. Under a moratorium, salmon that were no longer subject to harvest in the ocean would ascend rivers in increasing numbers, creating a bonanza for recreational fishermen. Such a situation would be unacceptable to those commercial fishermen who had suffered economic hardship. Thus the socioeconomic aspects of such a moratorium called for equality of sacrifice.

We believed that RASA's approach was as equitable as possible in this complex matter. Supporting this objective obviously meant that governmental agencies would have to severely reduce the angling catch in most rivers — more in some rivers than in others. Those rivers with healthy spawning runs would not require any moderation of harvest; in a number of rivers, however, a complete ban would be necessary for some time in order to rebuild runs. Thus all nations, according to their varying needs, would be called upon to pay for past overindulgences.

REFLECTIONS

Doomsday prophecy comes easily with Atlantic salmon. As the long downward slide progressed, RASA had foreseen and warned against the possibility of ultimate calamity. Perhaps the world had become so accustomed to creatures of all kinds becoming endangered that the absence of such an officially declared status for the salmon had lulled us all into a state of insensitivity and inaction. Or perhaps the time, energy, and money all of us were spending on the whales, polar bears, whooping cranes, and other splendid creatures prevented us from fully comprehending what was going on before our very eyes. Whether or not *Salmo salar* was or would be formally declared endangered was beside the point. For all practical purposes, this valuable, renewable resource most definitely was endangered.

Back in 1982, we in RASA had fully realized the difficulty of revolutionizing current trends. In international fisheries, traditional forms of behavior seem to persist even in the face of the certain knowledge that we are acting irresponsibly. Every now and then, something comes along that shocks us into a state of awareness. Ten years previously, it had been the devastating high seas overkill off Greenland. We had finally handled that, but would we handle this present crisis?

THE FIRST ANNUAL MEETING OF THE NORTH AMERICAN COMMISSION OF NASCO

On May 3–4, 1984, in Ottawa, the North American Commission of NASCO convened its first annual meeting. From the U.S. standpoint, the most significant issue discussed dealt with the recently published 1984 Canadian Atlantic Salmon Management Plan. Canada gave the distinct impression that this would be its contribution to salmon conservation — further measures under NASCO would not be required. The major elements of the Canadian Plan were:

1. The opening of the 1984 commercial fishing season for the province of Newfoundland would be delayed.

2. There would be shorter seasons for the commercial fisheries of the Maritime Provinces.

3. No new commercial salmon fishing licenses would be issued.

4. Only grilse could be retained by recreational fishermen in the provinces of Newfoundland, New Brunswick, Prince Edward Island, and Nova Scotia. Quebec would look into adopting this program.

5. For angling, the seasonable bag limits would be reduced to ten grilse.

6. It would be illegal to retain, or be in possession of, salmon captured incidentally in nonsalmon commercial gear.

From the start, the United States maintained that the Canadian plan did not adequately address the interception of salmon of U.S. origin and proposed that the Canadians implement more stringent specified management measures to satisfy our concern. The

U.S. proposal was rejected by the Canadians, but both parties agreed to recess this meeting and continue discussion on this issue at the upcoming full-scale First Annual Meeting of the Council and commissions of NASCO in July.

At this reconvened Annual Meeting of the North American Commission in Edinburgh the week of July 16, 1984, the head of the Canadian delegation, L. Scott Parsons, kept referring to the Canadian plan as "draconian measures." The management plan had tightened up some regulations to be sure, but they hardly added up to ones of draconian proportions. To warrant such a severe designation, the plan would have to call for something similar to the RASA proposal — complete moratoriums for specified periods of time and for specific locations. We drew attention to this point.

In crafting its 1984 proposal, the United States had sought restrictions for the upcoming fishing season that would reduce interceptions in Canadian areas during the particular months in which the United States suffered the greatest losses, with the least damage to stocks of Canadian origin. The Canadians maintained that scientific evidence as to the nature, location, and incidence of the interceptions had not been adequately reviewed, and until it had, it would be inappropriate to take any further action. This completely negative approach by Canada was also likely due to the fact that the government was already being besieged with protests from its commercial fishermen concerning the announced restrictions for the 1984 season.

Given the views of Canada, the United States sought assurances that Canada would take measures for the following year, 1985, that would specifically be designed to reduce interceptions of U.S. stocks. The Canadians gave no such assurances but agreed to an objective evaluation of such scientific data as did exist. The North American Commission was then adjourned. Thus, there was no progress at this second meeting.

GREENLAND QUOTA CUT BACK

The first annual meeting of the West Greenland Commission was held May 22–26, 1984, in Edinburgh. The representatives were unable to reach agreement on any management measure, due principally to the European Community's unwillingness to adopt restrictive measures for the Greenland fishery, since Denmark, acting for The Faroe Islands, had refused earlier, in the meeting of the North East Atlantic Commission, to cut back officially on that quota.*

The United States announced its objection to a linkage based solely on political grounds. The U.S. commissioners — Allen Peterson, Frank Carlton, and myself — had always been opposed to the concept of action in one commission being totally dependent on action taken in another commission. Linkage of this kind could have a paralyzing effect on the adoption of sound management measures. We were unwilling, however, to give up hope for action in the West Greenland Commission and were successful in securing approval of a recess rather than an adjournment.

Upon returning to the United States, we used customary diplomatic procedures through the offices of the U.S. Department of State and continued to press for movement on the part of the EC. Meanwhile, Canada was making similar overtures. All this bore fruit; after assurances by the EC that serious negotiations on a reduction of the Greenland quota would be entered into, the West Greenland Commission meeting was hastily reconvened on July 18, 1984, in Edinburgh, during the first annual meeting of NASCO.

The negotiations opened under widely polarized positions, with the EC still reluctant to accept a substantial reduction on the quota, and Canada demanding a dramatic cut to complement the stringent regulations it had adopted in its own home waters for 1984. The United States acted as the determined mediator, insisting that failure to reach agreement on an important reduction would result in permanent damage to the effectiveness of NASCO and to

---

* The Faroese authorities, acting under intense pressure to reduce their steeply escalated catch of 1,065 tons for the season ending 1981, did, however, decide to fix a voluntary unilateral allowable catch of no more than 625 tons for the 1984–1985 season. This was progress in itself.

the whole treaty effort. Finally, a conservation management measure was approved, reducing the total allowable catch of salmon at West Greenland from 1,191 tons to 870 tons, some 240,000 salmon.

The measure would be effective for the current 1984 fishing season, which was still possible even at this late date. Greenland does not normally open the salmon netting season until around August 10, and it extends into the fall until the quota is filled or stormy weather curtails further operations.

GREENLAND AWARDED HOME RULE FOR 1985

We had learned in Edinburgh that Denmark had endowed Greenland with home rule effective January 1, 1985, but not with responsibility for defense or foreign affairs. Therefore, Greenland would withdraw from the EEC and assume the status of an associated overseas territory. Denmark would take the place of the EC in negotiating for Greenland.

REFLECTIONS ON NASCO'S FIRST MEETING

During the flight from Iceland back to the United States, my initial feelings were ones of satisfaction over a good beginning. All concerned had exhibited a desire to make important and constructive moves to help the salmon. Then, as I relived the meeting, a certain sense of dismay — even of foreboding — came over me as I reviewed the makeup of the delegations at the meeting.

It came as a shock to realize that most of the delegates I had met and talked with were the same people who had represented their nations at meetings of the International Commission for Northwest Atlantic Fisheries (ICNAF). I should have anticipated this, but I had hoped that there would be at least a few members representing the sportfishing interests. The plain fact was that I could count on one hand the number of official representatives whose background was in sportfishing.

After the first flush of enthusiasm had died down, would the same brand of bureaucratic inertia roll over into NASCO that had existed in ICNAF? Could the sportfishing people expect any kind of a fair shake at the hands of people who normally dealt almost exclusively with problems of the cod, haddock, flounder, and herring? Their constituencies were the commercial fishermen.

This was the only important negative that came to mind, but it was a nagging one for several weeks. It was best to try to forget it.

REBUFFED AGAIN BY CANADA

Next year, at the meeting of the North American Commission of NASCO held in Boston in February 1985, the U. S. delegation advanced a new proposal to close the fall (September through December) fishery off Newfoundland and Labrador as a means of protecting U.S.-origin salmon.

Data that had been produced by U.S. scientists showed that a substantial percentage of the Canadian harvest of U.S.-origin salmon was accounted for by this fall fishery. The Canadian delegation questioned this proposal because, in its view, the scientific basis of the proposal was unsound. The data that formed the basis of the U.S. proposal were then submitted by the United States to a working group of the International Council for Exploration of the Seas (ICES). That organization confirmed the validity of the U.S. data, analysis, and conclusions. ICES estimated that such a management measure (closing the fishery from September 1 through December 31 each year) would reduce the catch of Canadian-origin salmon by only some 1 percent, but returns of U.S.-origin fish to home waters would be increased by approximately 23 percent.

We looked forward to positive action by Canada on the U.S. proposal at the second North American Commission meeting held during NASCO's second annual meeting in Edinburgh in 1985. But again, at this meeting, the Canadian delegation rejected this same proposal that had received the blessing of ICES. Canada then made it clear that positive action on this proposal was contingent upon acceptance of certain conservation measures under the purview of the West Greenland Commission. We again reiterated our strong disapproval of linkage between commissions.

To say that we were frustrated would be putting it mildly. We had provided the Canadians with what they had asked for — expert scientific advice — and they hadn't honored it. Other means would have to be sought.

RASA EXERTS SOME PRESSURE

With no definitive management proposals approved by Canada for 1985, the U.S. Commissioners came home from Edinburgh extremely disappointed but by no means discouraged. We were about to face another fishing season in which commercial netting off Newfoundland, Labrador, and West Greenland had historically taken several times the number of Atlantic salmon of U.S. origin that were returning to their natal streams in the United States.

We were still mindful of Canada's obligation to undertake regulatory actions in order to minimize interceptions. But how could we get Canada to reconsider its position? With this objective, we designed and implemented a number of important, high-level actions:

1. Early in 1985, RASA organized, together with the Connecticut River Salmon Association and Trout Unlimited, an Atlantic Salmon Committee with the objective of coordinating meaningful actions of the leading salmon organizations in the United States. We put out a special release describing the hang-ups and supplied some seven thousand of our members with the names and addresses of Canadian officials to whom letters might be written in support of it. The leading Atlantic salmon clubs in Maine joined in this effort, as did the National Wildlife Federation and the National Audubon Society. The Atlantic Salmon Federation-U.S. was invited to take part but did not respond.

2. RASA prepared a letter to be sent by the Committee on Merchant Marine and Fisheries of the U.S. House of Representatives, to Canadian Fisheries Minister John A. Fraser, requesting that the government of Canada adopt the U.S. proposal made at NASCO. This letter was signed by Walter B. Jones, Chairman; Norman E. Lent, Ranking Minority Member; John Breaux, Chairman; Don

Young, Ranking Minority Member; and the six New England congressmen of the Subcommittee on Fisheries and Wildlife Conservation and the Environment. No reply was received.

3. We persuaded all twelve U.S. senators from New England to send a similar letter to Minister Fraser on June 12. There was no reply. (See Appendix 5 for a copy of this letter.)

4. The United States Department of State, in late June 1985, sent a diplomatic note through its Ottawa embassy to Canadian Fisheries Minister John A. Fraser, requesting that the U.S. proposal be reconsidered. There was no reply to that letter either.

5. In the private sector, Atlantic salmon organizations urged their members to write letters to Prime Minister Mulroney and Fisheries Minister Fraser.

The response to the Atlantic Salmon Committee's special release was very encouraging and gave clear evidence that the matter of the Canadian interception of U.S. salmon stocks was very important in the minds of the general public as well as sportsfishermen. We received copies of many letters that were sent to Fisheries Minister Fraser. These were not ordinary form letters; they were individual expressions of genuine concern about the damage being done not only to the whole U.S. salmon restoration program by Canada's position but to friendly U.S.-Canadian relations as well.

The disheartening thing about all this was that there had been no answer from any official of the Canadian government — not to the State Department, not to the Senate, not to the House, and not to any conservation organizations. What were we to make of this apparent insensitivity? It was almost unbelievable. It must have been intended to tell us something, but what? And where was the United States to go from here? The only answer was to keep doggedly at it, which we did.

PUTTING OUR OWN HOUSE IN ORDER

A principal objective of NASCO was to minimize interceptions by one nation of salmon originating in the rivers of another nation. Clearly we needed a new approach to get the signatories started down this road. The strongest argument would be an exposition of what had already been accomplished. Conservation begins at home. Those of us who had played a major part in designing and drafting NASCO had this continually in mind and made sure that this principle survived the vicissitudes of four years of preparation and negotiations. Thus we had Article 9 of the treaty, which provides in part that "a Commission shall take into account...the efforts of States of Origin to implement and enforce measures for the conservation, restoration, enhancement and rational management of salmon stocks in their rivers and areas of fisheries jurisdiction."

This put-your-own-house-in-order provision could be an important means of making the treaty effective. Nowhere had this been more evident than in the June 1985 West Greenland Commission deliberations. Denmark (in respect of Greenland) took the position that before there could be any consideration of a further reduction in the 870-ton quota for Greenland, the Commission would need to reach an understanding and define the principle of "fair sharing" of the burden of conservation. Denmark requested that the other members, consistent with provisions of Article 9 of the treaty, make specific unilateral commitments for similar conservation measures.

In replying, Canada reported that, beginning in 1984, strict — in fact, draconian (as they continually described them) — conservation measures had been instituted, including drastic reductions in angling limits and commercial netting. Driftnetting was completely banned.

The United States demonstrated its substantial commitment to enhancement through the restoration of stocks. The United States recounted its substantial investments in hatcheries and fishways. At the instigation and urging of RASA, a new federal-state regional policymaking body, the New England Atlantic Salmon Committee, had encouraged the states to standardize their regulations that prohibited not only the taking of Atlantic salmon by any means other than angling but also the sale of any Atlantic salmon taken in the United States. Those New England states that had fisheries jurisdictions out to three miles were complying. The

National Marine Fisheries Service was undertaking to establish a management plan (subsequently approved) that would prohibit commercial salmon fishing in the area three to twelve miles offshore. A tagging program for the purpose of identifying stocks in the ocean had been approved and was in the process of being implemented with Canada and Greenland.

Then it was the European Economic Community's turn to satisfy Denmark that member states producing Atlantic salmon in large numbers were taking measures to comply with Article 9. In other words, where was the evidence of sharing the burden of conservation through the elimination of or substantial reduction in driftnetting and inshore netting and the imposition of strict limits on angling? The EEC was not forthcoming with assurances, since there was a lack of willingness and commitment to reduce or eliminate these abuses on the part of member states such as the United Kingdom and Ireland.

No quota was set for Greenland at this West Greenland Commission meeting in 1985, but Greenland subsequently adopted its own unilateral quota of 852 tons, which was easily reached early in the season. At least it was encouraging to know that the salmon were returning in substantial numbers to Greenland waters to feed, after a serious lack of availability in 1983 and 1984. There was still considerable support, however, for a reduction in the Greenland quota, simply because 852 tons represented 15 percent of the total world catch, a relatively high figure for a nonproducing nation. Since 1973, when the Greenland quota of 1,191 tons was first established, the world catch in home waters had fallen steeply from 9,802 tons to 5,610, a drop of 57 percent. Yet the quota during this period had remained the same — with one exception — until this 1985 quota of 852 tons. This was a reduction of only 43 percent.

AN OVERSEAS MISSION

During the early fall of 1985, it was my conviction that an effort should be made to educate the United Kingdom about the effect its reluctance to put its own house in order was having on progress under the treaty. I proposed that Assistant Secretary of State for Fisheries John Negroponte and I undertake a mission to exchange views on an informal basis with the nations particularly interested and involved. My two colleagues, commissioners Allen Peterson and Frank Carlton, enthusiastically approved of such an effort, as did John Negroponte. Nations signatory to the treaty were informed and supportive.

Negroponte and I met first with the top Danish fisheries officials in Copenhagen on December 16. This meeting was constructive in every way. The Danes were still on their "fair-sharing" kick, and they made the point that too much attention had always been focused on intercepting high seas fisheries and too little on self-serving domestic commercial catches by states of origin. They described the attitudes of many signatories, including those in the European Community, as highly unsatisfactory. On this particular point, we were on the same wavelength, and at the close of the meeting, the Danes expressed considerable appreciation for our visit and our overall purpose.

Our London meetings on December 17–18 could not have come at a more propitious time. The Queen, in her recent opening speech to the parliament, had made an unprecedented reference to the salmon, stating that Her Majesty's government would be introducing a bill containing certain measures on salmon, designed to update existing salmon legislation, which dated from 1868.

Whether this forward movement would go far enough and get translated into implementing actions was an entirely different matter. What didn't appear in the newspapers — and what the general public didn't realize — was that John Gummer, the Minister for Agriculture, Food and Fisheries (MAFF), was not about to phase out, much less close down, the driftnetting off the Northumberland coast. This was what was needed.

THE NORTHEAST ENGLAND DRIFT NET FISHERY

The international aspects of the drift net fishery were of central importance. As long as it was in operation, it would be impossible for either the EEC or the United Kingdom to exercise the influence it should in helping to control and, if possible, eliminate, the interceptory fisheries on the high seas, including the Greenland, Faroese, and Irish fisheries.

Tagging research, carried out from a research establishment of the English Ministry, had established that more than 94 percent of the salmon and grilse caught in the drift net fisheries off the English northeast coast were migrating toward the River Tweed and a number of Scottish rivers to the north. These drift net fisheries were therefore interceptory in the highest degree and indefensible by any proper management and conservation criteria.

These English fisheries were sometimes defended by Gummer because they were "traditional." In the sense that early on a few drift netters off Northumberland were taking about 2,000 salmon and grilse annually, they were "traditional." But they were not "traditional" in the context of the steeply escalated and expanded fishery that commenced in the late 1960s with the introduction of the deadly monofilament nets. But this is what Gummer was implying. This new method of fishing revolutionized the nature of these fisheries, with the result that the declared catch of salmon and grilse was multiplied twenty-five to thirty times. The figures speak for themselves:

| Average Declared Catches | |
Year	(Numbers of Salmon)
1950–59	2,162
1970–79	48,140
1984	77,220
1985	55,943
1986	63,425

It seemed incredible to us in the United States that steps had not been taken by the English Ministry to phase out these damaging interceptory fisheries. Internationally, the EEC and the

United Kingdom could not take a stand against interceptory fisheries in the North Atlantic without the appearance and, indeed, the reality of utter hypocrisy. The stage had been reached where only pressure on the United Kingdom government from governments of other North Atlantic countries, and particularly from the United States, would have any effect.

The Salmon Bill was introduced into the House of Lords in early December. On December 17 we met with David Clarke, Chairman of the Atlantic Salmon Trust (he was also a member of RASA's Coordinating Committee), and the Duke of Wellington, President of the Atlantic Salmon Trust. Lord Moran, a salmon conservationist and the leader of the effort in the House of Lords to strengthen the Salmon Bill by amendments, was also present. We received a thorough briefing on the British government's approach to the overall salmon situation. They asked for RASA's recommendations with respect to the proposed legislation. It was my suggestion that consideration be given to an amendment calling for the phasing out of northeast England driftnetting over a five-year period, the same type of treatment accorded the Danish high seas driftnetting off Greenland in 1972. The same rationale would apply.

On December 18, John C. Edwards, Assistant Secretary of MAFF, explained to us the United Kingdom's position on salmon. In particular, he pointed out that "Her Majesty's government does not see the overall balance quite the same as the United States does." He also stated that the recent declines in the North Atlantic had been confined largely to North American stocks, but that the United Kingdom had taken significant cuts over a long period. In addition, the significance of conservation measures taken by states of origin depends on the point from which efforts are measured. He cited the recent bill introduced in parliament as evidence of his government's resolve to strengthen enforcement measures.

Negroponte and I explained in some detail the Wishbone Syndrome principle, pointing out that the North Atlantic nations were uneasy in their criticism of the West Greenland driftnetting while driftnetting off northeast England continued. It was the same thing—indiscriminate.

Was it possible that MAFF either did not fully understand or chose not to adjust to the concept of the interdependence of world stocks of salmon? Overexploitation in the United Kingdom and Irish waters, legal and illegal, was a fact, and it translated into fewer salmon from their rivers migrating to feed off West Greenland. Thus the Greenland quota would be filled in greater measure from the Canadian and U.S. components. Or could it be that MAFF was so encased in problems of "whitefish" (cod, haddock, and flounder) as to be unresponsive to the geopolitical aspects of migratory anadromous fish like salmon?

Negroponte and I next met with Lord Gray of Contin, Deputy Minister of State for Scotland, who had introduced the Salmon Bill in parliament. He stressed that Scotland had a long and sustained record of serious salmon conservation, noting that Scotland had banned driftnetting twenty years ago. He said that driftnetting in England posed serious problems for conserving salmon in Scottish waters. With considerable enthusiasm, Lord Gray expressed his support for the U.S. efforts to move the NASCO process along and made it clear that Scotland would not soon be outdone on the conservation front.

The Salmon Bill had now been passed in the House of Lords and would go to the House of Commons, where final action should come sometime next summer or early fall, when Parliament would adjourn. Although the bill fell short of adopting the strict measures deemed necessary by conservationists, it significantly strengthened regulatory measures throughout the United Kingdom. Dealer licensing would be introduced to combat salmon poaching. This was in preference to tagging, which had been rejected by every Scottish salmon angling organization as impractical. The most influential opposition to tagging came, of course, from the fish farmers, who held that, with an annual output of some five million farmed salmon, tagging was impossible. The bill also would shift the burden of proof of the right to take and possess salmon from governmental authorities to those in actual possession of the fish. The allowable driftnetting effort would be reduced, but only slightly.

Despite its shortcomings, the bill represented long overdue action on salmon, the likes of which had not been seen in the twenty-five years or so since the Hunter Commission had made its forward-looking recommendations. It would give notice to Denmark of the United Kingdom's intent to start putting its own house in order, in compliance with the spirit of Article 9. There is no question that the efforts of the United Kingdom had been propelled by the events of the 1985 meeting of NASCO as well as unrelenting pressure by the Atlantic Salmon Trust in Great Britain and individuals such as Lord Gray and Lord Moran.

After our return from this trip, John Negroponte wrote to John Gummer, the Minister of MAFF, attempting to elicit an official expression regarding the British reaction to "fair sharing of the burden of conservation." Gummer's answer was a masterpiece of evasiveness, shifting all the responsibility for a discussion of conservation measures to the EEC. Quoted here is one pertinent paragraph:

> Although all parties to NASCO share the same conservation objective, national approaches can differ and, as you know, we participate in the work of the organization as a member state of the European Economic Community. NASCO is therefore an area of Community responsibility and the Community position has to take account of not only our interests but those of Ireland and France, who also contribute to the North Atlantic salmon resource. It would not be appropriate for me to try and predict what this approach might be though I am sure Mr. Gallagher would welcome an exchange of views on these issues.

Indeed, Gummer's intention appeared quite clear. The requirement that the EEC act for the United Kingdom on fisheries matters provided a convenient escape hatch. MAFF could just sit tight and do nothing about facing up to the realities of the driftnetting off the coast of Northumberland and how it was damaging the international effort.

This was depressing—a typical runaround. It led to the impression that we were up against an impenetrable bureaucracy.

BUY-OUTS: A NEW TOOL FOR SALMON CONSERVATION

At the conclusion of the December 17, 1985, meeting with the Atlantic Salmon Trust, David Clarke had been interested in finding out what I thought of a brand new development in salmon conservation—buy-outs of commercial salmon netting operations. The inventor and engineer of this buy-out approach was the Honorable Patrick Wills, an avid salmon fisherman, living in Whitchurch, England. His plan was to organize a small group of well-to-do salmon fishermen who would set up a charitable arrangement that would buy out netting stations along the northeast coast of Scotland, which harbored the legendary salmon rivers of the United Kingdom. His plans were well thought out, and I became very enthusiastic about the whole prospect. During the next half-year, Patrick Wills and I developed a close community of interest. He sought our advice on how best to organize such an ad hoc effort, since we had been through all this before with CASE and now with RASA. He and I became good friends as a result of all this collaboration.

Patrick worked ceaselessly at it, and by the spring of 1986, the approach was all set up. Here are excerpts from a news release on the subject:

> A new charitable trust, the Atlantic Salmon Conservation Trust (Scotland) declared its intention to launch a series of practical efforts to help lift the threat of extinction which it believed faces Scottish stocks of wild Atlantic salmon.
>
> The ASCT (Scotland)...has just concluded arrangements to take over 53 interceptory salmon netting points off the Moray Firth coast. Of these, 25 netting points currently being operated will be phased out by 1990....

While the Trust will initially concentrate its activities along the Moray Firth coastline, it feels that direct action on interceptory fisheries could ultimately provide a blueprint for salmon conservation throughout Scotland, replacing haphazard fisheries management with efficient controls linked to natural reproductive performance....

The Trust was organized on January 14, 1984, by Sir William Gordon Cumming, of Altyre, Morayshire; The Hon. Patrick Wills, of Whitchurch, Hampshire; and Mr. John Douglas Menzies, of Mounteagle, Fearn, Ross-shire. None of the three trustees has any personal interest in the ownership of salmon fisheries of any description....

The principal objective of the trust is to achieve the conservation and enhancement of wild salmon stocks through the acquisition of fixed engine and net and coble fisheries, and particularly interceptory coastal fisheries. Coastal fisheries purchased by the trust will be closed permanently, while estuarial and river nettings will cease until such time as stocks recover to satisfactory levels.

Wild stocks of Atlantic salmon are rapidly becoming an endangered species, largely because of a lack of political will by successive governments to introduce effective measures to encourage good management of the species.

We felt that there was a considerable opportunity for an organization dedicated to practical action. And such an initiative is not simply of national significance; in Britain we need to put our own house in order if we wish to be able to adopt a credible position in international negotiations on limiting salmon quotas in the high seas.

In acquiring any estuarial or river nettings, we plan to phase them out in consultation with local interests. Given the five-year life cycle of the salmon, the regeneration of stocks could take from five to ten years.

Once the appropriate river board considers stocks to be adequate, we will consider the reintroduction of netting... but only on a strictly controlled cull basis, linked to the adequacy of total river stocks....

It will take some time to implement and to produce results.... Initial responses have been excellent. We are in touch with the Atlantic Salmon Trust, the Salmon and Trout Association, and Restoration of Atlantic Salmon in America, Inc., who have all endorsed our plans.

Patrick Wills devoted his energies to acquiring the Scottish netting operations. It was a touchy business because of the competition, so to speak, between the commercial netters on one side and the sportfishermen and the rod-fishing industry on the other. But the tide was running in the trust's favor; the declining salmon runs had made commercial netting operations less profitable.

By the end of 1986, the trust had bought up fishing rights to, and closed down, a total of 245 interceptory fishing stations affecting the major salmon rivers in the Moray Firth area. It was estimated that all this would result in an annual increase in salmon runs up the rivers of over forty thousand salmon, about 25 percent of the total Scottish interceptory fisheries.

The cost of all this was substantial, amounting to nearly a million dollars. But this was only the start. The trust appointed Lord Hunter, head of the famous Hunter Commission, as its patron, and undertook a substantial fund-raising campaign.

RASA became closely associated with the activities of the trust, advising on international and geopolitical aspects of salmon conservation. We appointed Patrick Wills a member of the Coordinating Committee of RASA.

Almost immediately, runs to the rivers in Scotland that were now free of nets increased dramatically. This, in turn, helped Patrick and his associates raise more funds. Within the next few years, several million dollars would be spent retiring nets, with Buy-Outs occurring on such rivers as the Findhorn, Spey, Deveron, Nairn, Beauly, Conon, Dee, Don, Tweed, and parts of the Tay, to name but a few.

At this point, Patrick Wills felt that he had devoted all the time he should to this cause, and he retired from active involvement. His energies were tremendous, and he contributed greatly.

The principal reason that the Scottish Buy-Outs were so successful was that they were bona fide buy and sell agreements.

The sellers had something to sell — not only the fixed assets such as netting stations, engines, and boats, but also the fishing rights in the rivers bordering their properties. English common law, unlike that in other countries, granted these rights to the owners in perpetuity. The fishing rights in other countries are usually under the control of national or state governmental authorities.

These Buy-Outs in Scotland were entirely different from the Buy-Outs, or attempted Buy-Outs, that would become popular in later years, such as those in operation in 1992 with respect to the Faroese fishermen, and the 1993 approaches to Buy-Outs from the West Greenland fishermen.

WE WIN TWO FOR THE SALMON

The Third Annual Meeting of NASCO, held in Edinburgh, June 23–27, 1986, produced two important regulatory measures.

In the North American Commission, Canada formally agreed, as a regulatory measure under NASCO, to close the 1986 commercial fishery for Atlantic salmon in Newfoundland-Labrador on October 15. This was a compromise on the similar regulatory measure first proposed by the United States at the February 1985 meeting, which had been rejected by Canada.

The Newfoundland-Labrador area had been chosen carefully by the United States because that is where U.S. salmon stocks were known to congregate in the fall months, and closure at that time would give the most protection. It would also have the least adverse impact on the Canadian commercial netsmen, because most of the Canadian stocks would be in their rivers by that time, on spawning runs.

Canadian officials estimated that this regulatory action, together with other restrictions on commercial salmon netting in the Maritime Provinces, should result in at least a 30 percent reduction in the interceptions of salmon of U.S. origin. U.S. scientists believed that this estimate was on the high side.

Then, in the West Greenland Commission, Denmark, acting for Greenland, agreed to a quota of 850 tons for the two-year period 1986–1987. This represented a slight reduction from the 1985 actual catch of 864 tons, some 286,000 salmon.

Denmark also announced during the meeting that it had recommended a two-year quota period in the hope that a working group would be set up to attempt to arrive at a methodology of defining a "fair sharing of the burden of conservation," based on a new discipline rather than on the present hit-or-miss system. At the time, we in RASA believed that no science existed that was capable of defining a nonpolitical procedure for arriving at the harvestable surplus of world stocks, once the spawning requirements of the salmon-producing nations had been satisfied. Yet there was considerable sentiment in NASCO for undertaking such a study.

This third annual meeting of NASCO had indeed been fruitful.

THE THIRD INTERNATIONAL ATLANTIC SALMON SYMPOSIUM

The sponsors of the Third International Atlantic Salmon Symposium, held October 21–23, 1986, were the Atlantic Salmon Trust and L'Association Internationale de Défense due Saumon Atlantique. Its venue, Biarritz, France, offered easy access from the British Isles, the Republic of Ireland, and countries on the European continent, so there was a large and representative turnout. There were also a number of Canadians and Americans present, representing their organizations.

The title of the symposium was "Atlantic Salmon Planning for the Future," and the theme was legal and illegal salmon exploitation in the home waters of the salmon-producing countries. There were also sessions on science and management and the ocean life of salmon.

Early on, it was clear that the delegates were out to bite the management bullet; they were determined to promote greater emphasis on the benefits of salmon angling as opposed to commercial fishing for the species. Leading the charge in this respect were people like David Clarke of the Atlantic Salmon Trust; Wilfred

Carter, Executive Director of the Atlantic Salmon Federation; Jack
Fenety, of the Miramichi Salmon Association, New Brunswick;
John Mackenzie, Director of the Atlantic Salmon Trust; and Derek
Mills, scientist from the University of Edinburgh.

As a result, the symposium unanimously approved a resolution and recommendations, as follows:

Resolution:

In view of the greater income and employment potential
of salmon angling and its appreciably smaller harvest of limited
salmon populations, each national government of salmon-
producing countries is urged to declare a salmon policy which
will institute as a conservation measure, within its area of jurisdiction, management programmes to reduce commercial harvesting of salmon with a view to increasing salmon stocks and
improving recreational salmon fisheries.

Recommendations:

1. That NASCO investigates the value of a salmon tagging
    scheme such as is in operation in eastern Canada and Spain
    with the view that it recommends its adoption by all mem-
    ber countries for both a more reliable collection of catch
    data and a more effective control of illegal fishing.
2. That all methods of enmeshing salmon such as drift nets
    and fixed hang nets (excepting the operations off Green-
    land) should be phased out and the fishermen relying on
    these methods be given other opportunities to participate in
    the salmon fisheries of related industries, including salmon
    farming and ranching.
3. That we should support the recommendation of the Rap-
    porteur to the EEC Subcommittee on Fisheries that Com-
    munity funds should be made available to improve and
    coordinate national salmon fishery inspectorates.
4. Following the action taken by Canada, recommend that each
    nation, through its salmon conservation bodies and sport
    fishing organizations, encourage the introduction of a rea-
    sonable daily and season rod-catch quota, prohibit the sale of
    their catch, and consider the adoption of a catch-and-release
    philosophy.

I had been asked to deliver the closing address, and my purpose would be to treat the whole problem of salmon conservation in the North Atlantic. Where were we, and what should be done about it? After weeks of study and consideration, I had decided that it was time for someone to lay the cards on the table. My remarks presented a frank analysis of the principal problems at hand in salmon conservation. Here is the address, "Stewards of the Salmon," October 23, 1986:

> Ten years ago, the Atlantic salmon-producing nations had just secured a phasing out of the destructive high seas salmon fishery off West Greenland. Then came the extensions of fisheries jurisdictions for all species, generally to two hundred miles. And now the salmon begin to come under further control as we set regulatory measures under the new salmon treaty. Jobs well done. And the future can look bright indeed, but there are a number of "ifs."
>
> Man has the ability to produce salmon artificially in any desired numbers, but he has not shown an ability to hold his selfish instincts in check—with his nets in the ocean. Thus, it is not in the scientific area, but in the socioeconomic and geopolitical arena that the struggle to save the wild salmon must be engaged. How to divide up any harvestable surplus over and above the spawning requirements to perpetuate the species is the question that today plagues the governments of both the producing and user nations. These nations now realize that a continuation of the present overexploitation can only lead to exhaustion of the species, as being of any practical use to man. We are on a slippery slope, indeed, with the world catch in home waters off some 40 percent in twenty years.
>
> Whether or not these fish will be restored to their former abundance — and we should require nothing less — depends upon, first, a complete understanding of the nature of the interdependence of world stocks, and second, our willingness to reduce to a minimum ocean interceptions of salmon of foreign origin. Perhaps this message begins to get through, because, salmon-wise, a new wind sweeps over the North Atlantic today — a clearing wind from the west, carrying with it the seeds of a

new spirit of conservation. We want to see it become the prevailing wind, sweeping away the dense fog which envelops the northeastern waters of this great ocean which becomes ever more small, more interdependent. Today most nations are enthusiastically engaged in conserving stocks and restoring rivers — exciting ventures. We may have turned the corner towards important restoration. Where drastic measures have been introduced, salmon runs are increasing. Where not, there is not progress — and, occasionally, chaos.

Let's take a kaleidoscopic view of what the salmon nations bordering the North Atlantic Ocean have done recently to conserve inriver stocks and reduce ocean interceptions. These are the basic objectives of the new North Atlantic Salmon Conservation Organization (NASCO), the operating mechanism of the new multinational treaty to which we are all signatory.

In the United States, regulations permit the taking of salmon by angling only; salmon taken in U.S. waters may not be sold or offered for sale; angling is permitted only in rivers where restoration programs approach maturity. In Canada, the inriver angling catch limits have been drastically reduced; driftnetting has been banned; inshore commercial netting banned entirely in certain areas, and seasons cut back in others....

For the interceptory fishery at Greenland, Denmark, since the treaty became operative three years ago, has accepted two reductions in quota under NASCO agreements. The Faroe Islands, under pressures from within NASCO, has [sic] come to two separate cut-back agreements within the EEC. Iceland continues its exemplary example; driftnetting is not permitted, neither is commercial inriver netting, with the exception of several small traditional stations. In Norway, the government, influenced by steep declines in stocks...has announced that, as of January 1989, driftnetting for salmon will no longer be permitted; inshore netting seasons are to be shortened as of January 1988, and use of monofilament nets prohibited. And in France, efforts are under way in a number of conservation and restoration projects in rivers capable of supporting runs of salmon. Spain, like the United States at the tail end of a migration and interception chain, has dedicated its salmon fishery entirely to angling.

Russia has now become signatory to the treaty, inasmuch as its salmon often frequent the North Atlantic Ocean, migrating around the North Cape to feed in the Norwegian Sea. Like the United States, Russia has never permitted fishing for salmon in the ocean....

Now we come to the United Kingdom and the Republic of Ireland, for both of whom the European Economic Community negotiates under NASCO. Sad to say, in both these nations, which produce around 40 percent of the world supply, there has not been major forward movement. Driftnetting is condoned and illegal operations continue abated. In the U.K., the only governmental action consists of a new Salmon Bill before the parliament, which as recently structured provides no important reductions in catch, commercial or for angling. It does tighten up current law. But the indiscriminate driftnetting off Northumberland is not banned, nor are drastic measures taken to reduce substantially the inshore and inriver catch. The long downward trend in catch of salmon stocks demands a more urgent response than these timid proposals tabled in the Parliament.

Is it possible that the fisheries bureaucracies in the EEC-U.K.-Irish complex do not fully comprehend that the other NASCO members have already begun the long and arduous task of reversing the trend towards overexploitation? Do they realize their obligations to other signatories to the salmon treaty? Does the recalcitrance of this triumvirate in adopting modern principles of sound management have any serious effect on further progress under NASCO? The answer is definitely yes. Denmark, for instance, has indicated that it is not disposed to make further concessions until there is "fair sharing of the burden of conservation." And this, in fact, could kick up quite a storm.

There is no question as to the direction in which Denmark points the finger. So what might be the answer of these states of origin such as the U.K., for instance, to the question—What are you going to do about all this? It might very well be that the fisheries ministers would point out that NASCO is an area of the EEC's responsibility, and that it would be inappropriate to predict what the EEC approach might be. Are we to believe that these salmon-producing nations can so easily walk away from problems and responsibilities, hiding forever behind the cloak of Community representation?

And what might be the EEC's answer to the same question? It might be to the effect that all is as it should be. There is legislation in the producing states of origin with respect to conservation, restoration, and enhancement; money is being spent on management measures, and there is continuous reappraisal of their effectiveness. In other words, the claim is made that salmon conservation has been for centuries a successfully realized objective of the member states concerned.

If indeed all this can be considered a likely scenario, and if that great bard William Shakespeare were put down in the salmon world of today, he might even be tempted to exclaim once again, "A plague on both your houses."

All this "let-George-do-it" business appears clearly to be in contravention of the intent of Article 9(c) of the NASCO treaty. It states that, "in exercising its functions, a Commission shall take into account the efforts of States of Origin to implement and enforce measures for the conservation, restoration, enhancement and rational management of salmon stocks in their rivers and areas of fisheries jurisdiction."

True conservation is not fossilized, not static. The challenge has been accepted by most signatories. What is needed now is for these others to cooperate in designing and embarking on a long-term plan for the future enhancement of salmon stocks throughout the whole of their area of competence, including strict interim regulatory measures on an emergency basis wherever necessary.

All this is not to say that Denmark's territories Greenland and The Faroe Islands, which harvest but do not produce wild salmon, are entitled to annual catch levels which currently equal about one-quarter of the world catch in the home waters of the producing nations. How much is too much?

Now as to NASCO itself—the overarching bridge of mutual support and management regulations for the benefit of all. Those of us who played a part in conceiving, designing, and negotiating this new treaty did not do so with the thought of perpetuating an administrative status quo. There was the vision to perceive that arresting and reversing the decline in the world stocks requires the adoption of new directions and the acceptance of new disciplines. We look to the Council and Commissions of NASCO to develop creative new ideas. Thus any lack of progress under the treaty would be due to people, not the process. Actually NASCO has already established itself on a sound basis. Never before, between all the Atlantic salmon-oriented nations, have we had dialogue — that useful lubrication that comes from personal association and exchanges among negotiators. Conservation measures have been adopted. Dramatic progress will always appear to be too slow, yet important breakthroughs will be achieved from time to time. It was ever thus with international institutional arrangements, and particularly so with fisheries treaties. Examine the more important of these fisheries treaties, and it will be realized that NASCO ranks high with respect to forward progress in early years.

Looking to the future, what can be the role of research in achieving our objectives? The crying need here today is to be able to determine just what is the normal harvestable surplus of salmon stocks, and, when we have that answer, a means must be found to divide up that surplus on a rational, reliable, and equitable basis.... An end to pulling tonnage catch figures out of a hat and attempting to negotiate an acceptable compromise.... We also need scientific studies of such priority matters, for instance, as smolt mortality, the detailing of migration routes to show where stocks separate and to identify overwintering areas, the evaluation of net mesh sizes as a management tool, and the effects of varying levels of harvest at the feeding grounds of salmon.

We also must be constantly on guard to ensure that science is not used for the purpose of furthering existing political positions among nations. Science and biology are not a substitute for rational management — indeed they are the servants of rational management. Too often a lack of complete evidence is used as an excuse for delaying rational management decisions. Thus it often becomes necessary to take prudent reasonable action based upon the best scientific information available at the time.

So, here we are, bound together by a dependence on each other, yet split apart by the overlapping of jurisdictions and conflicting objectives of management and harvest. There simply will have to be less for all and more sacrifice by each, until we have the fish back in abundance. The challenge is, as usual in any common undertaking, for each to do his part.

We need always to keep in mind that we are the stewards of the wild salmon. We hold them in trust—for future generations.

Well, my closing remarks did indeed kick up quite a storm. Lord Moran requested—and of course received—approval to quote from it in a speech he gave in the House of Lords. He used parts of it to buttress his attempts to put more teeth in the Salmon Bill.

Numerous articles about it appeared in newspapers and magazines. An article in the *London Times* of December 4, 1986, entitled "Britain and Ireland Lag in Salmon Conservation," by Conrad Voss Bark, stressed the following points:

> Britain and Ireland were strongly criticized by an American Delegate at a recent scientific conference in France attended by all the major countries interested in salmon conservation.
>
> In his closing address, Richard Buck said Britain and Ireland had not progressed in conservation and the Salmon Bill in the UK Parliament provided no important reductions in catch levels, either commercial or angling.
>
> Buck went on to point out that a long-term plan of stock enhancement was needed, instead of the timid proposals put forward in Parliament.
>
> Other nations had done far better. In the United States regulations permitted Atlantic salmon to be taken only by rod and line. In Canada in-river angling catch limits have been drastically reduced, drift netting banned, inshore netting banned entirely in some areas and seasons cut back in others. Norway has agreed to stop drift netting by January 1989, inshore netting seasons are to be shortened by 1988 and the use of monofilament nets prohibited.
>
> Under the NASCO treaty there have been two cuts in the Greenland netting quota, and the Faroes have also agreed to two cut-backs in catches.

"Not only that," Buck said, while British and Irish Delegates listened gloomily, "even the Soviets, like the United States, have never permitted fishing for salmon in the ocean."

"Now we come," he went on, "to the United Kingdom and the Republic of Ireland, for both of whom the European Economic Community negotiates under NASCO. Sad to say, in both these nations which produce about half of the world supply [of salmon], there has been no major foward movement."

October 25, 1986, *The Field* (London) wrote:

> For a quarter of a century anglers here have watched and protested in vain as salmon stocks dwindled. The outcry mounted and little or nothing has been done by the Government, which alone can enact what is necessary.... The Government should be challenged again. Internationally, it is cheating.

Needless to say, the objective of the symposium had been achieved: wider international visibility for the salmon's plight.

REFLECTIONS ON THE FIRST THREE YEARS OF NASCO

NASCO was working. Geopolitically, the long-term outlook for the wild Atlantic salmon was still bleak, to be sure. The other side of the coin was that we were expecting too much too soon from this treaty. As a point of comparison, the United States was signatory at that time to six multinational fisheries treaties designed to protect mammals and fish of U.S. origin. Historically, none of these had shown substantial definitive action in the first few years with respect to reversing long-term trends of overexploitation. So NASCO was performing better than average.

Of one thing we were sure: NASCO represented the first time ever that there had been a multilateral body devoted exclusively to conservation of salmon of the North Atlantic Ocean. The widely polarized views of all the signatory nations were now being put under the microscope, examined, clarified, and debated. This uncovered and gave world visibility to the real abuses and road-blocks that for years had obscured and delayed the adoption of rational modern management techniques in home water ocean areas. Proposals for reforms were being made and quid pro quos established. As the pressures increased, effective regulatory actions would follow. Although still in its infancy, NASCO had demonstrated its worth.

26

The Mounting Crisis

Late in 1987, we in RASA set out to promote a new and greater emphasis on the advantages of recreational rather than commercial exploitation of salmon not only domestically but internationally. Here are parts of the position statement of October 5, 1987, that we released on the subject:

> WILD ATLANTIC SALMON IN THE TWENTY-FIRST
> CENTURY— A MASTER PLAN
> Restoration of Atlantic Salmon in America urges each Atlantic salmon-producing nation at this time to develop and commence to implement a long-term master plan for the conservation and restoration of the wild Atlantic salmon resource which will maximize recreational utilization, through reducing commercial harvest and also protect and preserve the health, genetic integrity, and productivity of wild strains, all with a target completion date of 2000 A.D.

The rationale for RASA's position was as follows. Governments, with a few notable exceptions, had not honored the principal obligation of any commercial endeavor utilizing renewable natural resources for private gain — the responsibility of maintaining the resource in at least as good a condition as it was when the exploitation commenced. Governments had not ensured adequate and sustainable spawning escapements in their own waters. With a few exceptions, they had not reduced their interceptions of salmon originating in the waters of other nations, as envisaged under the new salmon treaty. Yet the mandate was there. It was the lack of accountability — the resolve — that was wanting.

As novelist Saul Bellow so aptly put it: "Quite simply, when the center does not hold and great structures fall down, one has an opportunity to see some of the truths that they obstructed." Here are some of those truths:

1. Salmon fishing in the ocean was indiscriminate and unconservative. High seas fishing, being nonselective, might take from the very river runs needing particular protection. Proper management techniques required that salmon harvesting take place only at the mouths of streams or in the streams themselves. Only in this fashion could adequate stocks be maintained for each particular river run. Yet driftnetting was still permitted in the United Kingdom, the Republic of Ireland, and off Greenland. Long-lining was permitted off The Faroe Islands. Inshore netting along headlands was condoned. The result of all this overkill was that the 1986 reported total world catch was off about 32 percent from its peak some twenty years ago. And the illegal unreported catch was at least equal to the total reported catch.

2. Growing populations in the Atlantic salmon-producing nations required more recreational outlets. The size and importance of sportfishing emphasized this need. Thirty-four percent of Americans went fishing at least once in 1985. Report number 274 by the Sport Fishing Institute showed that in the United States, fishing was the preferred activity among 33 percent of the population, with the major motivation being the need to escape temporarily from stressful conditions.

3. Gamefishing would build a respect for nature and a commitment to conservation, which are necessary in the materialistic society of today.

4. Gamefishing would be the most productive use of the resource. Maximizing recreational opportunities would be a welcome source of new revenue for economically hard-pressed areas. In Canada, a study published by the Atlantic Salmon Federation showed that in 1985 an estimated 55,400 anglers fished for Atlantic salmon, spending a total of $84 million. Anglers accounted for 93

percent of the total economic activity generated by salmon fishing, yet took only 29 percent of the catch.

5. Farmed salmon would soon be able to supply the entire commercial demand for salmon. The total production of farmed salmon by Norway, Scotland, Ireland, and Canada in 1987 amounted to some 50,000 tons, or nearly six times the total world catch of wild salmon. Estimates for 1990 ran as high as 150,000 tons!

6. A final, most important reason for accenting recreational utilization was that reduction of commercial operations through closure or phasing out would relieve tensions between nations over fisheries. It would permit passage of migrating Atlantic salmon to home waters — a permanent solution to the long-standing and presently condoned practice of one nation's intercepting another nation's stocks.

The basic imperative common to the design of all master plans would be the setting up of strategic and operational procedures. Obviously there were different considerations and requirements that would dictate different approaches and emphases on the part of each Atlantic salmon-producing nation. There was, however, one particular area of concern that should be addressed in all master plans. The geopolitics of salmon of the North Atlantic was extremely complex because of a number of variables. All master plans should honor the primary responsibility of Atlantic salmon nations, which was to ensure that management regulations were compatible with those they had subscribed to under NASCO, the operating mechanism of the Atlantic salmon treaty.

It was only logical to expect, as nations continued to reduce commercial fisheries under master plans, that emphasized recreational opportunities, that the Greenland drift net and the Faroese long-line fisheries would come under increasing scrutiny. The total catch of these two fisheries was currently about 22 percent of the world catch in home waters. Would it then be reasonable for the Greenland and Faroese fishermen, in territories that were not wild salmon producers, to expect to be allowed to continue to fish commercially for salmon? Port aux Basques (Newfoundland) driftnet fishermen had already lost their licenses, and the Norweigan drift-netters would lose theirs by the end of next year. What about the fixed-net fishermen in the Moray Firth (Scotland), whose stations had been purchased and retired from operation? The Greenlanders and Faroese could expect to be asked to make the same sacrifices as the commercial fishermen of the salmon-producing nations. The resolution of these and other international transboundary questions would continue to be the province of NASCO.

The role of the private sector in furthering the master plans was clear. As was the case with the high seas overexploitation off West Greenland in the 1970s, leaving it to bureaucratic initiative was simply not enough. Fisheries problems were not high on the priority lists of governments. Enlightened fisheries ministries understood that support from the private sector could assist governments in undertaking innovative programs of political and sociological change that were necessary to salmon salvation. What was therefore required of the private sector was the fostering of effective partnerships throughout the salmon world that could be agents of constructive change.

We were already in the first phase of a genuine move toward conversion to recreation-intensive management regimes. RASA had shown that the rationale for continued progress was clear, because the benefits were so compelling.

Government and private sector alike were confronting the biggest issue in Atlantic salmon history: whether or not the wild salmon resource as we had come to know it could endure.

THE FIFTH ANNUAL MEETING OF
NASCO – 1988

Since Denmark had agreed to a three-year quota of 2,570 tons (i.e., an 840-ton yearly average) for the Greenland fishing seasons 1988, 1989, and 1990, the West Greenland Commission took no action this year.

THE SIXTH ANNUAL MEETING OF
NASCO – 1989

The North American Commission met in Edinburgh, June 13–16, 1989. At the previous year's Annual Meeting, the United States had proposed a cap of 416 tons for 1989 on the total catch in Zones 3 and 4. This is where the greatest concentration of salmon of U.S. origin is to be found during the summer and early fall. At that time, Canada indicated that it would study the proposal and have an answer at the regular interim February 1989 meeting. That meeting, held at Hilton Head, South Carolina, came and went with Canada delaying its decision, saying that its new five-year Atlantic Salmon Management Plan had not been finalized. Further assurance was given that a decision would be forthcoming at this June meeting.

The fact was that, beginning with the first annual meeting of NASCO back in 1984, there had been ten meetings of the North American Commission. At each one, a management measure was either proposed by the United States or on the table as a result of Canada's failure to act at a previous meeting. At only one of these meetings did Canada agree to a scaled-down version of a U.S. proposal, which had called for closing the fall fishery on October 1. In a unilateral action, without discussions, Canada had closed it on October 15.

At the opening of the June 1989 meeting of the North American Commission, Canada outlined the principal features of its five-year management plan and drew attention to the innovative establishment of an "allowance" (i.e., quota) for the Newfoundland-Labrador fishery and also to the testing of "zonal management," in essence a form of the River Harvest principle of regulation and harvest. The allowance for Zones 3 and 4 (from the Straits of Belle Isle eastward along northern Newfoundland) was set at 440 metric tons for 1989. This was 24 tons more than the 416 tons called for in the U.S. proposal. This was another unilateral decision by Canada, sprung on the United States—no preliminary discussion, no negotiations, simply a flat announcement. This Canadian figure was in no way a reduction. It was not even a hold-the-line regulation.

In an attempt to keep pressure on the matter of Canada's heavy harvest of U.S.-origin salmon in Zones 3 and 4, the United States made the following proposal:

> The United States congratulates the Government of Canada upon its decision "to explore the possibility of developing a plan for the implementation of zonal/river management for the future" and to "identify selected areas where it could be feasible to introduce zonal/river management starting in 1990." The United States therefore proposes that the Department of Fisheries and Oceans select Zones 3 and 4 as two of those in which to introduce for 1990 zonal/river management.... We would also like to offer to assist in any way desirable and feasible in furthering the successful outcome of this worthwhile and forward-looking venture on the part of the Department of Fisheries and Oceans.

Canada indicated that this informal U.S. proposal would be considered prior to and discussed at the next meeting of the North American Commission in February 1990, before any decision on the 1990 Atlantic salmon regulations was made.

The North East Atlantic Commission agreed to a new regulatory measure for the Faroese salmon fishery for the years 1990 and 1991. This measure reduced the Faroese catch to 1,100 tons over the two-year period. It also provided for more flexibility, in that the annual catch could exceed the average by 15 percent.

There was both good and bad news from Norway. The good news was the announcement that there would be a total ban on the drift net fishery for 1989. This fishery had landed about 50 percent of the total minimal catch in recent years. Also, there would be stricter regulations for all waters, sea and inriver, with respect to seasons, gear, and types of tackle permitted.

The bad news was in the following Norwegian statement: "Norwegian salmon stocks have for several years been under heavy pressure. The main problems are extermination of stocks due to heavy acidification, loss of salmon due to the parasitic fluke *Gyrodactylus salaris*, and a heavy exploitation, mainly on mixed stocks. This has reduced the spawning stock in many rivers and reduced the stock enhancement activity. Furthermore, the increased salmon farming is a potential threat to salmon stocks. For these reasons, in 74 Norwegian rivers, fishing is prohibited for a period of up to 5 years."

It was at this meeting that Allen Peterson, U.S. commissioner and head of the U.S. delegation, was elected to succeed Gudmundeir Eirikssen as President of the Council of NASCO. Gudmundeir had done a most effective job of building the administrative part of the organization into a smoothly running machine.

REFLECTIONS

Behind the curtain of the seemingly uneventful and nonproductive 1989 meeting of the North American Commission, a strange and disturbing drama was playing itself out. As the meeting progressed, the wide polarity between the two nations with respect to approaches to the treaty became ever clearer.

The Canadian representative, Wayne Shinners, had explained that Canada was open to consultation, advice, and discussion with user groups (i.e., local commercial and angling fishermen) on the Canadian position in NASCO, and in the light of those opinions the fisheries minister would make the best possible decision with respect to conservation. In a verbal exchange with the acting head of the U.S. delegation, Frank Carlton, Shinners reiterated Canada's commitment to maintain the dialogue with the United States, but made it clear that Canada would not "negotiate" its Atlantic Salmon Plan with the United States.

Thus, it appeared that Canada would treat any formal treaty proposal by the United States in no different a light from that under which it entertains suggestions from any of its constituents, such as clubs or a group of commercial fishermen.

The salmon treaty is a solemn agreement and undertaking between sovereign nations. Intergovernmental relations on Atlantic salmon matters are the province of NASCO, and the functions of the North American Commission are "to provide for consultation and cooperation — on matters relating to minimizing catches" (i.e., of fish of foreign origin) and "to propose regulatory measures . . . in order to minimize such harvests." Problems connected with minimizing catches of U.S.-origin Atlantic salmon should be addressed directly through consultation and cooperation under the mantle of NASCO, not obliquely as an adjunct to a domestic management plan.

The North American Commission had been ineffective in this primary objective of reducing interceptions. How ineffective becomes evident when its procedures and results are contrasted with those of the other two commissions, the West Greenland and the Northeast Atlantic). In those commissions, management proposals had been presented, negotiations — sometimes intense and heated — ensued, "walks in the woods" might occur, differences were ironed out, and compromises were reached. The result? The present West Greenland quota represented the third reduction in the allowable catch for this commission area. And the North East Atlantic Commission action in 1989 was the third reduction in quota for that area. These accomplishments were the essence of successful treaty relationships.

The United States had always gone to great lengths to ensure that U.S. proposals would not damage Canada's salmon interests. Every proposal made by the United States would actually increase runs to Canadian rivers. This, in turn, would help solve a problem about which Canadian fisheries officials had repeatedly expressed concern during the past few years — that the actual spawning requirements of multi-sea winter salmon (the big fish) were not being met.

We had continually emphasized that Canada and West Greenland together were taking more Atlantic salmon of U.S. origin than the total numbers running our rivers each year. How could the U.S. restoration effort ever reach its full potential under such debilitating conditions?

There was, however, a ray of hope for the long term. There was no question that, if rational management practices were followed under the zonal/river management experiment, runs to rivers in Canada would improve and the catch of U.S.-origin salmon would be substantially reduced.

Principle number 6 of the new Canadian management plan actually appeared to encourage a river harvest approach. This principle stated: "Interception of migrating salmon in mixed-stock fisheries will be minimized where practical and feasible, by adjusting seasons, gear, fishing area and the introduction of 'allowances'." River Harvest, the principle long espoused by RASA, dictated that all directed action against salmon, commercial or by angling, take place at the mouths of rivers or in the rivers themselves. "Adjusting...fishing area" could mean River Harvest.

There would be an added bonus to River Harvest management. With pressure on U.S. stocks reduced, the United States and Canada could forget their present difficulties and act together to persuade Greenland to phase out its destructive inshore drift net fishery, which took indiscriminately from virtually all salmon stocks in migrations throughout the North Atlantic Ocean. We made this point often in discussions with our opposite numbers.

THE SEVENTH ANNUAL MEETING OF NASCO — 1990

At this meeting, in Helsinki, June 12–16, 1990, it was confirmed by ICES that the total world catch of Atlantic salmon was down for the third straight year: 5,777 tons in 1989 — an all-time low! — compared with 7,714 tons in 1988 and 8,141 in 1987.

At the February 1990 regular interim meeting of the North American Commission in Halifax, Nova Scotia, the Canadian representative had pointed out that the total Atlantic fishery, principally Newfoundland (which includes Labrador) and Nova Scotia, was in a state of crisis. He had stated, "The steep downturn in northern cod stocks resulted in the closing of many fish processing plants, with at least 3,000 people out of work. This continuing basic problem will be with us for a number of years." To alleviate this situation, the Canadian government had announced a five-year rebuilding program of $575 million, omitting, however, any fixed allocation for salmon.

The total 1989 Canadian salmon catch, angling and commercial, had been 1,166 tons, compared with 1,311 in 1988 and 1,784 tons in 1987. The total 1989 Newfoundland salmon catch was 832 tons, against 972 in 1988 and 1,485 in 1987. Thus Newfoundland took about 80 percent of the total Canadian catch.

The Canadian representative at Halifax had admitted that Atlantic salmon are viewed in the context of all fisheries problems between Canada and the United States. He had even referred to a difference of opinion between the two countries over a Yukon River problem, where apparently the U.S. Commercial fishermen were under criticism by Canada for interceptions of Pacific salmon of Canadian origin — just the opposite of what was happening off Newfoundland. He had proposed that the U.S. Commissioners review this situation with Washington. This was the first time that Canada had admitted in such blatant fashion to such a linkage, which implied a trade-off. It was upsetting, and we so informed Canada.

In 1989, at the suggestion of the United States, NASCO had requested that ICES estimate the number of salmon of Maine origin that had been taken in Greenland each year. The reports showed that in excess of 4,500 Maine-origin salmon had been taken annually in Greenland — about equal to the total numbers running our rivers!

For 1989, the Greenland catch had been only 337 tons, a startling drop from 832 tons in 1988. The Greenland three-year quota of approximately 840 tons a year would expire this year. There was no indication as to what Denmark would propose for Greenland for 1991. Thus no formal action on management measures was called for.

RASA had always opposed anything other than a yearly quota, on the grounds that special circumstances in one year might require a change the following year. This was exactly what had happened. The United States and Canada would have had good reason to take the position that, because the causes of the steep 1989 fall-off were not clear, prudence required that the 1990 quota be much lower than the previous one of 840 tons.

The annual meeting of NASCO in Helsinki produced no definitive forward action in reducing the interceptions of salmon in oceanic commercial fisheries.

In April 1990, I voluntarily retired as a U.S. Commissioner of NASCO. For several years, I had been concerned over a subtle change that had come over NASCO. Gone was the sense of purpose and enthusiasm that had characterized the early years. NASCO seemed to have become more bureaucratized in recent years, more involved in matters of procedure than in the admittedly more difficult task of attempting to produce resolutions of conflicting interests. I chafed at my inability to do anything about this.

Thus it had become my conviction that whatever talents I possessed might be better utilized in the private sector. I recalled that Nat Reed, the former Assistant Secretary of the Interior, used to refer to me as the "watchdog of the Atlantic," and I yearned for that kind of involvement once again. Freed from the constraints of operating in the diplomatic arena, my efforts could be directed once again toward perceiving what was wrong, designing a potential cure for the deficiency, bringing it to government's attention, and organizing RASA to do something about it.

I sent my letter of resignation to President Bush on April 6, 1990, stating, "I feel that I can contribute more effectively to the advancement of the Atlantic salmon restoration effort as a private citizen, unencumbered by the admittedly necessary constraints attached to the position of a United States Commissioner to NASCO."

The President sent me a fine letter of commendation, but what particularly pleased me was to receive a citation by the Council of NASCO, dated June 1990, "in appreciation of his life long commitment to the conservation of Atlantic salmon and for his work to bring about agreement on the NASCO treaty and his consistent support and encouragement to the work of the organization."

To have been recognized by one's peers through an honor never before awarded by NASCO made me feel that all the toil and turmoil had been well worth it. At the same time, I felt humble, in the full realization that there were many others who had also distinguished themselves in their commitment.

President Bush appointed Clinton B. Townsend, President of the Maine Council, Atlantic Salmon Federation-U.S., to be my successor as U.S. Commissioner. As a lawyer, Townsend had a background of solid achievement in furthering the cause of salmon conservation in the state of Maine, particularly with respect to resisting the efforts of power companies to build new, or repair old, dam sites for the purpose of generating electricity—all of which would have increased the mortality rates of salmon on upstream and downstream migrations.

THE COALITION FOR THE ATLANTIC SALMON TASK

It had been my feeling for some time that the deteriorating Atlantic salmon situation in the North Atlantic was so serious as to warrant carefully planned input into the governmental decision-making process, both domestically and internationally, by private-sector organizations. As had been our experience with the Greenland overkill in the 1970s and later in organizing the NASCO treaty effort, we could secure the best audience and implementation of actions with a coordinated effort by private groups.

In 1989, RASA had organized the top officials of the leading salmon groups into a closely knit ad hoc association, the Coalition for the Atlantic Salmon Task (CAST), with a broad mandate of "helping restore Atlantic salmon to abundance in the rivers and waters of the United States." The members were David Berman, President of the Theodore Gordon Flyfishers; David Egan, Chairman of the Connecticut River Salmon Association; John Phillips, Executive Director, Atlantic Salmon Federation-U.S.; Gilbert Radonski, President of the Sport Fishing Institute; Andrew Stout, President of the White River Salmon Association; and me. I was elected chairman, and John Phillips secretary.

CAST would operate as a deliberative group, essentially a think-tank, calling upon the knowledge and experience of our associates. We also would take positions and make recommendations to U.S. federal and state governmental agencies and to top officials of foreign governments. Any positions taken or recommendations made by CAST would not imply or commit the support of any organization or federal or state agency with which the associates of CAST might be connected.

MORATORIUMS CALLED FOR

Although there had been no way of perceiving it at the time, back in 1987 the availability of salmon in the northwest Atlantic was in the early stages of a phenomenon that can best be described as the most sustained free-fall in Atlantic salmon history—four years of substantial back-to-back declines in the commercial catch off Newfoundland, Labrador, and West Greenland:

Year	Canada (tons)	West Greenland (tons)	Total (tons)
1987	1,784	966	2,750
1988	1,311	893	2,204
1989	1,166	337	1,503
1990	561	227	788

This was compelling evidence that the salmon had not been on their normal feeding grounds in the Labrador Sea and the areas to the west, south, and east of Newfoundland. This did not necessarily prove that there was a decline in the abundance of salmon throughout the entire western Atlantic. It could mean that, for reasons not known to scientists, some of the stocks may have split off to other feeding grounds — ones not available or not known to commercial netting operators.

It is important to point out that the cod fishery — many times the size of the salmon fishery — also went into a severe decline in these years. This caused severe economic hardship to fishermen and to those small local industries dependent on fisheries such as processing plants, freezing plants, and boat and equipment suppliers.

It was now clear that the northwest Atlantic was not a feasible area for commercial fishing for salmon. Rational management required that it be prohibited, and moratoriums would be an acceptable means to this end. Our CAST committee had been meeting regularly and involving itself in a number of domestic inriver projects, but we now felt strongly that action was called for with respect to this alarming situation in the northwest Atlantic.

We had recently received encouraging information to the effect that Canada might be in the process of developing a constructive new approach to the whole matter of the Newfoundland-Labrador fishery. On May 4, 1991, newly appointed Canadian Fisheries Minister John Crosbie, a Newfoundlander, met with the editorial board of the *Evening Telegram* and said that buying out commercial salmon licenses might be the solution to the province's weak salmon fishery. He reported that a decision on commercial buy-outs would probably be made sometime this year. The minister further commented: "I think we can get the money and if there is not huge resistance politically, this would seem to be a step that's necessary." He also said that it was difficult to predict how fishermen would perceive such a move, but it would probably be "received in a better spirit than that of four to five years ago."

In Canada, the Department of Fisheries and Oceans is responsible for regulation and management of fisheries. Yet the economic benefits derived from exploitation of these fisheries are realized by the particular province and its citizens. Therefore, the Canadian government manages renewable resources such as salmon in consultation and cooperation with provincial governments.

Currently the Progressive Conservative Party was in power at the federal government level, but in the province of Newfoundland-Labrador, the elected majority was from the Liberal Party. Thus, as Tom Humphrey, President of the private-sector Salmonid Council of Newfoundland-Labrador, put it: "Politics is kicking in." Yet Humphrey, who acted in the role of honest broker, believed that there was a better than even chance for agreement during the fall months between the two parties on the necessity and desirability of a buy-out of salmon licenses. This would be great news, for it had been estimated by our scientists that in recent years the annual Canadian exploitation rate of U.S.-origin salmon had ranged between 35 and 55 percent.

On May 26, 1991, CAST sent a letter to Commissioner Frank Carlton, acting head of the U.S. delegation to NASCO, making the following recommendations:

1. That the United States, in the North Atlantic Commission, propose that Canada declare and implement a moratorium on commercial fishing for Atlantic salmon in the waters of Newfoundland-Labrador.

2. That the United States, in the West Greenland Commission, propose that Denmark, in respect of Greenland, declare and secure implementation of a moratorium on commercial fishing for Atlantic salmon in the waters of West Greenland.

On purpose, CAST did not recommend any specified time frame for the moratoriums, believing that this could be more adequately addressed by the U.S. commissioners after they assessed the negotiating "climate" at the 1991 meetings.

As a means of encouraging Minister Crosbie to bite the management bullet, CAST wrote to him on August 1, recommending that he institute a moratorium in Newfoundland-Labrador (see Appendix 6 for copy of letter).

THE EIGHTH ANNUAL MEETING OF
NASCO — 1991

At the North American Commission meeting, the report of ICES was read. It stated that egg depositions and salmon returns in Canada in 1990 were generally reduced with only six Canadian rivers meeting spawning requirements, and that actual salmon landings totaled 870 tons, the lowest recorded level during the past thirty years. Seventy-four percent of the landings were taken by commercial fishermen, and the entire amount consisted of fish of Canadian and U.S. origin.

Later, Canada tabled a paper announcing its 1991 Atlantic Salmon Management Plan. Then the United States proposed that the 600-ton commercial quota set by Canada for the Newfoundland-Labrador area for 1991 under this plan should become a formal North American Commission regulatory measure. After considerable discussion, it was agreed to leave this subject open for further debate — which never happened.

No other formal management proposals were made by either party at this meeting. The United States, after discussions, did not press the matter.

RASA COMMENT

Under different circumstances, the U.S. 600-ton proposal would have been commendable. Its underlying purpose was to force Canada to relinquish a bad practice that had generally become standard operating procedure in NASCO: Canada would acknowledge a U.S. proposal and agree to take the matter under consideration; the year would pass with no action, and the next spring, Canada would announce its Atlantic Salmon Management Plan for the upcoming season. Thus, the United States never had an opportunity to enter into true negotiations over any new proposal.

This was no year, however, for the United States to waste valuable time on the floor of NASCO addressing an issue secondary to the overarching business at hand, which was the necessity of preventing further erosion of a renewable resource that, in the absence of evidence to the contrary, might be suffering severely from a basic lack of abundance. We in RASA were stunned to learn that the United States did not express itself forcefully in this respect by coming forth with a proposal that Canada implement a moratorium on commercial operations (as recommended by CAST) off Newfoundland-Labrador, to prevent further depletion of U.S.- and Canadian-origin stocks on migration.

CAST's recommendation to the U.S. Commissioners for a moratorium had also had a secondary and very important purpose — one designed to support Canada in its decision to deal decisively with the failing commercial salmon fishery situation. John Crosbie, Canadian Fisheries Minister, had stated on May 4, 1991, that "the need to conserve and protect valuable Atlantic salmon stocks is crucial. For this reason, we will review the commercial salmon fishery in Newfoundland and Labrador in mid-season and implement closures if necessary." Closures are akin to moratoriums — they accomplish the same objectives. So even if the Canadian representatives to NASCO had rejected a formal U.S. moratorium proposal, the United States would have sent a clear message to Minister Crosbie that he could expect the support of the United States should he decide on closures.

The United States permitted the opportunity at this North American Commission meeting to slip away. It adjourned without us taking one step forward in our diplomatic dealings with Canada on the U.S. problem in the northwest Atlantic.

Each year, Canada presented the United States with the fait accompli of its own plan for domestic management of all Atlantic salmon in Canadian waters. Thus, the United States had no input in this decision-making process with respect to protection of U.S.-origin stocks. Each year, the United States made proposals to comply with treaty objectives. These proposals had always been consistent with our desire and intention to recommend measures that were certain to benefit conservation and restoration not only of U.S. stocks but of Canadian stocks as well. Canada either rejected these outright or agreed to consider them, and that was the end of it. The United States proposes; Canada disposes.

Let us put the situation in proper perspective from the United States' point of view. Our government scientists had estimated the rate of exploitation of U.S.-origin salmon at West Greenland and Newfoundland, as demonstrated by an analysis of recaptured tags. This presented a grim backdrop to the following highly plausible scenario: For every ten salmon of U.S. origin at West Greenland, seven were caught there, and one would succumb to natural causes on its way home. A similar fate awaited U.S. -origin salmon at Newfoundland; five would be taken there, and one would be lost to natural causes. So, of twenty fish in the Labrador Sea and environs in any given year, twelve would be intercepted by foreign nets, two would expire naturally, and only six would return home to U.S. waters.

Under the Canadian Atlantic salmon management regime, the United States had been condemned to live with a dichotomy. On the one hand, we had a great respect and admiration for Canada as the leader among nations in keeping pace with the ever-changing realities of the Atlantic salmon world. This had been achieved largely through yearly adjustments and forward-looking improvements in the regulatory process. On the other hand — regarding our own salmon resource — the United States was being forced to suffer the continued aggravation of Canada's failure to operate within the spirit of the salmon treaty.

In the West Greenland Commission meeting, again the U.S. Commissioners decided not to put forward a substantive proposal designed to deal with the critical situation off West Greenland. They had rejected the CAST recommendation for a moratorium.

Denmark, in respect of Greenland, proposed a quota essentially extending the status quo of 830 tons. This was completely unrealistic, particularly in view of the fact that the Greenlanders had been able to take only 227 tons in 1990, the lowest since 1961. This proposal was defeated. Next, Canada proposed a 760-ton quota.

The United States voted against, as did Denmark; the EC abstained. Thus this proposal also failed. That was the end of it. The net result was that no restrictions on catch and no quota were agreed to at the meeting.

The Greenlanders could now fish as hard as they pleased, and should the salmon return in substantial numbers, Greenland might even impose its own quota, perhaps around 800 tons, just to make themselves appear responsible before the world community.

Denmark left the meeting the clear victor, diplomatically, in this exercise in futility. Yet by their intransigence, the Danes did stand condemned, guilty of showing no interest in the conservation and restoration of world stocks. Not being producers of salmon, their purpose was to take what was available.

But why had the United States not proposed a moratorium in Greenland — the only rational management measure certain to restore stocks? Even if the proposal had been made only for the record, it at least would have given support to Canadian Minister Crosbie in his upcoming decision.

The abject failure of nations signatory to the salmon treaty to agree on management measures guaranteeing instant relief for the resource left many people with a sense of foreboding. Here were all these delegations — with a crisis of major proportions staring them in the face — apparently willing to gamble that the salmon were still in abundance and that they would return in the future from parts unknown in sufficient numbers to warrant a continued pounding on what few stocks were still available. This was certainly not "rational management," a basic tenet of the salmon treaty.

TROUBLE WITH NEW ADMINISTRATION

There was now also an in-house problem of great concern. Beginning in 1991, it had become apparent that the situation between the U.S. Commissioners and the State Department had become tense, to say the least. State didn't talk with the Commissioners, and the Commissioners didn't talk with State.

Gone was the fine cooperation that State and CASE and later RASA had so carefully constructed and nurtured over the years. I had built personal and productive working relationships with each of the Assistant Secretaries of State charged with responsibility for oceans and fisheries and environmental affairs and/or their deputies and members of their staffs — fine people like Don McKernan, Roz Ridgway, Morris Busby, Tom Pickering, John Negroponte, and Ted Kronmiller. When Allen Peterson, Frank Carlton, and I became the first U.S. Commissioners to NASCO, we turned this State-RASA partnership into a triumvirate, which had had much to do with the early success the United States enjoyed in NASCO. Secretary of State George Shultz apparently had confidence in the U.S. Commissioners, because our positions had never been questioned.

This pattern prevailed until 1989, when it all began to fall apart with the retirement of Ronald Reagan and George Shultz. This unfortunate development was the result of an unusual set of circumstances, for which the initial responsibility rests with Secretary of State James Baker and, ultimately, with President Bush.

When a new president takes over, obviously one of the first things he does is appoint his cabinet and their assistants, usually assistant secretaries, administrators of federal agencies, and the like. Certainly, the position of Assistant Secretary of State for Oceans and International Environmental and Scientific Affairs had been one of the most important posts in the U.S. government. And it still should have been.

How did George Bush go about filling this sensitive spot in 1989? In the first place, believe it or not, the President did not make a permanent appointment to this post until early in 1990, his second year in office. This revealed something about the commitment of that administration to fisheries and the environment. And George Bush had announced publicly that he would be "the environmental President"!

How did it all play out from then on? Not at all well. The heads of private-sector environmental groups were eager to begin work with the State Department on programs for improving the lot of the Atlantic salmon.

I wrote to the new Assistant Secretary-Designate, E. U. Curtis Bohlen, for "the purpose of discussing the necessity for the State Department to involve itself importantly once again in the ocean affairs of Atlantic salmon." We met in April 1989 at his office, and he appeared to be interested in learning about the past history of the international affairs surrounding the treaty. On May 18, I wrote suggesting that there be a small think-tank meeting "to discuss strategy for a long-term objective and an operational plan under which the private sector can best support the efforts of your Bureau." I suggested sometime in early July. Time went on, and I received no answer.

I kept Bohlen up-to-date by letter on matters pertaining to the NASCO meeting in Helsinki in 1990. Then he scheduled a meeting with me for September 11, 1990, at which I presented CAST's recommendation that the United States consider the possibility of working together with Canada on the Greenland situation. His newly appointed deputy, David Colson, was present, and they both evinced an interest in this approach.

On September 26, 1990, I followed the meeting up with a letter (copy to David Colson) formally recommending a type of action, setting forth the rationale, and ending with an expression that "we are confident that this triumvirate, the State Department, the U.S. Commissioners to NASCO, and the private sector, realizes the importance of acting harmoniously, with each party feeling secure in its own talents and areas of competence and responsibility. We are well poised, ready to get at the extremely difficult job of phasing out or eliminating the Greenland salmon fishery."

I received no answer to this letter, nor any phone call from either Bohlen or Colson. I couldn't believe it. I waited as long as I could, three months — until January 2, 1991, to be exact — when I wrote a letter to Bohlen marked "personal," pointing out that "my associates in our CAST Coalition — and our own RASA members — are asking just what the U.S. is doing about the high seas netting."

I pointed out that the situation was becoming embarrassing and closed with: "I do need to know that you would welcome input from the private sector." I got no answer this time either. So I decided to give up trying to work with this new command, at least for the time being. And the State Department made no attempt to coordinate with the NASCO commissioners, either. A void existed.

Finally, in the summer of 1991, I decided to make one more try, because the interception crisis with both Canada and Greenland was getting nowhere. I wrote Bohlen a personal letter on July 19, 1991, sent registered mail, return receipt requested, setting forth, politely, the chain of events and saying that "such lack of consideration was a great disappointment." I then went on to state that "all the above is now past history," and "we, the CAST Coalition, wish to discuss a proposal that we believe gives promise of reducing and ultimately eliminating Canadian, and perhaps Greenland's interception of U.S. origin salmon."

This finally produced a response, but not directly from Bohlen or Colson. An official in the State Department (name withheld) called me to explain that the State Department had no record of my original letter of September 26, 1990, nor my letter of January 2, 1991. Apparently, they had been lost. Of course that could not have been true — all the originals and all the copies?

At any rate, I received an appointment for September, and this time I was smart enough to have David Egan accompany me. We were authorized to represent the CAST coalition of private-sector groups. Dave was President of the Connecticut River Salmon Association, very experienced on salmon, and a close friend of mine. Quite apart from his qualifications, it seemed desirable, based on my recent experiences, to have a witness.

The meeting covered events of the past year, and Dave Egan and I urged State to meet with Canada on the salmon matter, using the original CAST recommendations of September 26, 1990, as the U.S. position, which had proposed that "the United States Department of State initiate discussions with the government of Canada with a view to developing and implementing a common policy and unified approach with respect to the phasing out or eliminating of commercial fishing off Greenland for Atlantic salmon of Canadian or United States origin."

Bohlen and Colson found no fault with this proposed plan of action, and Bohlen closed the meeting with the assurance that the State Department would undertake discussions with Canada. That's the last we ever heard about the whole matter. Apparently, all the time and effort that the CAST committee had spent amounted to nothing. And on top of it, we did not even get the courtesy of a reply. What a way to run a railroad!

There is one more interesting facet to all this Bohlen business. The Earth Summit was held in Rio de Janeiro in the summer of 1992, and it is common knowledge that the U.S. representation there was ambiguous and ineffectual. Although the United States acknowledged the problems with the biodiversity treaty, it walked away from dealing with them. As a result, the United States lost considerable stature in the international conservation community.

All this came as no surprise to those of us in CAST. We had learned earlier that our "environmental President" George Bush had appointed Bohlen as Head of the U.S. delegation to the Earth Summit.

THE NORTH EAST ENGLAND DRIFT NET FISHERY

John Gummer's bureaucracy in the Ministry for Agriculture, Food and Fisheries (MAFF) had continued to postpone action to phase out or discontinue the indiscriminate and largely unregulated drift net fishery off the Northumberland coast of England. Putting it mildly, the private-sector groups and the salmon organizations in many countries were becoming impatient with the United Kingdom for its dilatory posture.

This fishery accounted for about 60 percent of the total salmon catch in all of England and Wales. In 1991, the fishery took 51,590 salmon, an increase of 10,173 salmon, roughly 40 percent over the 1990 figure. Scientists had estimated that about 75 percent of the fish taken in this English drift net fishery were on spawning migrations to their natal rivers in Scotland. This showed up in the Scottish catch, which in the same year suffered a decline of about 39 percent.

Finally, in October 1991, after studying the problem for about two years, MAFF presented to Parliament the overdue Review of the Northeast England Drift net Fishery, as called for under the Salmon Bill, which had become law several years earlier. Apparently, MAFF was willing to take some regulatory actions.

The plan would be to phase out the fishery over a long period. First, the National Rivers Authority (NRA) was invited to implement the phaseout of the fishery. The NRA proposed to halve the number of drift net licenses in ten years. A start would be made by encouraging the drift netters to transfer their operations to inshore locations. Also, the opening date of driftnetting would be delayed until May 1 in order to permit the early-run salmon unimpeded access to Scottish rivers.

There was a storm of protest over NRA's response to MAFF's invitation. The Atlantic Salmon Trust and the Salmon and Trout Association wrote letters outlining the inadequacy of the plan. So the frustration over the existence of this fishery would continue. It was having a damaging effect on the international cooperative effort to bring an end to ocean driftnetting.

ANOTHER NEW COMMISSIONER
Later in 1991, President Bush accepted Frank Carlton's resignation as a U.S. Commissioner. Frank, in his contributions to the work of NASCO, had an uncommon ability to perceive what was ineffective or inappropriate in any given situation and then to devise ways and means of putting it right. He also had the tenacity to continue searching for resolutions to vexing problems and conflicting interests.

David F. Egan, a lawyer specializing in public defender work, was appointed a U.S. Commissioner by President Bush to replace Frank Carlton. His qualifications were many and varied, through years of commitment to salmon restoration as President of the Connecticut River Salmon Association and also as Chairman of the federal-state-private sector Connecticut River Salmon Commission.

27

Buy-Outs

THE SUCCESS of the Atlantic Salmon Conservation Trust in buying out a substantial number of netting stations and fishing rights in Scotland led to interest in trying to do the same for the Faroese and West Greenland fisheries. As pointed out earlier, however, the two types of transactions differed widely. Under the Scottish projects, there had been substantial assets to sell, including the fishing rights. Neither the Danish government nor the Faroese long-line fishermen nor the native Greenlanders owned the fishing rights in the waters off their shores.

It was clear that a catch quota is not a saleable commodity. It is not owned by individuals but is determined in NASCO by agreement of the nations involved. It was not a separable fishing right to which there was legal title. Therefore, NASCO was the forum in which discussion of Buy-Outs should be held, for the international ramifications of these arrangements were of great importance. NASCO had to proceed with caution, however, because the final decisions had to remain valid with the passing of time.

There was nothing in the NASCO convention to prevent the inclusion of payment of compensation fees in a NASCO regulatory measure designed to conserve and manage stocks. Whether payment of a compensation fee for *not* fishing a NASCO quota would be acceptable to the governments concerned was another matter. Clearly this was a complex socioeconomic matter involving investment, legality, employment, and perhaps even the depopulation of distressed areas.

Then Orri Vigfusson of Iceland entered the picture. Vigfusson came from a prominent commercial fishing family in

Reykjavik and was an ardent salmon fisherman committed to salmon conservation. Vigfusson drew a great deal of internationa' attention in 1990 when he organized the Committee for the Pur chase of Open Sea Salmon Quotas. The objective was the buying out of the NASCO established quotas for the Faroese and West Greenland fisheries. All the salmon not taken in these fisheries would, at least in theory, return to their home rivers, spawn, and renew the life cycle, thereby helping to rebuild declining North Atlantic Ocean stocks.

The first target was the Faroese long-line fishery, which operated generally within two hundred miles of the islands. Through personal negotiations, an agreement to purchase the quota was reached early in 1990 between the Faroese fishermen (with the endorsement of The Faroe Islands government) and Vigfusson's committee. The agreement would cover the next three years, with a requirement that the Faroese government offer succeeding quota periods for sale on a similar basis. This was important because it would act to secure continuity of the program. The agreement had yet to be approved by NASCO, which would consider the matter at its June 1990 meeting.

Under the terms of the agreement, Norway would pay 55 percent of the funds, the United Kingdom 22 percent, Ireland 17 percent, and Iceland 6 percent. This formula was based on the ratio of tagged fish from those countries captured in the Faroese fishery.

This agreement marked a major step in salmon conservation, since it had achieved the effective cessation of an interceptory fishery on the Faroese fishing grounds, something that had never been realized through intergovernmental action or through NASCO.

At the 1990 meeting, the Council of NASCO considered the principles involved in the purchase of NASCO quotas. The three basic principles reviewed were (1) the compatibility with the NASCO convention, (2) the willingness of parties offered compensation to accept it, and (3) the willingness of other parties to pay it or to facilitate payment by other bodies.

On January 22, 1991, in London, the Council chaired a working group meeting of the contracting parties to further examine the principles involved. The working group had a general discussion about the principle of payment of compensation and the possible roles that NASCO could play in any quota compensation agreements. Iceland supported the principle and believed that such agreements should be considered as conservation measures, provided the quotas were not sold for fishery purposes in the area of jurisdiction of the party selling the quota. The EC questioned whether the proposed quota purchase was for conservation or economic reasons. However, the EC believed that it was the right of coastal states to dispose of their NASCO quotas as they deemed fit, provided the catch was maintained within the limits of the quota. Canada expressed concern that the exploitation rate at Greenland remained too high, and stated that a reduction in the West Greenland quota through NASCO would benefit the conservation of stocks. Moreover, Canada believed that compensation agreements as a method for resolving conservation problems should be actively discouraged. Denmark (in respect of The Faroe Islands and Greenland) accepted the principle that quotas could be sold but stressed that any arrangement for quota compensation must not imply a cut in an existing NASCO quota. The United States considered NASCO quotas to be based not on purely scientific advice but on political and economic considerations as well. Sweden supported the Buy-Out concept, and regarded it as a conservation measure. Norway supported the concept as long as a specified proposal could be accepted by NASCO as a conservation measure.

The answers to the three particularly pertinent questions that had been asked at the 1990 NASCO meeting were provided here at this 1991 working group meeting, as follows:

1. Can a party in possession of a NASCO quota receive compensation for not exercising its rights to that quota? It was generally agreed that there was nothing in the convention that would prohibit such compensation payments. A wide range of views was expressed on the desirability of this principle. Norway and Iceland

thought that this practice should be actively encouraged; Canada and Finland felt that the practice should be actively discouraged. Some concern was expressed about possible linkage between the setting of NASCO quotas and the financial aspects of the Buy-Outs. There were also different opinions as to how quotas could be sold. Though legally it might be possible for a NASCO quota to be sold to a third party that was not a NASCO member, it might not be desirable. There was, however, general agreement that there was nothing in the convention to stop a quota from being sold.

2. Would the parties concerned consider relinquishing all the quota or only part of it? Should the compensation agreement be a year-by-year arrangement, linked to the period of the NASCO quota, or a longer-term compensation agreement? The Faroe Islands and Greenland considered the amount of salmon being relinquished to be a matter for the parties involved in that agreement. Both governments believed that the period of the compensation agreement would have to be linked to the period of the NASCO quota.

3. Would the parties concerned, now or at some future date, be willing to enter into negotiations to pay compensation from public funds to a party to relinquish its NASCO quota? If so, should a formula be agreed among the contracting parties so that the cost is shared or should the funding be entirely voluntary? Most parties stated that they could see no justification for using public funds to pay compensation for NASCO quotas. Norway was willing to envisage this possibility and had set up some mechanisms for it. The possibility of the use of public funds by Iceland was not excluded. Since most parties did not intend to contribute, there was no need for a formula to be used.

Allen Peterson, who was President of the Council of NASCO at the time, tried to get NASCO to take a position on the private-sector Buy-Out of quotas. Regrettably, NASCO chose not to do anything about the matter. Allen Peterson felt, as I did, that this might come back to haunt us. As he put it in a letter of August

16, 1991, to me: "If we view that it is OK to sell the *right not to fish*, it is just as likely that somebody could sell *the right to fish* to someone who is willing to pay a higher price."

Initially, RASA was loath to take any position on the buying out of quotas because of the uncertainties involved. But with the passage of time, we became so concerned about the steep declines in catches of Atlantic salmon all over the North Atlantic and the possibility of exhausting the species that we concluded that it was most important to save as many fish as possible as soon as possible. We adopted a sort of "Pragmatic Sanction" and supported — as we still do — the Buy-Out efforts, with the caveat that any agreement be worded in such language as not to defeat the objectives and jurisdictions of the salmon convention.

Orri Vigfusson had also initiated talks with Greenland, and its fisheries minister had issued an invitation for the opening of formal talks with the fishermen. A meeting was set up for June 1990, and negotiations were planned for September.

It would be necessary for the Atlantic salmon-producing nations to come up with funding to pay for these Buy-Outs, and there was considerable interest on the part of private-sector groups in the United Kingdom, such as the Atlantic Salmon Trust, and in the United States and Canada by the Atlantic Salmon Federation. Discussions and planning for such an effort continued through 1991.

On April 27, 1992, a private institution, the North Atlantic Salmon Fund, was organized in Reykjavik, Iceland. According to a letter signed by the prime minister and dated July 18, 1991, the Icelandic government had agreed to support the establishment of a branch of the institution in Iceland, the objective of which was to pay compensation for salmon quotas that would be relinquished. The Icelandic government agreed to facilitate the operation of the fund in the field of currency and exchange.

The founders of the North Atlantic Salmon Fund included well-known salmon organizations and conservationists such as Perry

Bass, a significant contributor to salmon causes; Lord Tryon from the United Kingdom; Orri Vigfusson; and the Atlantic Salmon Federation.

In the United States, there was a lot of interest in Buy-Outs, particularly because at the June 1992 meeting of NASCO, the State Department had announced an objective of working toward the complete elimination of "ocean commercial interceptory fisheries for Atlantic salmon." This brought the support of the National Fish and Wildlife Foundation of Washington, D.C. The foundation made a grant of $750,000 to purchase the 1993 NASCO fishing rights from the West Greenland fishermen. In addition, it expressed an interest in working toward the objective of permanently retiring the West Greenland Atlantic salmon fishery and working with the State Department on the broader goal of ending all ocean interceptory fisheries.

It had always been apparent to me, from my early discussions with Einar Lemke, the veteran representative of Greenland at international meetings, that the Greenland government would not be satisfied with a simple Buy-Out of its fisheries. Salmon fishing had become a way of life for the natives there, so money alone would not solve the problem. It was politically important that alternative means of employment be found for the some 1,200 fishermen.

So, as of March 1, 1993, there was a three-way initiative under way:

1. The private-sector groups were negotiating a Buy-Out for the next two or three years, under which the local Greenland fishermen would be paid a number of dollars (as yet unspecified) not to fish for salmon, except for home use (i.e., not for export).

2. The U.S. State Department and others, such as the National Marine Fisheries Service, were actively attempting to secure seed money for the development of alternative means of employment — perhaps of a scientific research nature involving salmon — for the displaced fishermen.

3. There were active discussions among governments and

private-sector organizations about setting up a substantial international capital fund to generate sufficient income to underwrite a continued scientific research program involving the Greenland fishermen.

This was where things stood early in 1993.

COMMENT

There is a question of ethics in this whole buy-out business that has never been fully addressed. Who is responsible for the basic well-being of the Greenland and Faroese fishermen?

There is no doubt that the world Atlantic salmon resource would benefit by the elimination of the Greenland and Faroese ocean fisheries. And from a scientific point of view, prudence requires that they be eliminated now, for there is firm evidence of an increasing lack of abundance of stocks on ocean migrations. To be sure, the annual take of these two fisheries is not the sole cause of this lack of abundance of salmon in the Atlantic Ocean. Other factors are involved and are continually being addressed and acted on by the producing nations. Yet every single means of reducing mortalities of salmon is important in these crucial times.

The salmon-producing nations have been unable, however, under the framework of the salmon treaty — NASCO — to persuade Denmark to agree to bring an end to these indiscriminate fisheries. Hence the moves outside of NASCO to buy off the Greenlanders and the Faroese fishermen. But while the world Atlantic salmon community is considering the pros and cons of using Buy-Outs to accomplish this necessary relief, other pertinent questions have not been asked, yet have been on people's minds for years.

The elimination of these two ocean fisheries will cause serious socioeconomic problems in Greenland and the Faroes. In fact, these problems have already surfaced as a result of the steep decline in the availability of salmon and other species, such as cod, in the fishing grounds in the northwest Atlantic. Greenland and The Faroe Islands are both territories of Denmark, each with a high degree of autonomy — self-government — except for defense and foreign relations. Denmark already subsidizes these territories, so why is it not the responsibility of Denmark to come to the aid of these native fishermen?

The salmon-producing nations are investing large sums of money in the production and management of these fish. Why should they have to come up with more funding for two territories that only harvest but do not produce salmon, and thus make no contribution to the development and maintenance of the resource?

28

Fishing for Salmon on the High Seas

A PROBLEM that had been vexing NASCO nations for several years came to a head in 1990: salmon fishing in waters under NASCO jurisdiction by vessels not registered to NASCO signatory nations. Although such fishing was not illegal, it was undercutting the conservation efforts of the NASCO salmon-producing nations.

PIRATES OF THE SEA
During the winter, we learned that Danish vessels had been sighted conducting a high seas fishery for salmon in international waters of the Norwegian Sea north of The Faroe Islands. Three of these vessels had Polish registry, three had Panamanian registry, and one was unidentified. The boats used Polish or Panamanian flags in the hope of evading the restrictions of the NASCO convention because, although Denmark was signatory to the treaty, Poland and Panama were not.

Pursuant to the treaty provision that calls upon signatory nations to bring violations of the treaty to the attention of non-signatory nations, Iceland notified Poland of the situation. The Poles took swift action to end this abuse of their flag and assured Iceland that this fishery would be stopped. The United States approached Panamanian officials to ask that they cooperate with Danish authorities on a similar investigation.

To strengthen this existing NASCO procedure, at its seventh annual meeting in 1990, the Council adopted a resolution calling for action through diplomatic channels to ensure that fishing for salmon in international waters by noncontracting parties was halted.

These pirating operations, however, continued into 1991. All the sightings reported to NASCO were obtained by maritime patrol flights by the Icelandic and Norwegian Coast Guards. When fishing vessels are detected during airborne patrols, the aircraft descend from high altitudes to about five hundred feet so that details of the vessel and its activities can be obtained. Photographs are taken, although this is difficult at this latitude — during the winter months there can be almost twenty-four hours a day of darkness.

Information obtained from aerial surveys is restricted to the date of sighting, location, and, when visibility permits, the name and registration number of the vessel. From photographs provided by the Icelandic and Norwegian Coast Guards, it was clear that several of the vessels did not display their registration numbers. In addition, valuable information was received from Faroese authorities, as a result of one of the vessels calling at Torshavn Harbor for repairs, and from officers of Scottish vessels who boarded one of the boats near the Shetland Islands.

Although it was difficult to estimate the total catch taken by these vessels, the potential was well in excess of six hundred tons in any given year, which was more than the combined catch of The Faroe Islands and Greenland in 1990.

PROTOCOL FOR STATES NOT PARTY TO THE CONVENTION

To discuss this whole situation and to consider how to assess the nature and extent of these fishing activities and possible remedial actions, a special meeting of the Council of NASCO was held in London on January 14–15, 1992, and attended by representatives from all contracting parties.

At this meeting, a draft protocol that had been prepared by the United States was discussed. Following comments by the parties, the United States offered to prepare a simpler revised draft protocol so that a drafting session could be held prior to NASCO's annual meeting in June. Two revised draft protocols were subsequently circulated, and a final drafting session was held April 8–9 in Washington.

At its ninth annual meeting held June 8–12, 1992, in Washington, NASCO adopted the Protocol for States Not Party to the Convention of Salmon in the North Atlantic Ocean. The preamble to the Protocol drew attention to the Convention for the Conservation of Salmon in the North Atlantic Ocean and to the achievements of NASCO, and pointed out that the parties to the Protocol (i.e., the signatories to the salmon convention) desired "the creation of a legal instrument for States which are unable to become contracting Parties to the Convention." Selected nonmember states would be invited to sign the Protocol and observe its provisions. Then the terms of the Protocol made provision for the extension to non-NASCO nations of the NASCO prohibitions on salmon fishing in international waters and required the parties "to take appropriate action to enforce the provisions." It was not anticipated that any nonmember nation invited to do so would refuse to sign the Protocol.

UNITED NATIONS RESOLUTION ON LARGE-SCALE PELAGIC DRIFTNET FISHING

During the 1980s and early 1990s, the newspapers were regularly drawing attention to the large-scale high seas drift nets set by Asians in the Pacific Ocean and the carnage they inflicted on all species of fish. "Large-scale" netting is generally considered to be carried out by drift nets over twelve miles in length, but some vessels can set nets up to sixty miles long and 30 feet deep! Thus the fishing is indiscriminate and can take all species of fish.

Starting from zero in 1977, this Asian "super fleet," as it was referred to, expanded to over one thousand driftnet ships. The U.S. government reported that during 1990, this fleet killed more than 41 million sea creatures in the process of netting 106 million squid!

To fully appreciate the enormity of this fishery, the following statistics were drawn from reports of observers in only one of the five large-scale pelagic drift net fisheries in the North Pacific Ocean during 1990: According to the State Department, the by-catch included a mind-boggling 141,000 salmon and steelhead trout, 26,000 marine mammals, 700,000 sharks, 270,000 seabirds, 406 sea turtles, and 39,000 other fish.

Recognizing the overwhelming damage to marine life that was being done by the large-scale drift net fleets, the United Nations passed a 1991 amendment to an earlier resolution of 1989. This new document called for a worldwide moratorium on driftnet fishing beginning June 10, 1992.

Yet this UN action was no guarantee of getting the job done, because the drift net operators might simply choose to ignore the UN. Of the three worst offenders — Japan, China, and Taiwan — only Japan was a member of the United Nations. By the end of 1992, however, Taiwan, China, and others had announced that they would abide by the UN resolution. But what damage had already been done to future resources?

1992 RESOLUTION OF THE COUNCIL OF NASCO

Senator John Kerry (Mass.) reported early in 1990 that vessels from France, the United Kingdom, and Ireland were operating large-scale drift nets in the North Atlantic Ocean, principally in the Bay of Biscay. The Taiwanese were also known to be there.

This was a different kettle of fish as far as the salmon were concerned. It didn't take much imagination to realize the extent of the destruction that could be caused by such nets being set, for instance, across the migration route of salmon returning to their natal rivers in Ireland and the United Kingdom in the late winter, spring, and early fall of any given year.

The contracting parties to NASCO were quite concerned over the possible threat to migrating salmon by this burgeoning high seas driftnetting, and wanted to tighten all NASCO provisions opposing this practice. A resolution was passed to this effect at the Ninth Annual Meeting in Washington, June 9–12, 1992. The preamble simply drew attention to the prohibition on salmon fishing on the high seas in the NASCO Convention and the Protocol for states not party to the convention adopted at the same meeting. The Council then resolved that:

> All non-contracting Parties fishing for salmon on the high seas in the North Atlantic should be invited by NASCO to sign the Protocol to the Convention...NASCO should actively seek to encourage such non-contracting Parties to comply with the Protocol...should discourage its nationals and prohibit vessels owned by its nationals from engaging in any activity contrary to the provisions of the Convention...and should transmit to the Secretary of NASCO information concerning sightings of fishing activities on the high seas of the North Atlantic Ocean which may undermine the conservation measures of NASCO.

Now every available course of action or rule of conduct that could have been devised had been adopted under the regulatory procedures of NASCO. It was a pleasure to be able to point to one constructive action that could be freely addressed and agreed to by all parties to NASCO. It was in this kind of international situation that NASCO justified its existence as an instrument for protecting the salmon interests of its contracting parties.

POLAND ADMITS TO "SALMON LAUNDRY"

Orri Vigfusson, the mainspring of the North Atlantic Salmon Fund for buying out driftnetting quotas, wrote a summary letter of January 17, 1993; here are a few pertinent parts:

> During talks in Warsaw last week between representatives of the North Atlantic Salmon Fund (NASF) and the Polish Fisheries Department, Ministry of Transport and Maritime Economy, the Poles admitted to landings of Atlantic salmon in Poland for eventual transit to Switzerland.... Thus, NASF charges, the Polish government has broken an international assurance and diplomatic commitment on March 26, 1991, to Iceland to stop this international salmon "laundry."

During the past decade, 10–15 Danish vessels have been frequenting Atlantic salmon grounds in international waters between Iceland and Norway. The chief organizer of this illegal fishing is believed to be Mr. Hjarne Funch-Jensen, Danish born but currently registered in Austria (outside EEC jurisdiction).

A number of the "pirate" vessels have been brought to court in Denmark and their owners fined heavily (US $5 million). To escape further prosecution, a few boats subsequently changed registration from Denmark to Panama or Poland, which are not signatories to the North Atlantic Salmon Conservation Organization (NASCO) Treaty.

After considerable international pressure, Panama passed a regulation, January 23, 1991, prohibiting vessels carrying the Panamanian flag from salmon fishing in the North Atlantic. Similar regulations were believed confirmed by Poland to the Icelandic government, as well as the banning of all landings in Poland by vessels of other countries.

COMMENT

It seems apparent that this kind of pirating may be with us for some time, which is all the more reason for NASCO to hit it hard by addressing each case to the particular governments involved. The U.S. Commissioners should be working with the State Department in pressing objections to the offending governments.

These fisheries are, of course, of direct concern to the European nations. But they also affect Canada and the United States, for two reasons. More salmon taken in the northeast Atlantic translates to fewer salmon migrating to the West Greenland feeding grounds from Europe; with fewer European stocks available, North American stocks will be subjected to greater fishing pressure by the Greenlanders. For years the catch at West Greenland was spilt roughly 50-50 between North America and Europe. Recent catch statistics indicate a changing pattern off West Greenland. In 1991, 65 percent of the salmon taken at West Greenland were of North American origin.

A second reason this fishery is of consequence to North America is that its very existence has complicated quota negotiations for the West Greenland fishery. With some justification, Greenland has been able to point out that it makes no sense to impose a low quota at West Greenland as long as an undocumented, unregulated fishery exists in the northeast Atlantic Ocean.

29

The Turning Point

FOR YEARS on end, the conservation community had been subjected to depressing news about the salmon. We were entitled to a change. It came at just the right time, and it was momentous.

A WATERSHED EVENT

On March 6, 1992, John C. Crosbie, Canadian Minister of Fisheries and Oceans, and Walter Carter, Fisheries Minister for Newfoundland, announced a jointly funded offer of cash payments to commercial salmon fishermen who would voluntarily retire licenses issued in their name. This offer was the cornerstone of a major program to conserve and enhance the stock of Atlantic salmon.

Payments to commercial licensees would range from $8,000 to $50,000, depending on the level of their salmon landings in the best year out of the past three. Payments would be made after they had agreed to the terms of the offer and turned in their salmon fishing gear. Total cost of the retirement program was expected to be about $40 million, to be shared 70–30 by the federal government and the province.

Recreational salmon fishermen in all Atlantic provinces would also be observing new fisheries management initiatives in support of conservation and habitat renewal. They would be required to make a reduction in effort, with specific measures determined on a river-by-river basis. In accord with a previous judicial decision, known as "the Sparrow decision," handed down by Canada's Supreme Court, allowances would be made for the right of aboriginal peoples to fish for food.

"Salmon is a significant share of many fishermen's livelihood," said Crosbie. "We have made this retirement program as generous as possible so that those who accept it will have funds to invest in alternative economic activity. If the Atlantic salmon is to recover to the abundance of a generation ago, there is no alternative but to sharply curtail commercial salmon fishing," he said. "This is a voluntary program. However, I hope that the great majority of license holders in the province will choose to accept our offer."

Carter said that recent restrictions on the commercial sector, such as reduced seasons and quotas, had not rebuilt the salmon resource; therefore, fishermen would have to face further restrictions in the future. "In this context," he said, "this offer allows fishermen the option of accepting up to eight times the value of their best year's landings since 1989 and, given the current state of the resource, may be acceptable to many salmon license holders."

Commercial salmon fishing had been discontinued in Prince Edward Island, Nova Scotia, and New Brunswick nearly ten years ago. Newfoundland (which includes Labrador) was the only Atlantic province where it was permitted, and there were just under three thousand licensees still active in the province.

Despite prior license retirements and other conservation measures, preliminary figures for 1991 indicated a fourth consecutive year of declining commercial catches in Newfoundland and Labrador, with landings of 433 tons. This was 39 percent below the lowest catch in the 1980s (798 tons in 1984).

Coincidental with the retirement offer, a minimum five-year closure of the commercial salmon fishery for the Newfoundland portion of the province would take effect. At the time, the government of Canada further announced that "there is no guarantee that this fishery will ever reopen."

For Labrador, with its high dependence on salmon and limited prospects for fishery diversification, there would be no fishing moratorium. In order to increase stocks, however, those who chose to retain licenses would not be entitled to make up the catch forfeited by those who had accepted retirement. The allowable salmon catch in Labrador would decrease in the same proportion as licenses were retired. Continuing licensees would remain subject to restrictions on their catch, up to and including prohibition, for reasons of conservation. Fewer than one in seven of the commercial licenses outstanding in the province was held in Labrador, an estimated 418 out of a total of 2,979 licenses in 1991 for the whole province.

Some years ago, the New Brunswick and Nova Scotia salmon fisheries were closed on just such a basis, except that the minimum period was only one year and the "Buy-Out" terms were less advantageous. But most importantly, the salmon fisheries there were never reopened, presumably on the arounds that conservation needs of the species demanded permanent closure. So the implications of this "conservation" regulation certainly would not be lost on the Newfoundland and Labrador fishermen. It would be to their advantage to accept a lump-sum payment at this time rather than take the chance of not being able to fish for salmon at all in future years.

It was estimated that at least 80 percent of the Newfoundland and 60 percent of the Labrador fishermen would take advantage of this offer. Thus, the program obviously represented a substantial commitment on the part of Canada — estimated at the time to be as much as $40 million.

A momentous action of this nature immediately raised a number of diverse yet related questions and considerations, among which the following appear to be most important.

Pockets of Resistance. There were still a few situations here and there in the Canadian Maritimes that were, or might be in the future, out of sync with the seemingly overriding current trend. For example:

• Certain native bands were claiming historic rights to fish for salmon — mostly ad hoc inriver problems in a few locations. These claims had legal connotations and might be beyond the purview of governmental controls, but they were amenable to enlightened and reasonable resolution.

• There would be those Newfoundland and Labrador fishermen who would elect to keep their licenses, and this could pose a continuing problem. But the tide had been running so strongly in favor of restoring salmon runs that ways would undoubtedly be found to handle these isolated situations.

• Although the Province of Quebec was well along in its program of eliminating commercial salmon fishing, it was possible that a few fishing communities would hold out for retaining historic rights to continue commercial operations for salmon. But these situations should also be amenable to resolution, given time.

Increased Salmon Runs. This program should increase substantially the numbers of salmon returning to spawn in their natal rivers in Newfoundland, Labrador, Quebec, New Brunswick, Nova Scotia, and Prince Edward Island. In addition, our own U.S. scientists had estimated that the Newfoundland-Labrador commercial nets had been taking up to 70 percent of U.S.-origin salmon returning to their rivers annually. Commencing with the runs in 1993, the lifting of these nets should benefit the restoration program in New England.

A caveat. We need to keep in mind that this main move is technically a five-year closure of the Newfoundland fishery. Should salmon stocks recover dramatically, we can expect a move by commercial fishing interests for a reopening.

INTERNATIONAL IMPLICATIONS

There are important international implications attached to this Canadian action. For the past several years, RASA has been pressing for a reaffirmation of the U.S.-Canadian joint agreement on Atlantic salmon of 1971, which pledged a unified approach to problems of the species in the northwest Atlantic Ocean. This closure action by Canada should resolve most differences of opinion that Canada and the United States have had with respect to the Canadian

interception of U.S.-origin salmon. Thus we could and should act together to address the principal problem now facing both nations —
the West Greenland commercial fishery, which severely reduces
both Canadian and U.S. stocks.

It may take several years for the world Atlantic salmon community to fully digest the implications and ramifications of the
Canadian move, but all of a sudden it will come through loud and
clear that the entire North American continent can be considered
virtually free of commercial fishing for Atlantic salmon in the
ocean, because U.S. waters are not open to commercial fishing for
the species either. Thus, in view of the continuing steep decline in
the world catch of Atlantic salmon, North America presents a challenge to all the other NASCO nations to undertake additional management measures of major dimensions in their own waters.

Although Canada's action was one born, fundamentally, out
of necessity, it still took political courage. The Newfoundland
fishermen in particular — having suffered severe financial losses
through the failure not only of their salmon fishery but also of their
mainstay, the cod fishery — were initially resistant to the prospect of
losing their salmon licenses permanently.

There were a number of people in eastern Canada who
worked hard on this problem for some time, and they deserve our
thanks for what should turn out to be a permanent solution to it.
Minister Crosbie had to bear the brunt of the criticism and therefore deserves commendation for facing up to the challenge. There
was also the very able Walter Carter, the Newfoundland Fisheries
Minister from St. John's. I knew him in earlier days during my tenure as a U.S. Commissioner. We were usually on opposite sides of
the fence, for his constituency was principally the commercial
fishermen. Yet we always got along well and were often in agreement on the broader perspectives. He pressed his points well, and
he was fair; I always respected his integrity.

In the private sector, Canadian organizations such as the
Atlantic Salmon Federation, the Miramichi Salmon Association, and

others favored the moratorium and were supportive. Tom Humphrey, President of the Salmonid Council of Newfoundland and Labrador — representing angling clubs — worked tirelessly on the closure effort.

The importance of this major breakthrough in salmon conservation added up to the dawn of a new day for the salmon in the northwest Atlantic, clearing the horizon for the future.

30

NASCO Stumbles

AS THE REPRESENTATIVES of the contracting parties assembled in Washington in June 1992 for the annual meeting of NASCO, there were more uncertainties and conflicts hovering over the green table of negotiations than at any time during the history of the treaty. It is difficult to assess the extent of the adverse effect that these disturbances may have had on the competence and resultant performance of the U.S. Commissioners at this meeting, but it must have been considerable. There were two principal areas of confusion, one international and one domestic:

1. *Governmental negotiations on a bilateral salmon agreement.* A highly secret yet widely rumored venture to secure an agreement to phase out the Greenland fishery had apparently been occupying top officials of the U.S. government. It was even reported, unofficially, that Secretary of State James Baker had met with the Danish prime minister for discussions about it, but no details were forthcoming. Since that time, however, there had been a realignment of the Greenland home rule government, and what effect this would have was not clear.

2. *Relations between the State Department and the U.S. Commissioners to NASCO.* The lack of coordination and cooperation between the State Department and the three U.S. Commissioners to NASCO was still the order of the day. This year the State Department apparently felt that it should decide on the correct posture of the Commissioners in representing the U.S. position in NASCO. In a letter of May 4, 1992, Assistant Secretary of State Curtis Bohlen wrote to the three Commissioners to, among other things, inform them of the official position of the United States.

He wrote, "as NASCO Commissioners, you should state clearly that our target is to phase out commercial interceptory fisheries for Atlantic salmon in the next few years."

There was nothing wrong with this position per se, and the State Department certainly had the authority to design it, announce it, and implement it. In fact, its basic principle was similar to the position that RASA and our predecessor, CASE, had always espoused. But it was the dictatorial manner in which the whole thing was handled by the State Department that ruffled so many feathers. So it was not surprising that no one expected much in the way of progress. And that's exactly what we got.

THE NINTH ANNUAL MEETING OF NASCO — 1992

In the opening meeting of the Council of NASCO, Deputy Assistant Secretary of State Richard J. Smith announced that "the long-term policy objective of the United States is to work towards ending commercial fishing for Atlantic salmon." Smith indicated that the United States would "work through NASCO, bilaterally, multilaterally, and through any other appropriate forum." He stated, "we will continue to recognize the legitimate rights of subsistence users and personal use fisheries, and the fact that interceptions of salmon cannot be entirely eliminated."

At the Annual Meeting of the North American Commission, the United States made no management proposal with respect to the Canadian interceptions of U.S.-origin salmon in Labrador (Newfoundland was now under the moratorium). This was in line with instructions from the State Department to the effect that the U.S. Commissioners should make every effort "to develop a common policy with Canada." But in private discussions with the U.S. Commissioners, the Canadians apparently chose to let the United States carry the ball on matters of conservation — particularly with respect to the West Greenland situation. So with nothing forthcoming from the Canadians, it was not possible for the U.S. Commissioners "to develop a common policy."

It would seem that, in the best interests of forward progress in NASCO, the U.S. Commissioners should have been given a free hand in dealing with Canada — this had always been the case in previous years. Thus, they could have opened a dialogue on a management proposal to Canada. They could have requested that Canada give consideration to adopting a five-year moratorium on commercial fishing in Labrador, paralleling the one recently instituted in Newfoundland. The constraints imposed by the State Department should not have applied here, if indeed that is what was intended. Apparently, there was no communication at top levels between State and the Commissioners during the whole meeting.

This would have been a rational proposal made in the interest of consistency, inasmuch as the Labrador netting caused exactly the same type of mortalities of U.S.-origin salmon as the Newfoundland fishery. The United States could have explained that we understood the special sociological problems in Labrador, and we could have expressed sympathy that such a moratorium might inflict extra economic hardship on the Labrador natives.

It should always be kept in mind, however, that this salmon harvest was a part-time fishery, lasting only a few months. The cod fishery was the mainstay, and it was also critically depressed. Thus, the government of Canada had the whole fishery as a problem, and resolving the salmon part of it should not be at the expense of the U.S. restoration effort—through interceptions of U.S.–origin salmon.

It is probable that Canada would have rejected such a proposal, yet the U.S. concern should have been made part of the formal record, drawing attention to the inconsistency.

No definitive management proposals were put on the table by the United States at the annual meeting of the West Greenland Commission either. Canadian head of delegation Rawson pointed out that the Newfoundland moratorium and other conservation measures now in effect for Canadian waters were expected to cause a reduction in total Canadian catch — both commercial and angling

— of about 50 percent this year. The implication, of course, was that it might be appropriate for similar action to be taken by Greenland.

Here again, the U.S. Commissioners, under normal conditions, might have had an opportunity and justification for turning this Canadian situation into a formal proposal respecting West Greenland. The rationale would have been persuasive. The Greenland catch for 1991 had been 438 tons, so 50 percent of that would be a quota of some 200 tons, not at all unreasonable in view of the lack of availability of stocks throughout the entire northwest Atlantic.

As it turned out, the head of the Greenland delegation, Einar Lemke, reported an inability to negotiate any reduction in Greenland's self-imposed quota of 840 tons, apparently due to a political situation in his government back in Greenland. Lemke also pointed out that a whole new approach was needed — a long-term mechanism for handling the West Greenland problem — so that in years of abundant salmon, it would be possible to increase the quota.

Nothing was accomplished in this Comission either, and the Greenlanders could take as many salmon as they could catch in 1992.

In the North East Atlantic Commission, The Faroe Islands agreed to quota of 550 tons for 1992, a roll-over of the previous quota. So there was no progress here either.

It is important to note that the representative of the European Commission expressed the Community's concern about NASCO's failure to agree on regulatory measures for the second straight year. He called on the members of the Commission to reflect on the negative effects that persistent failure to resolve the situation would have on the future of NASCO. He suggested that the parties consider the need to confer before the next annual meeting in order to avoid another failure next year.

Allen Peterson's term as President of the Council of NASCO expired in 1992, and at the Annual Meeting he announced his decision not to permit his name to be put up for renomination.

He was succeeded by Børre Pettersen of Norway, who had been serving as Vice president.

Allen Peterson made substantial contributions during his incumbency, setting up a number of procedures that, in time, should improve the administrative processes in NASCO. In particular, he became engrossed with the problems of salmon aquaculture, and was active in developing NASCO's response to the possible threats inherent in the interactions between wild and cultured salmon. In all this work for the Council of NASCO, he was aided materially by the support of Malcolm Windsor, the conscientious and able secretary, who presides over the Secretariat in Edinburgh.

31

Where Have The Salmon Gone?

IT IS IMPORTANT to remember — in fact to emphasize — that the failed negotiations in NASCO that had been undermining the salmon conservation effort were being played out in 1992 against an alarming and perplexing backdrop — the lack of availability, or abundance, of the salmon in their normal feeding grounds in the northwest Atlantic Ocean. We had experienced six years of substantial declines of about 54 percent in the world catch of Atlantic salmon in home waters (and now one slight increase for 1992 — inconsequential as far as the broad picture is concerned). Here are the figures:

Year	World Catch (tons)
1986	7,737
1987	6,598
1988	6,573
1989	5,086
1990	4,333
1991	3,549
1992	3,720

This overall decline has certainly had an extremely damaging effect on the future spawning potential of the stocks of all states of origin.

The exact cause or causes of this phenomenon are shrouded in mystery. The explanation that first comes to mind is that we are now paying dearly for the overexploitation visited on the species over the past quarter century. To be sure, overkill has been a big factor in the lack of availability of stocks for harvest. You remove not only the fish you catch but also their ability to spawn and increase future generations. So the overkill feeds on itself — a double whammy, so to speak.

It is becoming apparent, however, that overexploitation by itself is not the sole cause for the absence of stocks from their accustomed feeding grounds. Other factors are involved. Scientists are now actively engaged in research projects that attempt to identify all possible causes of this depressing situation.

I recently asked two of our leading scientists this question: What in your opinion has been the cause of the recent lack of abundance or availability of salmon in the Atlantic ocean?

Dr. Kevin Friedland of the National Marine Fisheries Service at Woods Hole, Massachusetts, answered:

> The survival of Atlantic salmon has been poor in recent years and thus has stimulated considerable debate and some new research. Though a definitive answer, based on direct observations of salmon at sea, is still beyond our grasp, recent findings suggest survival is mediated by the ocean environment. For North American stocks, it appears that the first winter at sea is critical. Though the exact mechanism is still unknown, the amount and distribution of salmon habitat, as defined by sea surface temperature, appears related to overall survival. Survival of European stocks appears to be mediated by a different mechanism. There is some evidence that growth and survival are more directly related for European fish than observed for North American stocks. These findings definitely raise concerns over what impact global climate change may have on salmon marine habitat.

T. Rex Porter is a fisheries scientist at the Science Branch, Department of Fisheries and Oceans, St. John's, Newfoundland. He points out that the low population sizes cannot be explained by low numbers of spawners in preceding years. His reasoning is based on the fact that research being conducted on the Conne River and Northeast Brook on the south coast of Newfoundland indicates that the survival of wild salmon from the time they enter the sea as smolts until they return as grilse, one year later, has declined by about 67 percent between 1986 and 1992. So, for a given number of smolts, there were about a third as many salmon returning in 1992 as in 1987. Porter considers this quite dramatic in view of the fact that there were no commercial fisheries in Newfoundland in 1992.

The question can now be reworded: What caused the unusually high mortality of salmon at sea during the past few years? Porter reasons that certain inferences can be made from scientific knowledge of the salmon's marine life and the fisheries: (1) grilse are not harvested in the West Greenland fishery; (2) there was no commercial fishery in Newfoundland in 1992; (3) salmon are believed to occupy primarily the upper surface layers of the northwest Atlantic Ocean, where water temperatures are between 4°C and 12°C; (4) sea surface temperatures affect the distribution of salmon, so that during harsh winters and springs, when the northern ice floe extends farther south, salmon are also distributed farther south in the Labrador Sea and the Grand Banks area; (5) in years when the winter sea surface temperatures are below average, there appears to be lower population size the following year; and (6) oceanographic data indicate that, during the last three years, the ice conditions have been severe and water temperatures have been colder in the northwest Atlantic than in previous years.

A synthesis of this information suggests that the low abundance of salmon is in some way related to the unusually cold conditions at sea.

Porter points out, "It is difficult to postulate how the adverse environmental conditions actually caused the salmon to die. One possible explanation is that the salmon that died encountered ice crystals in the water which caused their gill filaments to freeze." It is also of interest that the biomass of other fish species such as cod and capelin has also decreased dramatically in the past three years, giving additional support to the hypothesis that the adverse environmental conditions have had a significant effect on survival rates.

All this fits with what we in RASA have come to believe about the scarcity of salmon. Colder sea surface temperatures would tend to force fish of all kinds — not just the salmon — to seek the more southern parts of the Labrador Sea, perhaps some of the warmer pockets of water formed by the eddy systems in this vast ocean area. Such an assumption is strengthened by the fact that there has also been a coincidental decline in recent years in the biomass of cod and capelin in their customary ocean habitats. This would explain why the salmon have not been as abundant in their accustomed locations. The stocks not only have suffered greater mortalities in the ocean but also have moved to areas not readily accessible to inshore fishermen in small boats.

It is encouraging to note that the conclusions of Kevin Friedland and Rex Porter are essentially in agreement as to the probable reasons for the decline in survival rates of the salmon in the Labrador Sea and environs. They are also consistent with the findings of David Reddin, an associate of Porter's in St. John's, Newfoundland (see Chapter 2).

It is obvious that much important work in this area remains to be done. It should receive top priority and commensurate funding from the Atlantic salmon research efforts of NASCO and the producing nations.

REFLECTIONS

We still do not know exactly where — in this vast expanse of water — the salmon now prefer to feed, given colder sea temperatures farther north. Perhaps, given our proclivity to turn knowledge of this kind to our own advantage and selfish interests, it is better that we do not know where these fish congregate. The important thing is that they return to their natal rivers in substantially greater numbers so that our stocks may be restored to their abundance of years ago.

32

A Judgment on NASCO

WHEN THINGS don't go right in NASCO, the first reaction of some is to blame the treaty, claiming that it is not structured correctly. This has always seemed to me to be too superficial and easy an approach. Let us view this whole question of the competence of NASCO from the standpoint of what is constructive about it:

• NASCO is the only international institutional arrangement that regularly provides a forum for people to consult and cooperate on all matters concerning the conservation and restoration of Atlantic salmon.

• NASCO provides the only mechanism for proposing and voting on regulatory measures for the management of salmon.

• NASCO is the only mechanism available for conducting inquiries into matters of a scientific nature of special interest to all salmon nations and making recommendations based on the results of scientific research.

• NASCO is the only appropriate forum for an exchange of views on international codes of practice and regulatory measures with respect to the aquaculture of salmon in the North Atlantic Ocean. (The treaty covers all species of salmon, not just Atlantic salmon.)

• NASCO is the only venue where opposing points of view on all aspects of Atlantic salmon management and harvest can be addressed by officials of governments and brought before the bar of world opinion.

• NASCO is the first line of defense for salmon in the North Atlantic Ocean against piracy on the high seas and indiscriminate large-scale driftnetting.

• NASCO is necessary to provide the collateral benefits customarily associated with institutional arrangements, such as the compilation of scientific or statistical reports and the enforcement of laws and regulations.

Keeping all the above in mind, let us now ponder for a moment what we would do without these avenues of expression and commitment. The answer is obvious. Without any NASCO — and thus no controls beyond national fisheries jurisdictions — it would be back to unrestricted salmon fishing on the high seas and the chaos of the 1970s.

The principal argument of critics of NASCO has always been that the voting procedure is based on unanimity rather than majority. This is an opinionated assessment based on a lack of understanding of the nature of international fisheries problems, which are geopolitical in nature. A number of years ago, nations went to great lengths to proclaim and protect their national sovereignty over ocean rights. They are therefore not about to give up control of their territorial seas, national fisheries jurisdictions, and exclusive economic zones. They would never agree to any provision in fisheries treaties, such as majority voting, that could jeopardize these hard-earned rights. The principle of unanimity in voting is embodied in all the fisheries treaties to which the United States is signatory, and it is reasonable to assume that this same principle would apply in the fisheries treaties of other nations.

Therefore, the responsibility for NASCO's inability to adopt what a clear majority might deem necessary to "rational management" has to be laid at the door of those nations that voted against any particular proposal. In the final analysis, it is people who are the obstructionists, not the treaty. If this is a reasonable assessment, then it follows that the policymakers of the signatory nations are responsible for any progress or lack of it in NASCO.

Another important assessment is whether the people currently in positions of authority in NASCO are qualified — through a background of knowledge and experience in Atlantic salmon matters — to make decisions about the particular kinds of fishery problems under scrutiny and consideration. Just what particular background of knowledge and experience is required?

In recent years, there has been a decided change in how different nations — and thus their representatives — view the viability, necessity, and desirability of continuing the commercial netting of Atlantic salmon. The result has been a decided shift by certain nations in support of the many benefits offered by salmon fishing for recreational purposes. These same nations are also many years ahead of the recalcitrant nations with respect to adopting and implementing management plans to accomplish these desired objectives.

The United States and Canada have clearly recognized that angling for Atlantic salmon — recreational sportfishing — is the wave of the future. In the United States, the New England states have always prohibited the sale of Atlantic salmon. Canada has now banned commercial fishing for Atlantics in all its provinces, with the exception of Labrador (part of Newfoundland) and in a few localized "native claims" situations.

As far as angling is concerned, the concept of "catch and release" became popular a number of years ago. These nations encourage this special conservation measure and have made it part of the regulatory process, often requiring the release of large salmon (the "multiple spawners") and retention of only a limited number of grilse (the "one sea-winter salmon").

It is important to note that in both the United States and Canada, governmental fisheries managers not only welcome private-sector salmon experts in their discussions on management measures but also often appoint them as participants in their decision-making actions. (In the United States back in 1983, when we were securing congressional approval of the enabling legislation for the salmon treaty, RASA was successful in including a requirement that two of the U.S. Commissioners to NASCO be from the private sector — with one from government — so long as they were knowledgeable and experienced in Atlantic salmon matters.)

In contrast, what is happening in the recalcitrant nations? In Scotland and England, the recreational salmon interests are still mired in the morass of the Ministry of Agriculture, Food and Fisheries, that commercially oriented and impenetrable domain of

John Gummer. The situation in Ireland is, in effect, the same—dominated by commercial interests.

But even if the Scots, the Brits, and the Irish could persuade their governments to take positions favorable to angling, they would still be subject to the influence, whims, and decisions of the European Commission, which speaks and acts for its member nations on fisheries matters. And who are the people running the show in the EC? We find about the same situation that existed years ago in ICNAF: The delegations are made up almost exclusively of bureaucrats in Brussels whose constituencies are the cod, haddock, halibut, flounder, and herring fishermen. How can they be expected to be knowledgeable and experienced in Atlantic salmon matters?

It also appears that the ministers and top officials in charge of these governmental agencies—all up and down the chain of command from Scotland, England, Ireland, and the EC—have not yet recognized the full impact of the message that is now common knowledge elsewhere: Salmon aquaculture has almost completely taken over the commercial world market for Atlantic salmon. And there are numerous authoritative studies from both sides of the Atlantic showing that recreational angling for salmon contributes far more to the economy of the salmon-producing nations than does commercial exploitation.

So, referring back to the original proposition, it is my conviction that any lack of progress in NASCO is due principally to a lack of commitment, qualifications, or both, on the part of the people involved. It is incumbent therefore upon each signatory nation to examine the competence of its representatives in NASCO. Are they qualified to address the requirements of the recreation-oriented Atlantic salmon world of the future? If not, the necessary adjustments should be made.

With such a revitalization program behind us, we should be able to proceed with more confidence to produce meaningful and constructive forward movement under the present structure of NASCO, just as we did in the early years of the treaty.

PART

VII

THE AQUACULTURE OF SALMON

33

Salmon Farming

AQUACULTURE IS BIG business worldwide. In recent years, Atlantic salmon aquaculture in particular has dominated the industry throughout the North Atlantic Ocean.

Atlantic salmon farming began in Norway in the mid-1960s and expanded rapidly after the company A/S Morvinkel started operations in the early 1970s in the waters off Bergen. It grew in Scotland also in the early 1970s, and, at about the same time, Seapool Industries set up a farm near Halifax, Nova Scotia. Efforts to raise salmon on the Maine coast go back to 1980, but environmental questions, difficulties with state regulatory agencies, objections from lobster, crab, and shellfish fishermen, and a lack of investment capital hindered early development.

The Canadian government, meanwhile, in accordance with its whole approach to the growth of its fisheries industries, undertook research and subsidies for salmon farming in an effort to become a leader in world markets. In New Brunswick, research on aquaculture was under way, and by 1974 scientists from the marine biological station at St. Andrews had successfully raised salmon off Deer Island in Passamaquoddy Bay. The federal government, in cooperation with industry, built a demonstration farm in St. George. Then a private firm, Sea Farm Canada, built a hatchery for the express purpose of raising smolts. In 1984, the province of New Brunswick set up a salmon aquaculture lease program, awarding grants to new farming enterprises. The whole picture was now complete, and the industry took off.

By the 1990s, farmed salmon had taken over almost the entire market in retail stores in the United States and Canada. The farmed product has important advantages over commercially caught wild salmon. Fresh-farmed Atlantics are of a uniform size, usually about six to eight pounds. They are available throughout the year, whereas the wild variety are generally caught only from early spring through late fall. The color of the flesh of farmed Atlantics can be controlled, and is therefore consistent.

Because of the tremendous increase in the production of farmed salmon, the price of fresh Atlantic salmon in the marketplace has fallen dramatically. This has put commercial salmon fishermen under heavy pressure, causing many to leave the business.

By the end of 1992, Norway, the pioneer, was farming 140,000 tons of Atlantic salmon annually; Scotland, 36,100 tons; Canada, 10,380 tons; Chile, some 12,000 tons; The Faroe Islands, up to 17,000 tons; Ireland, about 9,321 tons; the United States, 5,850 tons; and Iceland 2,100 tons. Thus, the total world production of farmed salmon in 1992 was about 232,660 tons (some 62,000,000 salmon). By comparison, the total world catch of wild salmon in 1992 — commercial and angling — by the producing nations was only 3,720 tons (about 1,300,000 salmon).

Salmon aquaculture is a two-phase operation: production of fry from the egg to the smolt stage in fresh-water rearing tanks in hatcheries, then transfer to sea water for culture and growth to marketable size. There are two approaches to raising the smolts to marketable size — farming and ranching — and each is just what the name implies. Salmon farming calls for containing and raising the smolts in "net-cages," and salmon ranching calls for releasing the smolts in the hope that they have become sufficiently imprinted with the aroma of that particular water to return there after feeding and growing one or more winters in the ocean.

Farming appears to be the more acceptable type of salmon aquaculture, simply because the fish are always contained in cages and thus under the farmers' control until marketed. With ranching, the salmon are released for ocean migrations and can range as they please. The salmon ranchers could even claim that their salmon were being harvested by others in the ocean and that they therefore

Net pens moored in Frenchman's Bay. Photograph courtesy of The Penobscot Salmon Company, Inc.

344 · Salmon Farming

have the right to harvest in the ocean what they had produced in the first place. As a consequence, fish of foreign origin would also be intercepted by these ranchers. All this obviously complicates and compounds international pressures already present with respect to harvesting in the ocean. In addition, not all the smolts planted at a certain point of departure will return to the doorstep of their release; there will be strays invading the rivers of other jurisdictions, perhaps bringing disease or populating river systems and interbreeding with native wild strains. Fortunately, salmon ranching has not taken hold in Canada or the United States, but it does exist in other countries, particularly Iceland.

We are fortunate in North America in that Canada and the United States possess the two finest locations for salmon farming in the whole North Atlantic. In Canada, it's the lower part of New Brunswick, in particular Passamaquoddy Bay. In the United States, just across the outflow of the St. Croix River (the international boundary with Canada), it's the Cobscook Bay area in Maine and the waters southwest along the coast as far perhaps as Rockland.

Canada and the United States share the following environmental advantages due to particular features of this habitat. First, tides of two to four knots per hour—with a rise and fall of at least sixteen and sometimes as much as twenty-eight feet—provide superlative flushing actions, removing fecal, urinary, and organic wastes from the area. Second, year-round water temperatures are ideal—not too cold in winter or too warm in summer. Third, the area has existing hatcheries nearby in northern Maine. All these factors mean that the Cobscook Bay region is already close to its capacity, but for the near future, there are other locations with good qualifications farther down the Maine coast.

A TYPICAL SALMON FARM
Just off Lubec, at the tip of Cobscook Bay, there is a typical salmon farm operating a total of thirty square-shaped net-cages set up in two large clusters called units. One unit is made up of eighteen

net-cages lashed together, each forty by forty feet; the other consists of twelve cages, each fifty by fifty feet. This is Treats Island Fisherys. It is run by Dan Marshall, who has an interest in the business, controlled by the Sea Farm Canada group of St. George, New Brunswick. Marshall estimates production for 1993 at some 700,000 pounds of salmon. Like most of the farms, this is not a fully integrated system. Treats Island uses both Penobscot River and St. John River strains — each as fine a quality stock as any in the North Atlantic community of salmon producers. He purchases the smolts from different hatcheries in the state, especially from Sea Farm Canada, the Canadian hatchery in St. George. Marshall is also doing research work, experimenting with the growing of halibut in net-cages.

He tells me that one of his greatest problems is continued attacks by that vicious predator of salmon, seals. They are numerous in the Passamaquoddy-Cobscook Bay area. Skillful hunters, they have developed the habit of "bagging" the nets — attacking from the bottom, battering the net up into a ball, and then sucking out the soft underparts, the entrails, of the salmon.

All farms have generally the same arrangement for hanging the cages and nets, which are on floating frames. There is a heavily weighted outside cage for predator control, the mesh of which is 5 ½ inches, usually of braided poly twine. Set about three feet inside these predator "baffle cages" is a second set of nets containing the salmon, with a mesh usually seven-eighths of an inch to two inches, the exact dimensions depending on the size of the smolts.

STATE OF THE ART

The Penobscot Salmon Company of Franklin, Maine, is just north of Ellsworth. It is owned by Hol Whitney, President, and David Miller, Vice President and Director, and has some fifteen full-time employees plus occasional part-time helpers.

It is a fully integrated system; that is, they own and operate the hatchery, processing plant, and net-cages. The hatchery and processing plant are in Franklin, where there will be a future capacity of 500,000 smolts. The net-cages are being relocated in 1993 to Johnson Cove, Eastport, Maine. It is a state-of-the-art operation.

The stocks being raised come from salmon eggs of either Penobscot River or St. John River stock. The net-cages are circular, about 235 feet in circumference, each with an initial capacity of 30,000 smolts — reduced to about 15,000 later on as they grow to marketable size. Miller plans on a future production of up to 4 million pounds of salmon from a total of forty-eight net-cages. It takes about eighteen months for the young fry in the hatchery to grow to smolt size, and another eighteen months to mature in the net-cages to a marketable size of about six to eight pounds — a total of roughly three years, as compared with five to six years for a wild salmon to reach the same weight.

The cost of one circular net-cage is about $50,000, including all the trappings such as buoys, anchors, metal chains, nets, and other gear, so this is not an inexpensive business. I recently asked Miller what his biggest problem was these days. His answer was, "foreign competition — marketing problems." He likened the whole situation to an unlevel playing field. The point is that foreigners are substantially subsidized by their governments, enabling price cutting to be the order of the day.

THE PRICE OF PROGRESS

The dramatic surge in aquaculture ventures in the North Atlantic since the early 1980s has added a whole new dimension to the conservation of salmon. Although salmon farming has already reduced the pressure on wild stocks, the other side of the coin is that it has also opened a Pandora's box of problems of domestic and international concern. Norway and Scotland, which were the first to rush into this business in a big way — without setting up protections for their native stocks against the impact of salmon farming — are now paying dearly for their oversights. Salmon farming can bring environmental degradation, the spreading of disease, and adverse interactions with wild stocks, such as the loss of genetic integrity.

All over the North Atlantic, salmon held in net-cages escape accidentally, averaging perhaps as much as 10 percent of production yearly. Violent storms, damage from heavy floating objects such as logs, and loss from loading and unloading the fish from net-cages are the principal culprits. These escapees can invade nearby rivers and intermingle and interbreed with wild salmon.

In August 1989, for instance, it was reported by David Shaw, under the pen name Schiehallion in the English *Trout and Salmon* magazine, that some 100,000 farmed salmon escaped from a farm in Loch Canon, in Wester Ross, Scotland, due to the ravages of a storm. At about the same time, about 200,000 salmon escaped at Loch Eribol and entered nearby rivers. Shaw went on to say that "farmed salmon are about in every river in the Highlands," and "a few have far more than 50% farmed to wild."

In Norway, increasing numbers of escaped farmed salmon have been observed in the home water fisheries and among the spawning population in many rivers. It was reported back in 1988 that at least 600,000 to 700,000 salmon escaped after net-cage breakage.

In the United States, we have had relatively few serious losses of this nature. The farmers are always concerned, however, about predators like the seals. Cormorants also do a lot of damage, diving into the net-cages, which are usually open at the top.

In general, it is accurate to say that Maine's salmon farming industry is different from that of the European nations such as Norway and Scotland. Environmental and disease problems in those regions are linked to a huge and crowded population of salmon farms, the likes of which Maine will never have, if for no other reason than the paucity of suitable farm sites. Our habitat and environmental conditions are exceptional in quality because of Maine's colder water temperatures, stronger currents, and generally clean water — conditions all beneficial to the growing of salmon.

In recent years, the entire industry in the North Atlantic has suffered from a severe oversupply due to the proliferation of salmon farms worldwide, particularly in Norway, Chile, the United

Kingdom, New Zealand, and, to a much smaller extent, Canada and the United States. This oversupply has caused stiffer competition and falling prices, forcing a number of farms out of business, particularly in Norway and the United Kingdom. This situation is in the process of adjustment and should work itself out, bringing higher prices and a more profitable industry for all concerned.

ENVIRONMENTAL IMPACTS

Most of a salmon's weight is put on in salt water, so the greatest impacts on the environment occur in the ocean habitat.

It has been estimated that a twenty-acre salmon farm produces as much organic waste as a town of ten thousand people. The salmon produce fecal and urinary organic wastes; unused feed pellets are also lost from the cages. Thus, too many sea cages crowded in close proximity can cause an area to exceed what is referred to as its "carrying capacity." In the state of Maine, the Department of Marine Resources carefully monitors a salmon farm's performance in this respect, and the agency has the authority to shut down the farms, which are under lease from the state.

Brian Rogers, President of Sea Farm Canada and of Sea Farm Lubec, is one of the most experienced sea-farm owners in the business. Here are some of the more pertinent points in his paper on the subject of pollution:

> Experience has taught us that successful fish farming is totally dependent on high quality waters. The fish's environment must be as clean as possible with oxygen levels inside the cages not only acceptable for survival but more importantly growth.
>
> The deposits from any farm are directly related to what the fish are eating, and its dispersal, or lack of it, is a direct function of the husbandry and tidal influence at the site. We know that cage sites with heavy fouling of their nets will have less dispersal of the waste than farms which change their nets regularly. Further, farmers that pay strict attention to their feeding practices will have less feed which passes directly through the cage and is not eaten at all, and consequently less wastage.

It is clear that many industry critics cloud an emotional objection to fish farming with concerns about pollution, antibiotics and genetic pollution of wild stocks. Yet it is not a simple issue of now you have pollution and now you don't, but rather it is totally controllable by the farmer and his or her practices.

The issue of antibiotics is also discussed too generally. From a purely business point of view, these treatments are very expensive. Thus, it's in a farmer's best interest both economically and practically to keep his fish as healthy as possible. However, when a farmer does have a bacterial or viral infection, the use of these antibiotics is strictly controlled both in their availability and application and also closely monitored by our insurers.

The seabeds of most of the areas where salmon farmers seek to lease sites are adjacent to or bordering prime habitats for lobsters, crabs, and shellfish. It is only natural that fishermen who have been fishing these waters for years, perhaps generations, are very concerned about the water being polluted to the detriment of their operations. They worry about contamination to nearby bottoms from salmon droppings, antibiotics used in the cages, and chemicals used in the fish food.

Most fish farms employ divers who regularly check the buildup of wastes under the cages. As a further protection against permanent damage to the seabed, many farms move their sites from time to time to other parts of their lease area, which may consist of several acres.

It is apparent that fish farmers in the State of Maine get high marks for avoiding excessive pollution of their sites and the surrounding waters. To be sure, it is in their best interests to do so, but it requires constant attention.

SCENIC DEGRADATION

Not every seaside community approves of salmon farming in the waters off its shores. One such place was Vinalhaven, Maine, an island reached by ferry from Rockland. The residents resoundingly rejected a 1988 proposal for a lease of twenty-five acres of sea bottom off the town. Vinalhaven has some 1,200 year-round residents and a summer population of nearly 6,000. It was principally the summer people who reacted with considerable emotion to the idea of having to look out from their waterfront homes and view a commercial operation of this type. Their view would be spoiled by a large cluster of pens and all the activity involved. A public hearing on the matter was held, with the voters rejecting the idea five to one. The company withdrew its proposal.

34

Interactions — Cultured and Wild Salmon

BACK IN THE 1980S, next to overexploitation in the oceans, the introduction and transfer of nonindigenous salmon and trout ("alien species," RASA calls them) posed the greatest threat to conservation and restoration of wild salmon in the Atlantic Ocean. This was a tremendously complex problem. In the United States, for instance, strains of Pacific salmon and steelhead trout were readily available to willing Fish and Game Commissioners of other states, who were eager to satisfy what they saw as the needs and desires of a growing body of anglers.

Another source of alien species in coastal rivers was the salmon farms. It has always been estimated that, as far as the whole industry was concerned, an average of 10 to 15 percent of the total number of salmon held in net-cages in any given area escape accidentally. These fish, not being imprinted to any particular river, would invade and populate rivers in the vicinity of the net-cages from which they escaped.

Little thought was given to the probable consequences of all these actions and accidents. Strict controls needed to be adopted to prevent damage to native wild salmon in the form of disease, loss of genetic integrity (through interbreeding), and decreased productivity (due to upsetting the ecological balance in the habitats).

DISEASE
A major concern of the salmon farmers is the possibility of the spreading of disease in the net-cages. The most common diseases

of Atlantic salmon are furunculosis, vibrosis, and kidney disease. All are bacterial and endemic in native stocks, and are subject to treatment with antibiotics, vaccines, and medications. Apparently, there are no diseases of Atlantic salmon to which humans are susceptible.

The interesting thing about this whole disease question is that biologists believe that, although the transmission of disease agents from farmed salmon to wild salmon in the rivers could occur, it is very unlikely. In fact, the opposite is more likely — that disease can be transmitted from wild salmon to farmed salmon. For instance, a number of years ago, when furunculosis was found in several salmon farms, the origin was traced to a federal hatchery in New Brunswick.

By far the most extensive and damaging outbreak of disease in Atlantic salmon took place in Norway, caused by *Gyrodactylus salaris*. Here is an excerpt from a letter of August 12, 1989, sent to me on this subject by Lars P. Hansen, a leading scientist of the Norwegian Directorate for Nature Management:

> The fluke attacks salmon parr and a very high proportion of those attacked subsequently die. It reproduces both sexually and asexually and the number of individual flukes in an area can rise very rapidly. The fluke is probably spreading from parr to parr. This parasite was first observed in 1976 in a river in northern Norway. A survey of parr from 212 Norwegian salmon rivers and streams in 1980–1984 revealed that 28 rivers were infected. The geographical distribution of the infected rivers is correlated with releases of young fish from infected hatcheries. Parr densities in these rivers declined seriously during these years and this has resulted in a great decrease in returning adults. The annual salmon loss is estimated to be 250–500 tons. There are strong indications that the parasite has only recently been introduced to Norwegian rivers, probably from another geographical area. The dramatic effect on the infected salmon stocks might be explained by a possible lack of resistance in the salmon parr to the parasite. The parasite has had no effect on brown trout and

the sea trout populations in the infected rivers have increased. Furthermore, salt water is a barrier for the parasite. At present there is no good solution to the *Gyrodactylus* problem. Otherwise, we have since learned that entire juvenile salmon populations have been virtually eliminated by *Gyrodactylus* in a few years. Catches of adult salmon in 18 infected rivers have dropped to zero, while in most other Norwegian rivers catches have been stable or increased. Rehabilitation methods involved burying fertilized salmon eggs in streams and complete eradication of fish populations with rotenone. About 8 small rivers have been reclaimed this way.

American salmon farms were importing substantial numbers of Norwegian Atlantic salmon eggs. The only comforting fact was that *Gyrodactylus* is not present in salmon eggs; it affects only the fish to which it is attached.

Internationally, there was practically no protection against diseased salmonids — fish or eggs — being transmitted from one country to another. In the United States, for example, the only federal regulation in effect was a Title 50 certification that the importations were free of two specified diseases — the "whirling disease" and a virus causing septicemia. Yet no less than eight specific diseases are recognized by federal and state biologists as possibly being dangerous to salmon. This Title 50 certification is signed in the country of origin by a designated official acceptable to the Secretary of the Interior as being qualified in fish pathology, or in the United States by a qualified pathologist designated by the Secretary of the Interior.

Domestically, importations and transfers from one state to another also lack adequate controls. As one State Fish and Game Commissioner told me recently: "Most states have the authority, in their overall mandates, to control importations, both foreign and domestic, with respect to disease, but in the real world, the exercise of that authority is quite another matter. Would the disciplinary action hold up in court?"

LOSS OF GENETIC INTEGRITY

Perhaps the greatest danger in breeding salmon through aquaculture is the indiscriminate crossbreeding of different river stocks from different sources. In the 1980s, fish farmers were scouring domestic and international markets for brood stocks, all of which could involve the scrambling of gene pools that may have taken thousands of years to evolve.

The Norwegian government estimated that an average of 12 percent of fish in sea cages escape. In light of these developments, Norwegian authorities took steps to protect natural salmon stocks. The Norwegian Salmon Act was revised, providing a legal basis for management of salmon at a given population level. No further importation of live salmon would be permitted.

A salmon gene bank of frozen sperm was started, containing genes from a number of threatened Norwegian stocks. On this subject, Lars Hansen was quoted as saying, "Even farmers can benefit from returning to nature to draw on hereditary features that have more or less been lost in the process of changing Atlantic salmon into farm animals."

Thus there was growing concern in Norway about the extinction of local indigenous salmon stocks and the erosion of genetic resources. Scientists began monitoring the occurrence of reared (that is, hatchery-bred) fish, principally fish-farm escapees, in sixty-two river systems. Approximately 20 percent of the returning adult fish were found to be of reared origin, and in some rivers it was as high as 80 percent. There was circumstantial evidence that such fish could breed, meaning that interbreeding between wild and farmed stocks was likely.

In Canada, in the 1989 autumn issue of *The Atlantic Salmon Journal*, John M. Anderson, Vice President, Operations, Atlantic Salmon Federation, had this to say on this whole subject:

> There is good evidence supporting the view that each river in which Atlantic salmon reside contains genetically distinct stocks of fish. In other words, the salmon in these rivers have, through

natural evolution, adapted to these rivers by subtle genetic means. Escaped, aquacultured salmon, with a [different] genetic heritage...could mate with local salmon and thereby pass on traits not [suitable] for survival...in [a] wild environment....

There is almost no information on the nature of the interactions these fish have with local, wild stocks.... After several generations of selective breeding for traits related to sea-cage life, it is possible that domesticated, aquacultured salmon would not be able to compete successfully with local salmon in the wild....

A more certain way of ensuring that no genetic consequences ensue from the interactions of escaped and wild salmon would be to insist on the use of sterile salmon for farming. Resolving the issue of the biological impact of salmon sea-cage escapees is of paramount importance. The scientific community has its work cut out for it.

It is also important to maintain the ecological balance and productivity of salmon rivers. The tremendous increase in fish-farmed stocks means hundreds of thousands of excess parr and smolts being sold for restocking. Who is to ensure that the environmental conditions for a restocking exercise are satisfactory? For instance, is there enough food available to ensure the survival of both the new and the indigenous stock? The little scientific literature that does exist on this subject indicates, for instance, that Cohos and Chinooks, which spawn later than Atlantics, could disrupt Atlantic salmon spawning beds.

Finally, in February 1990, we got positive proof that escaped farm salmon do indeed interbreed with native wild strains. Here are excerpts from a report entitled "Study of the Behaviour in Rivers of Wild Salmon and Salmon of Farmed Origin" by John Webb, Fishery Biologist of the Atlantic Salmon Trust, England:

Between the end of October and the middle of December 1989, a detailed study of the riverine behaviour of wild and farmed adult salmon in the River Polla in northwest Sutherland was made. The study relied on both the direct observation and telemetric monitoring of the behaviour of radio-tagged and conventionally Floy-tagged fish together with periodic sampling of groups of fish by netting and electrofishing various areas of the river.

Farmed and wild fish could be distinguished by their appearance, farmed fish tending to have deformed fins. Many of the identified cases were subject to subsequent confirmatory analysis in the laboratory by testing samples of gonad and muscle tissue for the presence of canthaxanthin, which indicates that the fish is probably of farmed origin.

Whilst the wild fish distributed themselves throughout the length of the river system the farmed fish tended to be more restricted in their distribution. The greatest numbers of farmed fish at spawning were within the lower two kilometres of the river. All of the farmed fish that were inspected were found to be sexually mature. Some randomly selected farmed fish were crossed artificially and the eggs held in a hatchery until eyeing. All the crosses made proved to be fertile.

Farmed fish of both sexes were observed to spawn. Most of the farmed females spawned in the lower reaches of the main river. In some of these areas, farmed females cut redds on areas of gravel that had been previously used by wild fish. Farmed and wild fish were observed to cross.

A thorough electrofishing survey of the larger holding pools in the lower reaches of the river was carried out in mid-December. All the farmed and wild fish captured during this operation were in a spent condition.

CANADA AND THE UNITED STATES COOPERATE

The U.S. Commissioners to NASCO, working with their opposite numbers in Canada at the June 1986 meeting of the North American Commission of NASCO, set up a Bilateral Scientific Working Group to study and make recommendations on this whole subject. The group reviewed management structures currently in place, internationally as well as within Canada and the United States, that protected against adverse effects from salmonid introductions and transfers.

As a result of the working group study, the North American Commission at its annual meeting in June 1987 adopted a Common Policy on the "Introduction and Transfer of Nonindigenous Species of Salmonids." The Policy was to "encourage that introductions and transfers of salmonids to the rivers and coastal waters of eastern North America occur only if the risk of adverse effect on fish health, genetic integrity and/or productivity of wild Atlantic salmon stocks is minimal and in accordance with standards established within the North American Commission."

This policy also encouraged the federal, provincial, and state agencies of the members of the North American Commission to adhere to the following action plan:

• Submit to the commission, in a timely fashion, proposals for introductions and transfers to be reviewed for potential adverse impacts on Atlantic salmon populations.

• Discouarge the rearing and prevent the release of diseased fish.

• Eradicate fish disease wherever practicable.

• Prevent the introduction or transfer of fish infected with disease agents that may have genetic or ecological impact.

• Use local-origin salmonid stocks in aquaculture and restoration.

• Protect selected wild stocks from hybridization with hatchery-cultured fish or foreign stock and from overfishing, thus ensuring the fullest possible protection of the genetic integrity of such stocks.

• Where necessary, develop legislative authority and regulations to allow the control and possible eradication of fish diseases and to control the introduction and transfer of fish that may adversely affect the genetic integrity and/or productivity of Atlantic salmon stocks.

It is important to note that the protocols of the action plan were not cast in concrete; they were, and should be, dynamic, not static. The objective was to encourage the states to adopt early-warning systems, alerting all concerned to any possible problems. Applications for permits to operate could then be processed and handled on a case-by-case basis.

RASA INVOLVEMENT
RASA was no stranger to these troubled waters. In 1975, after a two-year struggle, we had been able to persuade Robert M. White, Administrator of the National Oceanic and Atmospheric Administration (Department of Commerce) to drop a proposal to stock the waters of New England with one million Coho (Pacific) salmon yearly for three years. Two states, however, New Hampshire and Massachusetts, went off on their own and continued, without any important success, to persist in trying to establish different species of Pacific salmon.

RASA supported the NASCO policy and action plan and remained centrally involved in the development of it. We urged private-sector organizations and individuals to join us in a coordinated and cooperative effort to help governmental agencies solve problems associated with the introduction of alien species.

RASA believed that one possible means of alleviating the whole situation would be "to build a fence around New England," prohibiting the importation or exportation of wild Atlantic salmon stocks in any form, either domestically or internationally. Following Norway's example, we could establish a gene bank from the presently excellent U.S. strains. We discussed this with officials of the U.S. Fish and Wildlife Service. A basic question, of course, was whether sufficient stocks could be made available to fish farmers for establishing their own brood stocks, after federal and state requirements for the U.S. restoration program had been satisfied. The initial reaction was that such might be possible within five to ten years.

DOMESTIC IMPLEMENTATION
Under the NASCO common policy and action plan, an embargo was recommended on all transfers of salmonids from west of the

continental divide in North America and from Asia to prevent the introduction of fish diseases from those areas to eastern North America.

This is where we ran into serious trouble with the Maine Sea Run Atlantic Salmon Commission, which sets statewide policy on Atlantic salmon matters. In a letter to me of November 10, 1987, David Locke, Superintendent of Hatcheries, stated, "embargoes such as proposed are not the solution to disease control. Tough importation requirements that are enforced such as is currently done in Maine, and thorough searches for safer alternative sources make embargoes unnecessary." And in a letter of January 5, 1988, to my fellow U.S. Commissoner Allen Peterson, William Vail, Commissioner of the Maine Department of Inland Fisheries and Wildlife, had this to say: "The rapidly expanding aquaculture industry has created a demand for salmonid seed stock that cannot be fulfilled at the present time with stocks of local origin. Consequently, it will be necessary to allow the transfer of salmon eggs from nonindigenous sources until sufficient local supplies of disease-free stock are available. The fish health status of each source will be carefully reviewed before importations are permitted, but the risks of adverse genetics impacts may not be fully considered."

There we had it — the beginning of a serious difference of opinion between NASCO and the State of Maine on this subject. At the time, I recognized no fewer than four distinctly different influences that may have governed the state's approach to the problem.

First, there was the age-old question of quantity versus quality. The state was not ready to delay approval of licenses until such time as hatchery supplies of local stock might become available, which could take as long as five to ten years.

Second, there were the socioeconomic aspects of the problem. Washington County, Maine, in which most of the aquaculture ventures would be located, for years had been considered one of the poorest counties in the United States, with high rates of unemployment. Fish farming ventures and their related pursuing power would help alleviate this situation.

Third, here was a prime example of the age-old argument of states' rights versus those of the federal government. State O' Mainers can be a proud and stubborn people; they simply don't relish being told how to conduct their affairs.

Fourth, the plain fact was that the specialists responsible for administering all aspects of aquaculture management were experienced, knowledgeable, and careful — people like David Locke, and Lew Flagg and Ken Honey of the Division of Marine Resources. They knew and appreciated the consequences that would result if they let down the bars on rigid screening of applicants for licenses and rigid inspection practices.

But we in NASCO had to be concerned with the overall national problem of what might happen under future state administrators — officials who were perhaps less competent and commited. Allen Peterson and I met with certain members of the Maine Sea Run Salmon Commission on November 30, 1987, at which time Commissioner Bill Vail informed us of Maine's concerns about provisions of the NASCO common policy.

The situation continued with no resolution for some time. In 1989, Allen Peterson had to point out what appeared to be serious infractions of the intent of the policy. He informed William Brennan, Commissioner of the Maine Department of Marine Resources, in a letter of May 26, 1989, that it had been documented in reports to our scientific working group that "entities in the State of Maine have imported over 2.5 million Atlantic salmon eggs from European and Icelandic sources."

Vail responded in a letter of June 5, 1989, in which he stated that adequate numbers of eggs certified as free of disease had not been available in 1987 or early 1988 from either U.S. or New Brunswick sources, so "one importation was made in December 1988 from a source in Scotland that meets our fish health requirements." Vail again pointed. out that Maine's concerns about the provisions of the policy had been conveyed at the November 1987 meeting. He went on to say, "we had also urged NASCO and its subgroups to identify any deleterious genetic stocks and to develop guidelines to prevent introductions that could produce undesirable impacts upon the genetic variability of existing salmon stocks in this area." His letter closed by reiterating that "there will be times when our programs and local needs may conflict with your ideas."

Allen Peterson, in a reply of June 8, 1989, quite aptly pointed out that the "role of the U.S. Commissioners is to represent the interests of the United States in the international management of salmon. To do our job effectively we need to have factual information. We cannot and will not deal with allegations in NASCO nor will we ever make judgments on any domestic issues based on allegations."

NASCO ADDRESSES GENETIC PROTOCOLS

At its 1989 annual meeting, the Council of NASCO accepted the draft report by the Subgroup on Genetics of the Scientific Working Group entitled "Genetic Protocols for the Maintenance of Genetic Variance in Atlantic salmon." Among the points covered were the following:

• Transfers or introductions of Atlantic salmon stocks or strains from any continent to North America are not recommended, because the greatest genetic differences are found between North American and European stocks. The best planting results are obtained when using local stocks.

• Introductions for purposes of enhancement are a potential threat to the integrity of wild stocks.

• The potential negative impact of aquaculture escapees on wild stocks is of great concern. Therefore, fish farms should be encouraged to use domestic strains derived from local stocks where available. Where not available, they should be developed from an appropriate nearby stock.

• Sterilization techniques hold promise for aquaculture stocks and for reducing the genetic risks they pose to wild stocks.

• In hatchery management, cultured brood stocks held in captivity for several generations and used for aquaculture should not be used for wild fish management. Single use of progeny derived from annual egg collections from wild fish is the preferred strategy.

• Fishery resources agencies should consider the use of gene banks for stocks of Atlantic salmon already highly depleted as a result of overharvest and/or habitat loss.

1990 NORWAY MEETING ON INTERACTIONS

A very important meeting on the subject of interactions between cultured and wild stocks was held in Loen, Norway, April 23–26, 1990. It was attended by scientists and managers from nearly all North Atlantic nations with salmon interests. Here is part of a published summary of the more important conclusions reached at the meeting:

> There are still gaps in our knowledge of the impacts of the genetic, disease and environmental interactions between wild and farmed salmon. Research will take many years to complete and if the international community awaits the firm conclusion of this work the changes, which are potentially irreversible, will have already taken place. On the evidence available to date it should be assumed that there is a real risk to the native salmon until it is proven that there is no such risk.
>
> There is evidence that fish produced in hatcheries may show marked changes in fitness. Interactions can therefore be damaging to the wild stocks and one solution might be to make the cultured salmon unfit [i.e., sterile] for survival to breed in the wild. . . .
>
> The conditions of farming can favour the outbreak of disease and the transmission of pathogens, increasing the risk of infections being passed between wild and cultured fish. Good husbandry and health management of farmed fish are therefore of great importance, and appropriate controls are desirable. There is full support for investigations on the transmission of diseases and parasites between wild and cultured stocks. A major goal should be control of disease in salmon farms.
>
> The development of codes of practice used by the farming industry, which would include measures to minimize

escapes...is to be encouraged. For example, zones free of aquaculture could be established near stocks which are designated for conservation reasons, or are threatened.

ZONING OF RIVER SYSTEMS

Finally, in 1991, the U.S. commissioners to NASCO and the state of Maine were able to arrive at a satisfactory resolution of their different approaches to the problem of introductions and transfers.

At the 1992 annual meeting of the North American Commission of NASCO, the Scientific Working Group presented its Draft Protocols for the Introduction and Transfer of Salmonids into the North American Commission Area. These were approved by NASCO. The objectives of the protocols are:

1. To minimize the introduction and spread of infectious disease agents (fish health);

2. To prevent the reduction in genetic variance and prevent the introduction of nonadaptive genes to wild Atlantic salmon populations (genetics); and

3. To minimize the intra- and interspecies impacts of introductions and transfers on Atlantic salmon stocks (ecology).

The Report on Protocols was divided into four parts, the first of which introduced a zoning concept. Three zones were designated based on the degree of degradation or manipulation that had occurred on the wild Atlantic salmon populations. (See the map on page 364 of eastern Canada and the northeastern United States, showing the three zones proposed for implementation of the Protocols.)

Description of Zones

Zone I. Zone I includes Northern Quebec, Labrador, Newfoundland (west coast), and Anticosti Island. Rivers are classified primarily as class I. They are pristine rivers with no significant man-made habitat alterations, no history of transfers of fish into the watersheds, and no fish-rearing operations in the watershed.

Zone II. Zone II includes Quebec rivers flowing into the Gulf of St. Lawrence south of Pointe des Monts, the Gaspé region of

SALMON AQUACULTURE - U.S./CANADIAN ZONES

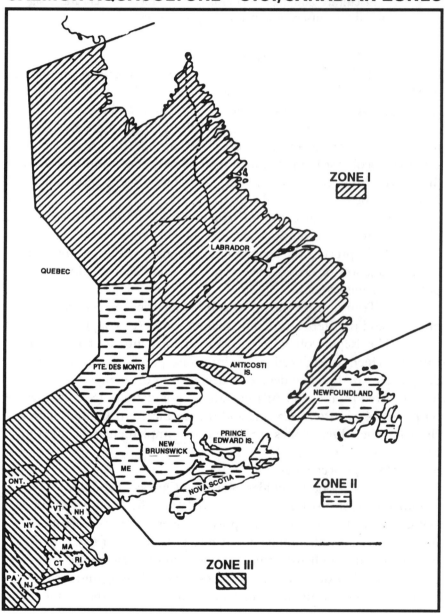

Quebec, Magdalen Islands, Prince Edward Island, New Brunswick, Nova Scotia, Newfoundland (except the west coast), St. Pierre and Miquelon Islands, and the state of Maine east of Rockland. Rivers are classified primarily as class II watersheds in which one or more of the following conditions occur: the habitat has been altered, nonindigenous wild or hatchery-reared Atlantic salmon have been released, or aquaculture has been conducted in marine cage culture. Other species may be present in land-based facilities.

Zone III. Zone III includes Lake Ontario, southern Quebec rivers draining to the St. Lawrence River, the State of Maine west of Rockland, New Hampshire, New York, Connecticut, Massachusetts, New Jersey, Rhode Island, and Vermont. Rivers are classified primarily as class III watersheds in which habitats have been altered, fish communities are destabilized, or exotic species are present.

Protocols Applicable to All Three Zones*

1. Reproductively viable Atlantic salmon of European origin (strain), including Iceland origin, are not to be released or used in aquaculture in the North American Commission Area.

2. No live salmonid fishes, fertilized eggs, gametes (reproductive cells), or fish products are to be imported from infectious hematopoietic necrosis (IHN) virus enzootic areas, unless sources have an acceptable history of disease testing demonstrating the absence of IHN. IHN-infected areas currently include the states of Washington, Oregon, Idaho, California, and Alaska and British Columbia.

3. Prior to any transfers of eggs, juveniles, or brood stock, a minimum of three health inspections of the donor facility will be undertaken during the two-year period immediately preceding the transfer, and the inspections must reveal no evidence of either emergency or restricted fish pathogens in the donor population.

---

* There are additional and voluminous protocols applying to each of the three zones. These are contained in Report NAC (92) 19 and may be obtained from the Secccretary, NASCO, 11 Rutland Square, Edinburgh, EH1 2AS Scotland, U.K.

4. Prior to any movement of non-native fishes into a river system or rearing site inhabited by Atlantic salmon, the agency with jurisdiction will review and evaluate fully the potential for inter-species competition that would adversely affect the productivity of wild Atlantic salmon populations. Such evaluations should be undertaken, as far as possible, using information on the river in which the introduction is to occur and from similar situations.

5. Hatchery-rearing programs to support the introduction, reestablishment, rehabilitation, and enhancement of Atlantic salmon should try to comply with the following measures:

a. Use only progeny from wild stocks.

b. Derive brood stock from all phenotype age groups and the entire run of a donor population.

c. Avoid selection of the "best" fish during the hatchery-rearing period.

d. During spawning, make only single-pair matings from a brood stock population of no fewer than one hundred parents.

Effective implementation of these protocols, developed through the international cooperation of NASCO, will be possible only when affected user groups in Canada and the United States have been fully informed and understand that these measures are necessary to protect all wild salmon stocks. In support of such an effort, it is desirable to secure the support and backing not only of the Canadian provinces, the New England states, and New York State but also of the respective federal governments. Toward this end, early in 1993, the U.S. Commissioners and agencies of the federal government began drafting implementing legislation for federal and congressional approval.

RASA INVOLVEMENT

From the beginning, RASA has been actively involved in support of the sea farming of Atlantic salmon, for the principal reason that it will take the pressure off the overexploited wild stocks. Our hope was that the extensive work being done in Canada and the United States would be understood for what it was intended to be — a protection not only for the superior strains of Atlantic salmon but also for the burgeoning salmon-farming industry. It has never been our intention, nor in our interest, to denigrate the serious and industrious commitment of the community of fish farmers. The fish farmers themselves have more to gain from the protocol protections than do governmental agencies. If, for instance, a fish farmer has a serious fish-kill due to disease, he may go out of business. Federal, provincial, and state governments would not.

We wanted to do something positive and useful by spreading and, if possible, demonstrating the message that, with respect to introductions and transfers of nonindigenous salmonids, it was not sufficient simply to protect against disease and loss of productivity due to competition in the habitat. Genetic calculations, cautious thought, and a mind toward the future are even more serious considerations if we are to restore to abundance the wild Atlantic salmon as we have come to know it.

The international situation with respect to salmon farming is desperate. We have only to reflect on what has happened in Norway, Scotland, and Ireland to realize that the interactions between cultured and wild fish can be devastating. In those countries, hundreds of thousands of farmed salmon have escaped from their cages and invaded rivers populated by wild salmon, with the certain result being a spread of disease and loss of genetic integrity. Only the imposition and enforcement of adequate controls on both sides of the Atlantic can prevent these scourges from becoming a greater threat to restoring salmon runs than indiscriminate netting in the ocean.

VIII

WILD SALMON — THE FUTURE

35

Leadership by Example

THE BRITISH

AROUND THE MIDDLE of the twentieth century, it was the British who refined the management of their rivers into the state of the art. Their standards and regulations established models that still command the respect and attention of those governmental ministers and private owners who hope to build their salmon fisheries into renewable resources of great recreational value. This was what was needed at the time — skills, particularly of a scientific nature, that would ensure the productivity of the rivers.

Along with this, the British wrote the book on fly-fishing for salmon. Their precepts are still followed in salmon rivers all over the North Atlantic as well as in other parts of the world. It was also these pioneers who laid the foundations upon which organizations and governments would build their opposition to overexploitation of salmon in the ocean. We owe the British a deep debt of gratitude for these traditions that are now available to all.

Soon after World War II, however, new and sophisticated techniques of fishing the oceans were developed, requiring completely different approaches to the problems — principally geopolitical in nature — arising out of steeply increased interceptions of salmon on ocean migrations. The British at that particular time — still suffering all kinds of losses inflicted on the nation during the war — were understandably neither equipped nor poised to embark on this kind of mission.

THE AMERICANS

Beginning around 1968, certain individuals and organizations in the United States became convinced that timely action was necessary if

our burgeoning Atlantic salmon program was to survive the incess-
ant pounding by commercial netting interests in the northwest
Atlantic Ocean. The Americans could unfurl the banner more
readily than any other producing nation simply because we had had
to start from scratch to rebuild a resource that we had destroyed. We
Americans had no excess baggage such as being weighed down by
the political power of commercial salmon fishermen. It also took an
enthusiasm and determination that are the special assets of Yankees
who feel unjustly treated. Fortunately, we made the right moves.

Americans led the crusade to bring an end to the overkill of
salmon on the high seas by driftnetting in the northwest Atlantic.
Next, Americans designed and led the negotiating effort to produce
an international institutional arrangement — the salmon treaty — that
could open the doors of rational management through reductions in
the take of interceptory fisheries. All this made a more universal
protection of the species on ocean migrations possible — a prerequi-
site to enhancement in the rivers. Americans were to dominate the
international diplomatic scene on salmon for some twenty years — a
generation.

But now, as we look ahead, there is the need for a sober assessment of whether the United States still possesses the attributes
that caused and enabled it to coordinate the efforts of the world
Atlantic salmon communities. Sad to say, it is obvious that it does
not. The United States is wanting today in the disposition, aptitude,
and capacity to continue in the role of leader in this effort. This is
due to a complex set of circumstances. The basic problem today is
that in recent years conservation of the wild strains of Atlantic
salmon were no longer a major concern of federal agencies. Thus,
these salmon have been subjected to a kind of double whammy.
The State Department permitted the international conservation effort on behalf of wild salmon to slip way down on the priority list of
fisheries problems. The wild Atlantic salmon has also lost its ranking position with the Fish and Wildlife Service of the Department
of the Interior; it was the hatchery-bred Atlantic salmon — the
"prefabs" — that drew its attention.

Perhaps, under a more conservation-oriented administration in 1993, this inattention can be reversed.

As if these negatives were not enough to cope with, the past ten years have brought into being a new and insidious influence — the all-powerful political action committees (PACs), probably the most effective lobbying force of all time. Those organizations that contribute the most to congressional candidates are going to get the most favorable treatment at the hands of legislators and others. The Atlantic salmon interests do not have that kind of money. And even if they did, they would not spend it this way — thank goodness. The American system of democracy is being adulterated. So where and how do we enlist the aid of government?

There is another area in which the salmon restoration effort is deficient — and badly so: the commitment of the private sector. It is accurate to say that the big, important moves over the years — particularly in the international arena — have usually been initiated, and then actively supported, by the salmon conservation organizations. But we no longer have the leaders — intelligent, capable, hard-working individuals who can and will devote their efforts to building meaningful, productive, and enduring relationships at the highest levels of government.

Compare the shortage of qualified movers today with the situation in earlier years. Chapter 11 of this book, for instance, demonstrates that it was possible to get fourteen of the most prominent conservation organizations in the United States involved in a special mission — and to stay involved for some fifteen years. Not so these days. We can count on the fingers of one hand the number of organizations whose leaders are ready and capable of undertaking top-level direction of salmon missions.

Where are these men and women now in their prime who should have been coming along to take over from us, the seniors and the elderly? Unfortunately, they were summoned by a more persuasive influence, Mammon, that false god of riches and avarice — the "I've got to make a million before I'm thirty" syndrome.

We do know that the rising generation of young men and

women today have expressed a greater interest in environmental matters than did their immediate predecessors. But it appears that these new hopefuls are without direction as yet. The groups and organizations that do exist appear to be splintered and without specific goals. Perhaps that's our fault. Yet we fervently hope that our future leaders will decide to throw in their lot in the service of environmental affairs. Our job now is to get involved in the training and encouragement of these future leaders. To be sure, there's no big money to be made in conservation work, but those of us who have had the experience of helping the salmon have found it engrossing—sometimes frustrating, sometimes exciting—and in the end very rewarding.

The realities of the situation demand that leadership in Atlantic salmon affairs now pass to that nation best equipped to show the way internationally. The Americans can step aside for the time being. We have a lot of work to do at home before the train will be on the tracks again, and this is where our efforts should now be directed. But there should be no misunderstanding. There is no intention of giving up the struggle—that's not the American way. We will continue to support the all-important work in the area of ocean affairs of salmon and, it is hoped, be back in the fray before too long.

THE CANADIANS

Who are the people to assume the mantle of protection for Salar? We must look to a society that has a substantial resource of wild salmon and a proven record of well-reasoned management under the trying socioeconomic conditions that are inflicted on fisheries managers. In particular, the call should go out to a nation that has chosen to undertake a program of enhancement of this renewable fisheries resource whose value is second to none; a nation that has given evidence of skillful handling of its salmon affairs, including the courage to do away with the age-old shibboleth of the rights of citizens to exploit salmon on their front doorstep. Here, the finger points only in one direction: to Canada.

Let us look at the characteristics that nature has bestowed on Canada. These gifts are of the highest quality. First, the geographical locations of nearly all the salmon rivers are positioned to avoid the excessive fishing pressures associated with densely populated metropolitan areas, a handicap that can cause untold regulatory problems. Next, the topography of nearly all these rivers is such that there are very few steep gradients. The rivers do not descend from their sources by such degrees of slope as to call for the building of locks for transportation; nor do they encourage the building of dams for the development of hydroelectric plants, which in turn would have required the construction of fish-passage facilities, with concomitant upstream and downstream fish mortalities. Finally, the climate and, in particular, the water temperatures in eastern Canada are normally conducive to a healthy existence for free-living salmon, a cold-water species.

Canada's management of its salmon resource has been exemplary; that is well known. But certainly of greater importance is the fact that Canada has been the agent of change—a sea change of historical significance. The transition from a dying commercial Atlantic salmon fishing industry to the more rational and productive pursuit of salmon as a gamefish is at hand. It will not be easy—building for the future through fundamental change never is. Careful planning at the start should provide opportunities for growth down the road, easing the transition for those adversely affected. Also of great importance is the fact that a successful program of change will act as a spur for recalcitrant nations. This is the collateral challenge to Canada.

Yet there are additional, and conclusive, qualifications necessary to the assumption of leadership. Here the old maxim applies: Is Canada ready, willing, and able? From all the above, we know that Canada certainly is able. What about the other two?

As to readiness, Canada appears well poised to show the way. In fact, Canada is already doing so in some important areas. Canadian scientists are a knowledgeable lot, continually searching for new answers to explain why salmon act the way they do in the ocean and rivers. These scientists make important contributions to the many seminars and symposiums held in various parts of the salmon world. Of the private-sector groups in Canada, the Atlantic Salmon Federation is the acknowledged leader, coordinating the efforts of the many regional and local salmon clubs into an effective medium for expressing concerns and making recommendations to government about programs and projects designed to improve the lot of the fish. The Miramichi Salmon Association is an old-timer in the business of supporting sound conservation, and there are many other clubs and organizations committed to the salmon effort.

Is Canada willing to assume the extra burden of international leadership? This would involve a full realization that the salmon, including those of Canadian origin, must be made safe all over the North Atlantic before it is certain that they will be able to return in sufficient numbers to their rivers of origin and renew the life cycle. We do have some reservations here, in the light of past history. Back in January 1972, when we were forcing the Danes to give up the high seas fishery off West Greenland, the Canadians exhibited a lack of resolve by pulling out of the negotiations at the last moment. And throughout the four long years leading up to the signing of the Atlantic salmon treaty — 1979 through 1983 — the Canadians continually exhibited a recalcitrance and indecisiveness that inhibited the whole treaty-making process. At one point, when they boycotted the negotiations, they nearly ruined the chances of securing a salmon treaty. Are these shortcomings a fundamental characteristic of their whole approach and posture in foreign relations, ones that are endemic to the Canadian body politic?

This whole situation brings to mind an observation attributed to a prominent Canadian author, Mavis Gallant. She is reported to have commented, "Canada is a nation in search of an identity." This is an expression of considerable wisdom, and it may be as good an answer as any to the questions posed above.

At any rate, Canada does appear to have an identity today when it comes to its Atlantic salmon resource. Its action in 1992 in calling for a moratorium on commercial netting off Newfoundland

and the offer of permanent Buy-Outs to the Newfoundland and Labrador fishermen took considerable courage, considering the political factors involved. In setting this example, Canada evinced the qualities of leadership. Yet maintaining and strengthening this Atlantic salmon identity in Canada will require continuing attention at the highest levels of government. Leadership in developing universal, sustained moves to save these free-living fish requires nurturing—it does not spring up full-blown overnight.

What is needed now is for Canada to continue to exhibit a clarity and consistency of purpose and action in the international affairs of the North Atlantic salmon community of nations.

Can—and will—Canada deliver under such exacting conditions? We hope so, but the answer is not yet clear. We'll just have to see how it all plays out over the next few years.

Of one thing we are certain: It is that—figuratively speaking—the future well-being of this salmon resource beckons to our good neighbor to the north as never before.

36

Atlantic Salmon in the Global Environment

SUPPOSE ONE WERE standing before a large globe of the world, rotating it slowly, and all the while musing on the sweeping changes that have come over this planet of ours, especially during the last half of the twentieth century. These changes have necessitated a redrawing of the boundaries of many nations. Out of the former USSR, for instance, have come fifteen new countries. Religious, tribal, and cultural pressures have caused ethnic conflicts and the springing up of nations such as Rwanda and Swaziland in Africa and others elsewhere.

Tremendous changes have also occurred in the global environment. The biosphere — all forms of life and everything that supports life on land or in the ocean — has been altered, and not for the better. The mind searches for explanations, and out of this comes the impulse to characterize the effect of these environmental changes with one word: depletion.

Continents and oceans, forests and lakes, fields and ponds, rivers and streams, air and minerals — all depleted in one way or another. It is the same with creatures of all kinds — depleted through overexploitation or loss of the particular qualities and characteristics that made them unique. Some were driven the whole way — to extinction. Others still hang on, exhausted, against great odds. Set apart, of course, is that paragon of creation — Man, euphemistically dubbed "sapiens," the wise one. We go the other way — overpopulating — thus becoming the agent for this very same depletion that is the cause of our discontent and frustration.

WORLD CATCH OF ATLANTIC SALMON IN HOME WATERS 1967-1992

(Excluding Greenland and Faroese Fisheries)

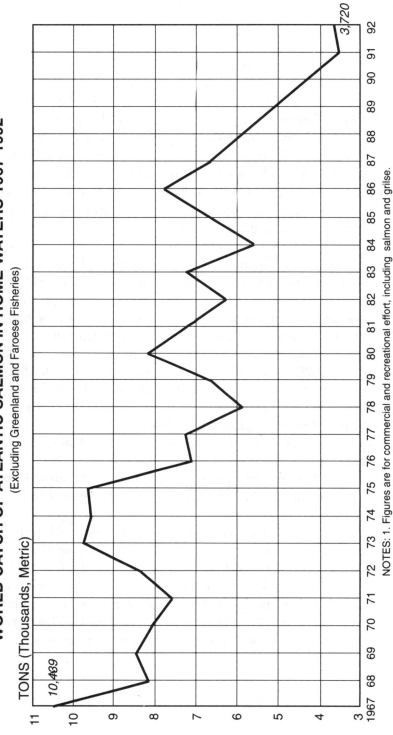

TONS (Thousands, Metric)

10,489

3,720

NOTES: 1. Figures are for commercial and recreational effort, including salmon and grilse.
2. Figures do *not* include production by aquaculture (salmon farming or ranching).

SOURCE: Chart prepared by RASA (Restoration of Atlantic Salmon in America, Inc.), P.O. Box 311, Dublin, N.H. 03444, USA.
Figures compiled by ICES (International Council for Exploration of the Seas), FAO, United Nations

The contemplation of all this is sobering and frightening. A sense of moral indignation comes over us as we watch many of our precious natural and self-renewing resources become threatened, then endangered, and ultimately go down the drain.

Today some enlightened governments are aware of these threats and take novel and decisive actions to protect species that are either peripherally or actually endangered. In many nations of Africa, for instance, citizens are forbidden to hunt rhinos and elephants, even though these animals are encroaching on — and ravaging — the agricultural lands that the natives work.

And what about that particular creature of which we are speaking — the Atlantic salmon? It is also depleted, and badly so. It is obvious that the sea of troubles inflicted on this wild fish is but a microcosm of what has been visited on many other creatures. The question of utmost importance now is, how many opportunities will we have to save Salar from ultimate exhaustion as a resource of any aesthetic or practical value, if not from absolute extinction?

With many other species, we have had such opportunities, with differing degrees of success and failure. Let us look at the destinies of a few examples of those free-living beings whose fates can be traced to overexploitation or loss of habitat:

- Some we lost completely — the dodos, the passenger pigeons.

- Some are now at the precipice — the snow leopards, the cheetahs, the gorillas, the giant pandas, the spotted owls. Will they go over?

- Some were approaching the precipice and we pulled them back — the whales, the polar bears, the whooping cranes. Yet even now they cannot and should not be considered safe.

- Some were approaching this same precipice and were pulled back to the point where they can now be considered saved and protected — the grizzly bear, the bald eagle. These are the success stories — proof that it can be done if we have the will.

It serves no useful purpose here to speculate on which particular category the wild Atlantic salmon fits into these days — approaching the precipice or at the precipice. Of one thing we are certain: It cannot be said that they are saved. Using past history as the criterion, we would all have to agree that if we let down our defenses, the innate greed of Man would once again be in the ascendancy. So how do we go about ensuring the permanent protection of these fish from exploitation in the ocean?

Let us face up to it — the broad picture. We are at the point of no return.

It is no longer a matter of ethics, such as whether or not this group or that group has the right to fish for salmon in the ocean. It is simply a question of whether or not the North Atlantic nations are determined that this species must be returned to its former abundance. If the answer is in the affirmative — and we believe it will be, then it should be obvious to all that no one should fish for salmon in the Atlantic Ocean.

If we are to achieve this objective, RASA recognizes full well that there is a pressing need for sterner self-denial to be embraced by all, under an entirely new perspective, discipline, and commitment. And in order to strengthen our resolve in this regard, we have come to realize that there is what we call "The Moral Imperative" involved in such a challenging enterprise.

Here we give expression to it, by justifying it and defining it.

THE MORAL IMPERATIVE OF ATLANTIC SALMON RESTORATION

The one distinguishable and measurable factor — among others less easily identified — in the reducing Atlantic salmon stocks to dangerously low levels is the practice of commercial fishing in the ocean for this species. Yet such exploitation is unscientific. Discrete stocks intermingle in the ocean, and no gear, no science known to man, can separate them out. Thus, this fishing can take indiscriminately from the very river stocks requiring special attention. It is also wasteful because fish are taken before they attain full growth and netting often injures or kills fish without capturing them.

Thus prudence requires that salmon migrating to, and from, and on their feeding grounds in the Atlantic Ocean must be granted free and innocent passage without exploitation, commercially or recreationally, in order that they may return to their natal rivers to be managed scientifically and rationally by the State of Origin for the purpose of permitting adequate escapement upriver for spawning and renewing the life cycle.

This is The Moral Imperative.

Those nations that have already accepted this concept and are implementing it are to be commended. Those nations that have not yet embraced the discipline are urged to shake now the shackles of outmoded custom and political expediency, and come down on the side of the resource. The need is compelling, and time is of the essence.

Finally, there is the basic proposition. Even though the Law of the Sea Convention recognized that a producing nation may have the "primary responsibility" for the salmon throughout its range in the ocean, some have maintained that this is not an exclusionary right. So who does own the salmon?

These fish have been around from time immemorial. They have served the imagination, emotions, and reverence of men and women during all that time. Yet it is only in the last half of the twentieth century that they have been "discovered," that is, increasingly exploited in the ocean, commercially and recreationally. It is clear that, whatever else can be said about ownership of these fish, these wild Atlantic salmon do not belong to the present generation alone. We are the stewards of these salmon, holding the resource in trust. As trustees, do we then have the right within a short span of years — scarcely more than a generation — to deplete this splendid creature in such a way that future generations can never turn to it to be enriched, uplifted, and sustained?

The question, then, is still before us: Will we save the wild salmon of the Atlantic? Will we make it the symbol of successful restoration of fish? We can, if we will.

In the meanwhile, Salar, keep swimming upstream, as you have done so bravely over the centuries — against all obstacles and against all odds.

Keep swimming upstream.

APPENDICES

Appendix 1

U.S.-Canadian Joint Statement on Atlantic Salmon

The United States and Canada today issued the following Joint Statement on Atlantic Salmon. The statement was prepared at a meeting of American and Canadian fisheries officials in Washington, November 22-23, and was released simultaneously in Washington and Ottawa following approval by both Governments. Officials of the Departments of Commerce, Interior, and State participated in the meeting and three Departments approved the statement.

Joint Statement on Atlantic Salmon
"The Governments of Canada and the United States have viewed with grave concern the failure of the North Atlantic fishing nations to agree completely on a ban on the high seas fishery for Atlantic salmon (Salmon salar), particularly through the International Commission for the Northwest Atlantic Fisheries (ICNAF) and the North-East Atlantic Fisheries Convention (NEAFC). Under these two Conventions, the North Atlantic fishing nations are pledged to cooperate in protecting and conserving the fish stocks of the North Atlantic. Their failure to do so effectively thus far calls into grave question the survival of the valuable Atlantic salmon stocks and requires a renewed effort on the part of those nations.

"The Governments of the United States and Canada consider the Atlantic salmon to be a particularly valuable natural resource, and note the unique dependence of the species on the rivers of origin for survival — a dependence found among very few species of the world, and even fewer in the North Atlantic. The Governments of Canada and the United States also note the heavy burden borne by those nations where these rivers are found in maintaining the rivers in a suitable condition to maintain the salmon runs, and otherwise in taking action to preserve the species. The investment in maintaining and increasing Atlantic salmon runs in North America is counted in the millions of dollars, and the two nations plan to increase their investment in this resource in coming years.

"Moreover, the Governments of the United States and Canada note the utter impossibility for a high seas fishery to differentiate between those runs which are in need of particular measures in order to ensure their survival and those runs containing salmon which can be harvested to provide food, recreation, and income for mankind. This fact alone is sufficient scientific justification to restrict the harvesting of Atlantic salmon to areas close to or within the rivers of origin, where scientific criteria can be applied to the harvest permitted to be taken from each run.

"The issues involved in a ban on high seas salmon fishing have been thoroughly examined by all of the governments involved since Canada raised the proposition in ICNAF during its 1967 meeting. A two-thirds majority on both Commissions has found the ban to be justifiable in terms of the powers and criteria of the two Conventions, and the ban has been in legal effect for twelve members of ICNAF since early 1970. Nonetheless, a few governments continue to oppose the ban, and through their actions have nullified the effect of the ICNAF action and have prevented the NEAFC action from having any effect. Subsequent compromise actions taken by the two Commissions do not address the basic problem that high seas fisheries are applied indiscriminately regardless of the scientific needs of individual runs. Nor do they address the question of equity whereby a few nations make virtually all of the investment to conserve and protect the Atlantic salmon while others reap a significant portion of the return on the investment while making little or no investment of their own.

"The Governments of Canada and the United States have vast experience in managing large salmon resources in the North Pacific. Thus far there has been nothing whatsoever to suggest that this experience cannot be applied to the Atlantic. On the contrary, as knowledge of the biology of the Atlantic salmon is increased, the two nations are led more and more to believe that the vast scientific experience in the Pacific is directly applicable to the Atlantic.

"The ban on high seas salmon fishing must be considered a unique conservation tool, not generally applicable to most other species of fish found in the ocean, because of the unique dependence of anadromous species on positive action by the state of origin to maintain them.

"The Governments of the United States and Canada believe that the evolution of fisheries management has proven incontrovertibly that to postpone conservation action until such need has been fully proved by scientific evidence can only lead to depletion of resources.

"Accordingly, the Governments of Canada and the United States affirm their belief that the rational method of managing the Atlantic salmon resource is by limiting the harvesting to the extent practicable to the country of origin of the salmon. In addition, the two Governments agree to cooperate in research and in maintenance and in enhancement of Atlantic salmon stocks with the objective of maintaining the species at the optimum level of abundance in the rivers of the two nations.

"The Governments of the United States and Canada call upon all nations fishing in the North Atlantic to cooperate fully in the protection and conservation of the Atlantic salmon. They urge that immediate action be taken by all concerned to end the high seas fishery for Atlantic salmon throughout the entire Atlantic. They re-affirm their commitment to continue working toward this end until the goal is achieved."

Appendix 2

Responses to 1981 CAST Initiative

Mr. Richard A. Buck
Chairman
Restoration of Atlantic Salmon
    in America, Inc.
Box 164
Hancock, New Hamsphire 03449

Dear Mr. Buck:

Thank you for your recent letter regarding the status of efforts to implement a new multilateral treaty for the protection of our Atlantic Salmon. I certainly appreciate the efforts of you and your organization, Restoration of Atlantic Salmon in America. Inc. (RASA), in this endeavor. I understand from Deputy Assistant Secretary Kronmiller that RASA has provided him with invaluable technical assistance as he pursues the comprehensive treaty we all believe necessary.

I'd also like to thank you for enclosing the *National Geographic* article on the problems of the Atlantic Salmon stock. Please be assured that the Members of the Fish and Wildlife Subcommittee are following this issue with interest.

Thanks again for taking the time to write and keeping me informed on your perspective of these important negotiations.

Sincerely,

JOHN B. BREAUX
Chairman
Subcommittee on Fisheries
and Wildlife Conservation
and the Environment

JBB/sf

Mr. Richard A. Buck
Restoration of Atlantic Salmon
   in America, Inc.
Box 164
Hancock, New Hampshire
USA 03449

Dear Mr. Buck:

Thank you for your letter of September 21, 1981 concerning Canadian participation in the development of an Atlantic salmon treaty.

I appreciate your organization's concerns and wish to assure you that the Government of Canada shares your desire for the establishment of an organization which will contribute to the conservation and restoration of the Atlantic salmon.

Your suggestion that Canada is not actively participating in the negotiations is most puzzling. The reasons for our non-participation in the Geneva meeting this summer are well known: this action was taken as a "last ditch" effort to stop Denmark and the EEC from upsetting an international arrangement in place (thanks in large measure to you) since 1972, and to emphasize the sensitivity of the 1190 m.t. figure, with a view to protecting it for incorporation into the Atlantic Salmon Convention.

Following the Geneva meeting we have been extremely active in the ongoing negotiations, through diplomatic channels and through personal discussions with U.S. and EEC authorities. We believe these bilateral negotiations to be a fundamentally important part of the negotiating process, as we wish to avoid a situation where a diplomatic conference fails because necessary bilateral understandings were not reached beforehand.

I am fully aware of the influential position you and your organization have in the development of U.S. policy on this question. Your assurance of U.S. flexibility regarding the proposals which have troubled Canadians is, accordingly, most welcome. I would very much appreciate anything you can do to persuade your authorities to respond positively to the proposals we have made, so that the decks can be cleared for a joint Canada/U.S. approach at a diplomatic conference. I am totally convinced that the best interests of salmon conservation can only be served if your country and Canada work in close cooperation in the final stages of these most important negotiations.

Yours sincerely,

Roméo LeBlanc

Appendix 3

Letter to Members of Parliament

Dear Mr. Member of Parliament:

I am writing you on behalf of the Atlantic salmon and this Association's concern about the position that Canada has taken with respect to an International Atlantic Salmon Treaty.

It appears that Canada has withdrawn from the negotiations at a critical time, when a treaty is in its final stages before being submitted for finalization to a diplomatic conference.

The Executive and Directors of this Association feel that Canada should participate fully in any conference or treaty that deals with Atlantic Salmon.

One reason Canada has withdrawn is because she feels that having other countries make recommendations on internal fishery matters is an invasion of sovereignty. This Association does not understand that point of view and feels that in the interest of salmon, any serious recommendations on fisheries management should always be welcome. Canada should also be positioned to make recommendations to other countries on their salmon fishery management, both in the interest of salmon and in her national interest. Salmon is by nature an international fish because it travels through the waters of many countries... hence what takes place in one country very much affects the salmon of another country.

We would appreciate you making the appropriate approaches to get Canada back to the negotiating table. Can we have a commitment to this end from you?

Sincerely,

W. Michael Price
Executive Director

WMP/fd
bcc: Mr. Dick Buck

Appendix 4

Testimony Before the Senate Foreign Relations Committee

by Richard A. Buck, Chairman
Restoration of Atlantic Salmon in America, Inc., (RASA)
on the NORTH ATLANTIC SALMON CONVENTION
Washington, D.C. — August 10, 1982

Mr. Chairman, and Members of this Committee: My name is Richard Buck, a Member of The Ocean Affairs Advisory Committee, United States Department of State, and of The U.S. Negotiating Team on Atlantic Salmon. I am also Chairman of Restoration of Atlantic Salmon in America, Inc., known as "RASA." RASA is the organization that developed the concept of a multilateral treaty for Atlantic salmon, and has been involved in this effort from the beginning.

I appear to testify in favor of the proposed North Atlantic Salmon Convention.

Atlantic salmon from nations rimming the North Atlantic Ocean migrate to the waters off Greenland to feed before returning to natal rivers to spawn and renew the life cycle. All along the migration routes, these fish have been and are subject to heavy interceptions, in the form of ocean netting, both legal and illegal. In the years 1964-1972, the Danes, Norwegians and Faroese escalated a Greenland "high-seas" fishery to a point where scientists feared for the survival of the species. Catches in the home waters of the salmon-producing nations plummeted. A movement spearheaded by the private sector in the United States, working closely with the

U.S. government, secured the U.S.-Danish Atlantic Salmon Agreement of January, 1972, which called for phasing out the "high-seas" fishery by 1976, and establishing an 1190 ton quota on the "inshore" fishery by native Greenlanders. This Agreement was later in 1972 incorporated verbatim into an ICNAF (the International Commission for Northwest Atlantic Fisheries) Agreement. The terms of this Agreement were, in general, adhered to.

But then ICNAF was terminated in 1976, leaving the Atlantic salmon without protection in the ocean. There are international treaties for those other highly migratory species, the tunas, the whales, the seals, and Pacific salmons, but none for the Atlantic salmon.

In 1975, our organization RASA became the first to call for a multilateral treaty, and by 1978 it had persuaded the U.S. Department of State to introduce the draft of a Convention to interested nations. Since then, five Working Group Meetings of the Consultative Parties have been held, in Washington, Brussels, Ottawa, Oslo and Geneva. A full Diplomatic Conference in Reykjavik, Iceland, produced the Final Act on January 22, 1982, which adopted a "Convention on the Conservation of Salmon in the North Atlantic Ocean," with votes of the following: The United States, Canada, Iceland, Norway, Denmark (for The Faroe Islands), and the European Economic Community (EEC), acting for its ten member states (of which the United Kingdom, the Republic of Ireland and France are producers and harvesters of salmon, and Denmark only a harvester).

There are four principal reasons why the United States should ratify this treaty.

First, stocks of salmon in the North Atlantic Ocean are interdependent, and thus the present overexploitations on one side of the Atlantic have their indirect effect on the other. What RASA calls "The Wishbone Principle of Atlantic Salmon Exploitation" provides the rationale for a multilateral approach. If an imaginary "wishbone" is superimposed on a map of the North Atlantic Ocean, with Danish Greenland as the apex, then Labrador, Newfoundland,

Nova Scotia, and New England waters become the left-hand "migration bone," and Ireland, Scotland, England, France and Spain waters the right-hand "migration bone." These are the routes followed by the salmon returning to home waters.

Greenland for the foreseeable future will continue to insist on taking a fixed quota of Atlantic salmon annually, in return for permitting these fish to forage in its waters. So, if Canada permits the "migration bone" to be cracked through overfishing, for instance, fewer Canadian and United States salmon would be going to Greenland, and Greenland would be filling a greater percentage of its quota from European stocks. Thus, the European Community nations want a chance to comment on the impact of Canadian domestic management measures on the number of fish available off Greenland. The opposite also applies. If Ireland, for instance, overexploits, Greenland then fills its quota in larger measure from the Canadian and United States components, so Canada and the United States need an international forum in which this inequity can be addressed.

It is this interdependence, this "Greenland connection," that makes multilateral agreement and action necessary, rather than the current fashion of short-term, ad hoc, regional fisheries agreements, which are self-serving, often conflicting, and constantly subject to the winds of political change.

Another reason for U.S. commitment to the treaty is that the United States has a rapidly growing Atlantic salmon resource to protect. Once plentiful in the rivers of New England, the Atlantic salmon had virtually disappeared by the middle of the Nineteenth Century, due to river pollution and the building of dams for hydroelectric power. Then, some hundred years later, in 1967, a Compact of Federal and State Governmental Agencies undertook to restore salmon runs. To date, more than $149,000,000 has been spent under this program on the construction of Fish Hatcheries and Fishways, and on management. This is exclusive of the hundreds of millions of dollars invested by industry and municipalities in water and sewage-treatment plants on rivers under Atlantic salmon restoration programs. Pollution has been reduced to a point where salmon can inhabit, migrate and spawn in the rivers. These efforts of the private sector, government and industry have been successful, and there are now substantial and increasing runs of salmon in the rivers under restoration.

This program is still in its infancy. Yet already it can be said to be successful. On the Penobscot River in Maine, for instance, this year as many as 1,000 people a day have been known to fish for the salmon returning there. Thus, a substantial restoration will bring long-term economic and social benefits of great value to the United States.

A third reason for approval of the treaty is that the world resource is in serious trouble. Now, in place of the Greenland over-kill of the 1960's, almost all of the major producing nations of the North Atlantic community in recent years have permitted an equally damaging escalation. This has served to continue the long downward trend in the world catch in home waters of the producing nations. In 1967, the peak year, 10,417 metric tons were taken. By 1981, the catch had fallen to 7,301 metric tons — a drop of over 30% in 15 years.

A final reason for ratification is the fact that the treaty has been a U.S. effort all the way. Americans originated the concept, introduced the draft, controlled the negotiating process in the face of resistance, and made the final moves that enabled the Diplomatic Conference to be convened, and the Convention adopted. The Atlantic salmon nations look to the U.S. to continue to lead the way.

It is not unrealistic to prophesy that, unless present trends are sharply reversed, the species Atlantic salmon will, in the not too distant future, become, not necessarily extinct, but so exhausted as to be of no practical use to man. Not much of a legacy to leave to future generations. A growing world population requires more, not less, protein. More, not less, opportunity for recreation. And the proposed treaty offers the most practical and rational means of persuading nations to conserve and restore the stocks.

Mr. Chairman, allow me to express my appreciation for being granted the privilege of appearing before this distinguished Committee. Thank you.

August 10, 1982   Richard A. Buck

Appendix 5

Letter to Minister Fraser

June 12, 1985

The Honorable John A. Fraser
Minister of Fisheries and Oceans
Ottawa, Ontario, Canada K1A 0E6

Dear Mr. Minister:

We are writing to let you know of our concerns over the international management and conservation of Atlantic salmon.

As parties to the North Atlantic Salmon Conservation Organization (NASCO) and as members of NASCO's North American and West Greenland Commissions, the United States and Canada have the opportunity to share their common goals and resolve outstanding problems regarding the conservation and management of Atlantic salmon.

We are therefore disturbed that Canada has rejected a U.S. proposal to close the fall fishery off Newfoundland and Labrador as a means of protecting U.S. origin salmon. As you know, the United States has invested a great deal in the restoration of the Atlantic salmon to its rivers and spends $100 million a year to support conservation and enhancement programs. Unfortunately, we have not yet realized increased harvests of Atlantic salmon despite these efforts, in large part because a substantial portion of all U.S. fish are intercepted off the coasts of West Greenland and Canada before they make the return trip to their spawning grounds in U.S. rivers.

At the February, 1985, meeting of the North Atlantic Commission of NASCO, the U.S. put forward its proposal to close the

Canadian fishery based on scientific evidence later validated by a working group of the International Council for the Exploration of the Seas. Following initial questions from the Canadian delegation, the U.S. addressed every concern expressed by Canada prior to NASCO's Second Annual Meeting in Edinburgh. To our dismay, at that meeting the U.S. proposal was rejected by the Canadian delegation, which stated further that any positive action on the proposal would be conditioned on acceptance of conservation measures to be considered by the West Greenland Commission. We believe this type of linkage is unfortunate and recall that Canada in 1984 decried a similar move to link conservation actions by the Northeast Atlantic and West Greenland Commissions.

It is our strong belief that Canada, as a party to NASCO, is obligated to adhere to Article 7(1)(b) which requires regulatory actions as a means of minimizing interceptions. We therefore respectfully request that you abide by the U.S. proposal regarding the closing of the fall fishery off Canada's eastern coast.

With best regards, we are

Sincerely,

George J. Mitchell	William S. Cohen
Claiborne Pell	Warren B. Rudman
John H. Chafee	John F. Kerry
Gordon J. Humphrey	Lowell P. Weicker, Jr.
Patrick J. Leahy	Christopher J. Dodd
Robert T. Stafford	Edward M. Kennedy

Appendix 6

Letter to Minister Crosbie

August 1, 1991

Mr. John A. Crosbie
Minister of Fisheries & Oceans
240 Sparks St., 8th Floor West
Ottawa, Ontario K1A OE6
Canada

Dear Mr. Crosbie:

Our organization is writing to urge you to announce and implement at this time a moratorium on commercial fishing for Atlantic salmon in Canadian waters.

Our Coalition, known as "CAST," consists of the top officials of the leading Atlantic salmon-intensive organizations based in the United States. In the past we have enjoyed what we believe has been a productive dialogue with your predecessors, and we hope that such an exchange of views may continue under your term of office.

Our particular concern has to do with the fact that the North American and West Greenland Commissions of NASCO at the Annual Meeting in June of this year failed to approve management measures which we believe were, and still are, necessary to prevent further declines in the abundance of salmon in the Northwest Atlantic. In this connection, please review the enclosed Position Statement of July 1, 1991 by Restoration of Atlantic Salmon in America, Inc, which CAST endorses whole-heartedly.

The NASCO nations, in their failure to approve additional international controls for the Northwest Atlantic, have left the door open for governments, which are always under political pressures from their own commercial fishermen, to set their own quotas and thus enable their constituents to benefit materially out of adversity and uncertainty.

We want it to be clearly understood that our Coalition does not single out Canada in this respect, for we certainly do not exonerate the United States from its share of blame in permitting the NASCO Meeting to adjourn without any constructive forward movement for Atlantic salmon in the Northwest Atlantic.

The only rational recourse at this time for the Government of Canada — if it is to protect the resource and maintain its credibility — is to call a moratorium on commercial fishing for Atlantic salmon for an unspecified period of time, during which the planning and implementation of the "buy-back" program that has been under active consideration for some time can be undertaken.

Such action would certainly be within the competence of the 1991 Atlantic Salmon Management Plan as previously announced by you, which stated, inter alia, that you "will review the commercial salmon fishery in Newfoundland and Labrador at midseason and implement closures if necessary."

It also would have a very important collateral benefit. The setting of such an example by Canada would not be lost on Danish Greenland, and the governments of the United States and Canada could then hold informal discussions with that country towards the same end.

So we urge you, Mr. Minister, to put such a moratorium in effect at this time.

For The Coalition for the Atlantic Salmon Task.

Very truly yours,

Richard A. Buck
Chairman

maf
Enclosure

Bibliography

Carson, Rachel. 1968. *The Sea Around Us.*

Gingrich, Arnold. 1971. *The Joys of Trout.*

Hasler, Arthur D. 1966. *Underwater Guideposts.*

Netboy, Anthony. 1974. *The Salmon — Their Fight for Survival.*

Netboy, Anthony. 1968. *The Atlantic Salmon: A Vanishing Species.*

Reddin, D. G., 1985. "Atlantic Salmon (*Salmo salar L.*) on and East of the Grand Bank of Newfoundland."

Reddin, D. G., 1986. "Ocean Life of Atlantic Salmon (*Salmo salar*) in the Northwest Atlantic." Presented at the Third International Atlantic Salmon Symposium.

Reddin, D. G., and K.D. Friedland. 1992. "Marine Environmental Factors Influencing the Movement and Survival of Atlantic Salmon." Presented at the Fourth International Atlantic Salmon Symposium.

Reddin, D.G., and W. M. Shearer. 1984. "Sea-surface Temperature and Distribution of Atlantic Salmon (*Salmo salar L.*) in the Northwest Atlantic."

Reddin, D.G., W. M. Shearer, and R. F. Burfitt. 1984. Intercontinental Migrations of Atlantic Salmon (*Salmo salar L.*)."

Reddin, D. G., and P. B. Short. 1981. Postsmolt Atlantic Salmon (*Salmo salar*) in the Labrador Sea."

Warner, William W. 1977. *Distant Water — The Fate of the North Atlantic Fisherman.*

Index